History at the End

History, Climate Change and the Possibility of Closure

History at the End of the World?

History, Climate Change and the Possibility of Closure

Edited by Mark Levene, Rob Johnson and Penny Roberts
in association with Rescue!History

http://www.rescue-history.org.uk

𝓗𝓔𝓑 ☼ Humanities-Ebooks, LLP

First published by Humanities-Ebooks, LLP,
Tirril Hall, Tirril, Penrith CA10 2JE

The PDF Ebook (with the facility of word and phrase search) is available from http://www.humanities-ebooks.co.uk and to libraries from Ebrary, EBSCO and MyiLibrary.com

ISBN 978-1-84760-166-7 Ebook
ISBN 978-1-84760-167-4 Paperback

Contents

For Saul (1984–2008)
And all his generation

An individual may be told, she, he, is to die, and will accept it. For the species will go on. Her or his children will die, and even absurdly and arbitrarily – but the species will go on. But then a whole species, or race, will cease, or dramatically change – no, that cannot be taken in, accepted, not without a total revolution of our deepest self.

— Doris Lessing, *Shikasta* (1979)

Notes on Contributors

Dr Robert Biel lectures in international political economy and sustainable development at the Development Planning Unit, University College London. His *The New Imperialism – Crisis and Contradictions in North-South Relations* (2000) has recently appeared in a revised edition in Spanish and Arabic. He is also an activist in the allotment movement and keen experimenter in low-input farming.

Dr Chris Callow is Lecturer in Medieval History at the University of Birmingham. His main research interests are in the history, archaeology and literature of medieval Iceland.

Dr Jonathan Coope gained his PhD in History from Southampton University in 2008. He has contributed to *Visionaries of the 20th Century* edited by Satish Kumar (2006) and *Earthographies: Ecocriticism and Culture* (2008). Jonathan previously trained as an engineer at Imperial College London and the BBC.

Dr Elaine Fulton is a founder-member of the Birmingham University Centre for Reformation and Early Modern Studies. Her most recent publications include *Catholic Belief and Survival in Late-Sixteenth Century Vienna* (2007). She is currently working on the perception of natural disasters in early-modern Europe.

Dr Tehmina Goskar is a medieval historian primarily working on the relationship between economics and culture in the Mediterranean. She is broadly interested in causes of cultural change, is also a museologist and, currently, a part-time lecturer at the University of Winchester.

Dr Rob Johnson is a historian at the University of Oxford, interested in conflict studies in a global or regional setting. He is the author of *A Region in Turmoil: South Asian Conflicts Since 1947* (2005) and *Oil, Islam and Conflict: Central Asia Since 1945* (2007).

Dr Roman Krznaric is an independent consultant and scholar specialising in multidisciplinary approaches to climate change, human development and social policy. He is co-editor (with Theodore Zeldin) of *Guide to an Unknown University*, author of the Oxfam report *How Change Happens* (2007), and is currently writing a history of the art of living.

Dr Mark Levene is Reader in Comparative History at the University of Southampton, specialising in the study of genocide. He is founder of Rescue!History, co-founder of the Crisis Forum and most recently, with David Cromwell, editor of *Surviving Climate Change, The Struggle to Avert Global Catastrophe* (2007).

Nicholas Maxwell is Emeritus Reader at University College London. He has devoted much of his working life to arguing the urgent need for an academic revolution. The author of five books, most recently *What's Wrong With Science?* (2009), he is the subject of *Science and the Pursuit of Wisdom: Studies in the Philosophy of Nicholas Maxwell* (2009).

Dr Jean-Francois Mouhot is Research Fellow at the University of Birmingham working on the history of UK Non-Governmental Organisations since 1945. His background is as an Early Modern Historian. He is the author of *Les Acadiens réfugiés en France (1758–1785): l'impossible reintegration?* (Quebec, 2009).

Prof. Peter Middleton is a Professor of English at the University of Southampton. He has published widely on modern poetry and fiction, and has a longstanding interest in science fiction. His most recent book, *Distant Reading*, is a study of the way poetry is circulated in public culture.

Dr Kate Prendergast runs the Oxford consultancy ISIS which specialises in public and independent sector communications. A freelance writer with an interest in climate change and the current development crisis in Africa, she has taught prehistoric archaeology at Oxford and the University of East London, and is currently collaborating on a volume on Neolithic rock art.

Dr Penny Roberts is Associate Professor in History at the University of Warwick. Her research specialism is the sixteenth-century French religious wars, but her wider interests span the late medieval/early modern divide (c.1300–1700).

Chris Shaw is a mature PhD student who has been working as an associate tutor in the Sociology department at the University of Sussex whilst writing up his thesis on how and why the climate change debate has become defined by the idea of a dangerous limit.

Dr Bryan Ward-Perkins teaches History at Trinity College, Oxford. He has practised both as an archaeologist, and as a historian. He is the author of *The Fall of Rome and the End of Civilisation* (2005), which won the Hessell-Tiltman prize for History and has been translated into six languages.

Prof. Dave Webb is Professor of Engineering and co-founder and Director of the Praxis Centre, established for the Study of Information and Technology in Peace, Conflict Resolution and Human Rights at Leeds Metropolitan University. He has published widely on the application of engineering modelling, nuclear disarmament and the militarisation of space.

Acknowledgements

This is a book which has come out of Rescue!History, an independent network of radical academics, independent researchers and committed campaigners. Since its inception, in late 2006, the network has sought to put its expertise and skills towards alerting not just academics and students but also a wider public of the dangers inherent in the human present and future by way of a better understanding of our past. Necessarily, our work focuses on anthropogenic climate change, the most urgent but also all-encompassing of challenges now facing humanity. We do not receive any long-term funding or research grants to pursue this work and thus acknowledge, with gratitude, the help we received from the Humanities school at the University of Southampton and the School of Historical Studies at the University of Birmingham to support a small conference the network hosted at the Birmingham and Midland Institute, in April 2008.

The success of the conference, 'An End to History? Climate Change, the Past and the Future', proved the launching pad for this book. We had a number of other potential essayists for this volume over and above our final band of sixteen. Thanks to Jens Justinussen, Cleo Paskal and Rachel Pope who ultimately were unable to contribute.

More centrally, both Colin Feltham and Richard Maguire played leading roles in the inception of this volume, both at the conference and beyond. We owe to both a debt of warm gratitude. A further inspiration was Stefan Skrimshire, whose volume *Future Ethics, Climate Change and Apocalyptic Imagination* (Continuum, forthcoming) complements, in key respects, our own. Behind the scenes, Colin Richmond, as always, provided grist to the intellectual mill. From a different perspective, Crisis Forum, out of which Rescue!History developed, has provided moral and more immediate practical support. My deepest thanks to David Cromwell, just for being there in the background and, above all, to Marianne McKiggan who stepped into the breach at a critical moment to get us to, and beyond, that final hurdle. Finally, to my co-editors, Rob Johnson and Penny Roberts, a heart-felt salute for their conscientious efforts, not to say sheer grit and perseverance.

To overcome the emergency humankind now faces will require a much broader engagement with the issues that Rescue!History raises. A thank you to all students, colleagues and fellow travellers who have helped this small contribution to the greater task.

ML
Kineton, Warwicks
December 2009

Introduction: A Chronicle of a Death Foretold?

Mark Levene

Recently, I ran an undergraduate class on the nuclear arms escalation of the early 1980s. None of the students present were born before 1990 so it was all history to them. To try to bring home the sense of underlying angst which pervaded the Cold War I asked them if they might be able to elicit any memories or experiences from their parents. Rather tellingly, almost as if that earlier generation had either blotted out the memory or had had little awareness of what was going on at the time, the exercise proved a damp squib. A few weeks later, however, one student kindly emailed me with some information she had gleaned from her father who had been in the Royal Navy:

> He said for a lot of the 1980s he was based on a naval ship and that 'he spent half his career being trained in what to do if there was a nuclear war', he remembers being told that if the Russians did attack their life expectancy on board was 15 minutes.[1]

It may seem rather odd to begin a book which purports to be about climate change harking back to the nuclear threat. But it may offer a necessary reminder that we have been living under the shadow of our own self-destruction now for some sixty years, and the manner in which we may finally arrive at that point—or, alternatively, avoid it—contains multiple dimensions and possible directions.

Premonitions of an end to the human are in themselves nothing new. They are in-built into the human psyche, along with spectacular notions of the sky falling in or the earth being ravaged by fire or flood. Quite correctly so, as natural disaster could—indeed can—strike at any time. But whereas in the ancient past a cosmic order was always dependent on outside forces, and our own part in the drama was to propitiate the gods for fear of incurring the full weight of their

---

1   Thanks to Emma Hemsley.

displeasure, our own time is fundamentally different in the degree to which we imagine ourselves to be the true masters, if not of the universe, then certainly of this planet.[1]

Even a few centuries back, as Elaine Fulton and Penny Roberts develop in these pages, crisis on earth, climatic or otherwise, had as its corollary a collective, religiously-based recognition of human *limitations* in the face of divine judgement. The repeated response was to repent. If we really are now in a state of terminal crisis, central to that condition is our assumed ability to dispense with such ideas as superstitious nonsense. Why should we need to abase ourselves before an imaginary God, or gods, when we have proven our ability to control the environment as we see fit? Yet, perhaps, this is the reason why at the heart of the present human condition lies a profound paradox. The historical moment when 'we'—or at least the hegemonic elements within that 'we'—have come closest to assuming a complete break with *natural* history, proves to be exactly the same moment when the potential for nature's blow-back is at its most total and devastating. And, as Dave Webb attests in his chapter, *both* nuclear weapons and anthropogenic climate change are the two strongest—as well as closely interrelated—contenders for pushing humanity to that brink.

To be sure, there are obvious differences. The actuality of nuclear war would obliterate millions in an instant. From where we currently stand, the effects of carbon emissions leading to global warming seem more like a slow strangulation, the outcome of which might more closely mirror T.S.Eliot's ending of the world, 'not with a bang but a whimper'.[2] Even so, from different directions they bring us up short on this critical point: the level of technical sophistication which has enabled the harnessing of the energy of the universe—now unravelling at speed—is founded on a social formation which has lost either its fear or understanding of the necessity of restraint. Or put another way, divested of the usually religiously-based ethical injunctions which have historically provided that safety net, we are—at the time

1   Divine displeasure was almost always provided through the gods' ability to wreak environmental devastation. See for example, Norman Cohn, *Cosmos, Chaos and the World to Come, The Ancient Roots of Apocalyptic Faith* (New Haven and London: Yale University Press, 1993).

2   T. S. Eliot, 'The Hollow Men' (1925).

when the need is greatest—emotionally and culturally as ill-equipped as we ever have been to deal with catastrophe.

As Jonathan Coope later explores, this amounts to a pathological condition. But it also may explain why the trajectory towards self-destruction is likely to accelerate. Unable or unwilling to read backwards into deep human experience we assume that there will always be some scientifically-ordained technical fix by which we can punch our way out of whatever mess we have made for ourselves. In relation to climate change the most extreme rendition of this thinking, to date, are various proposed geo-engineering schemes designed not to decelerate global warming but rather to all the more tightly 'manage' the climate, albeit again for hegemonic needs. Dependent on extraordinary combinations of technological precision, scaled-up material resources and military-style planning, they represent just the sort of high-stakes technocratic problem-solving which began with the atomic bomb-building Manhattan Project.[1]

Another contemporary tendency is to assume that there must be some opportunity at hand to be wrested from the encroaching disaster. For instance, as the Arctic ice cap melts, the fossil fuels (the sequestrated solar energy) underneath will become accessible, thereby staving off for a few more years a scarcity of the very resources central to both developed and developing economies. The fact that emissions from fossil fuels are the major driver of global warming is likely to play little or no part in such calculations, especially as these will be determined in terms of national-cum-corporate interest, probably precipitating a militarised scramble for the Arctic.[2] Humanity at its twilight may well be one characterised by the calamitous geo-engi-

1   See Jay Michaelson, 'Geo-engineering, A Climate Change Manhattan Project', http://www.users.globalnet.co.uk/~mfogg/links.htm. More generally, Dave Webb, 'Geo-engineering and its implications' http://www.crisis-forum.org.uk/events/workshop1_resources.php. Significantly, as I write, the Royal Society is publishing its own report supporting in principle a range of geo-engineering techniques. See Catherine Brahic, 'Top scientists call for geo-engineering plan 'B,' *New Scientist*, 1 September 2009, http://www.newscientist.com/article/dn17716-top-science-body-calls-for-geoengineering-plan-b.html.

2   Scott G. Borgerson, 'Arctic meltdown: the economic and security implications of global warming,' *Foreign Affairs*, 87:2 (2008), pp. 63–77. Also Naomi Klein, *The Shock Doctrine, The Rise of Disaster Capitalism* (London: Penguin, 2008).

neering effects of iron fertilisation of the oceans, or spraying sulphur aerosols into the stratosphere, resulting in an even more rapid collapse of the global commons with world-wide starvation ensuing. Or, yet again, by an unregulated and rampant social Darwinism in which the most powerful players in the international system struggle against each other to hold or conquer all residual energy and food resources. In such circumstances the likelihood of nuclear confrontation is high. Global warming could yet be trumped by nuclear winter.[1]

But reading the near-future in such bleak terms must seem decidedly perverse. And surely its effect can only be counter-productive? Not only does it fly in the face of all the UN sponsored, NGO-abetted, national, EU and other collective-state efforts to arrive at an internationally agreed deal on halting and reversing carbon emissions, it also, more parochially, would seem to be at odds with the purpose of this book. After all, its creators came together under the aegis of the Rescue!History network whose name does not suggest a misanthropic celebration of the end to history.

Even so, one premise of *History at the End of the World* is of our need to step up to the plate and consider the strong possibility of human foreclosure as a consequence of practices, economics, technologies and socio-cultural behaviour which we might otherwise take to be normative, even benign. Until we have done so, our ability to move onto a new and safer path which might genuinely meet the challenges posed by the encroaching crisis is highly unlikely to succeed.[2] Whether governments and other ruling elites can—in the wake of Copenhagen—facilitate an orderly, non-violent retreat from the carbon economy is something upon which contributors to this book may not necessarily agree. What is being proposed, however, is that the task requires a much more all-encompassing vision of the possibilities and pitfalls of human society, and *societies*, than that currently on offer. And who better to guide us in this direction than those who study the past?

---

1   See Webb's chapter, 'On the Edge of History, the Nuclear Dimension'.
2   See David Cromwell and Mark Levene, eds, *Surviving Climate Change, The Struggle to Avert Global Catastrophe* (London: Pluto Press, 2007), for further development of this theme.

Historians and other students of the past: are they any use?

Having set up the proposition, however, what evidence is there to suggest that the present cohort of academic historians, or those working in similar fields, are those to whom a wider public might turn for inspiration or, failing that, for a half-decent epitaph on our species at its demise? Far from running with the issue, as one of our contributors proposed at a recent historians' conference, he was met with a largely negative response rather more suggestive of a desire to avoid the issue at all costs. Here, for instance, is the gist of how one participant responded:

> Surely climate change is too contentious an issue at present: too scientifically contested and too politically controversial for historians to deal with. Surely historians need to wait some time, maybe even decades, until the science is secure enough and we, as historians, are in a position to look back at global warming coolly (as it were) and view it with the kind of dispassion worthy of a proper scholar.[1]

Even the most cursory glance at the rapidly burgeoning *scientific* literature proves such commentary to be not only misplaced but entirely redundant. Far from being a matter of decades away the science is quite firm that carbon dioxide accumulated in the atmosphere from anthropogenic sources over previous decades is already at dangerous levels.[2] In addition, there is an increasingly prevailing view that future emissions, unless brought down to something close to zero, have the potential to engender *irreversible* earth system feedbacks which for most of the planet's biota, including ourselves, could herald mass extinction.[3]

The fact is that except for the small handful involved in environ-

---

1 Post-graduate historian's conference, Aberystwyth, 2008.

2 See Kevin Anderson and Alice Bows, 'Reframing the climate change challenge in light of post-2000 emission trends', *Philosophical Transactions of the Royal Society*, 366:1882 (2008), pp. 3863–82.

3 David Wasdell, 'Radiative Forcing, Climate Sensitivity & Boundary Conditions of Runaway Climate Change', December 2008, http://www.crisis-forum.org.uk/events/Workshop1_presentations/wasdell_talberg_revised.php

mental history, most historians are not much interested in the *natural* world.[1] Like the rest of humanity, they take for granted the provision of the necessities of life: water, food, light, and breathable air. They may be students of the past but they equally assume a future into which they, too, can retreat. As a consequence, they are as prone as any other group to deny that climate change is a clear and present danger, with all the standard prevarication or shirking of responsibility for doing something about it.

Two things need to be said here. The first relates to what one might call professional *amour-propre*. The second genuinely matters for the rest of us. On the first count, by ducking the issue, historians, and those in related disciplines, are in danger of proving their irrelevance while others have to get on with a practical response to the spiralling emergency. And it is significant that the historians' deficit on this score is already evident. Think of recent volumes which consider human behaviour and interactions as a consequence of historic climate change, or the related impact of humankind (locally or globally) on the biosphere, and one will be hard-pressed to find a mainstream historian. There are a handful of notable exceptions such as the consciously world historical father and son duo, William H. and John R. McNeill, whose holistic approach always sought to relate technologies with geo-politics, and microbes with macro-history.[2] More often than not though, it is earth system physicists, evolutionary biologists, environmental scientists or, as in the case of Jared Diamond, all of these and more rolled into one, who have made the running.[3] For all the academic rhetoric about the value of interdisciplinarity, there are actually relatively few scholars from humanities' backgrounds willing or able to make the leap across the necessary boundaries. As a result, where genuine synergy does arise on the relationship between

---

1   Archaeologists are more generally exempt from this charge. They are, after all, as a general rule, ready to get their hands dirty.

2   See J. R. McNeill, *Something New under the Sun: An Environmental History of the 20th century World* (New York: Norton, 2000) idem and W. H. Neill, *The Human Web* (New York: Norton, 2003) for among their works.

3   Jared Diamond, *Collapse: How Societies Choose to Fail or Survive* (London: Penguin, 2005); also William F. Ruddiman, *Plows, Plagues and Petroleum* (Princeton and Oxford: Princeton University Press, 2005)

man and planet it nearly always involves, on the humanities side, archaeologists, anthropologists, geographers, or the small band of environmental historians usually seen as being at the margins of our core discipline.[1]

More critically, however, and this brings us on to our second point, current efforts to find routes out of the climate change crisis are either largely wanting or inherently dangerous *because* they are products of highly solipsistic, not to say hegemonic, criteria or methodologies. But supposing we were to demonstrate the case that the methodologies themselves are self-limiting (as Nicholas Maxwell argues), while the global political-economic system which they support is inherently unsustainable (for which read Robert Biel). Back in 1992, Francis Fukuyama published what was in effect a paean to the system: *The End of History and the Last Man*.[2] The irony of its title, not to say the closeness of it to our own, should not belie the fact that Fukuyama was offering an absurdly roseate version of the future. How was he able to do this? By offering a dramatically foreshortened historical perspective beginning with the Enlightenment and ending with the post-Cold War triumph of American-style corporate capitalism, while ignoring, *tout ensemble,* the impact of a fossil-fuel driven, Western-led human aggrandisement at the expense of the global commons.

This book, by contrast, argues that what is needed now is not the prospect of an end to history, *à la* Fukuyama but rather a genuine *return* to understanding the past. Indeed, only by such a return might we begin to see outside the baroque goldfish bowl construction which we have been lured into believing represents our safety and well-being. Could that be the impetus to our breaking out of the bowl altogether in order to become free, independent actors in our own right? Yet in the context of climate change it is difficult to imagine how any struggle of the commonweal, not only for a temporary survival but a long-term resilience and sustainability, could proceed without some deeper

---

1   See for example, Roderick Mackintosh et al., eds, *The Way the Wind Blows, Climate, History and Human Action* (New York: Columbia University Press, 2000); Robert Constanza et al., eds, *Sustainability or Collapse, An Integrated History and Future of People on Earth* (Cambridge, MA: Dahlem University Press, 2007).

2   Francis Fukuyama, *The End of History and the Last Man* (London: Penguin, 1992).

awareness of the full panoply, complexity and variety of human experience across time. Surely, before it becomes too late, this demands the full mobilisation of students of the past in support of the exercise? With their assistance, the rest of us might perceive more closely how tightly circumscribed the strictures and categories of current modernist thinking are. And with the recognition that we no longer need to be duty-bound to the notion that only this society works, can work and will continue to work into the foreseeable future, we might venture onto fresh yet also historically-informed paths geared towards enabling us to work with nature and each other.

However, this can hardly be simply a question of cherry picking history and prehistory for what looks most promising to present needs. Before we can even start using the past as an agent for transformation, we urgently need to know how and why we have arrived at our present impasse. If, as the atmospheric physicist Paul Crutzen puts it, we are now in the era of the anthropocene in which the impact of human beings on eco-systems is the prime factor determining the behaviour and perhaps ultimate fate of the biosphere, then we surely need to pinpoint the societal and economic processes by which this has arisen.[1] Is it a function of the advent of the industrial revolution, and hence of an emergent capitalism whose origins also lie in the peculiar rise of the West? In which case is the 'damage' done by the last two hundred years of historical trajectory, in any sense, containable or reversible? Or is this assumption itself flawed, the advent of coal-fuelled steam machines far from being an unfortunate wrong turn rather the logical consequence of pre-existing factors, most obviously a scarcity of wood or peat for the energy needs of an inexorably rising European population?[2] In which case, the issue at stake might be less one of a *long durée* of renewable energy versus the short-term rupture of the carbon economy, but rather of a relentless human trajectory towards a seeming mastery of the planet set in motion by the ending of the last great Ice Age. Such a thesis would certainly seem

---

1   Paul J. Crutzen, and Eugene F. Stoermer, 'The "Anthropocene,"' *Global Change Newsletter*, 41 (2000), pp. 17–18.
2   See Joachim Radkau, *Nature and Power, A Global History of the Environment*, translated by Thomas Dunlap (Cambridge and Washington DC: Cambridge University Press, 2008), especially pp. 136–42.

to knock the idea of human agency on its head, the leap of human endeavour towards 'civilisation' being no more than a function of ephemeral climatic conditions which were bound to end sooner or later with, for instance, the advent of a new glacial epoch.

An argument such as this would represent something of a cul-de-sac for our purposes. While it might invite a more open-ended philosophical, or possibly theological, set of speculations about the limits of free-will set against climate realities, the underlying determinism would further serve to marginalise the role of critical historical analysis of either the causes or prognosis for the anthropocene. Yet the very complexity of elements out of which the modern, carbon-fuelled world emerged would hardly suggest an inevitability of process. Certainly, as Jean-Francois Mouhot asserts, one might acknowledge that, once set on that path, withdrawal from our carbon addiction has become increasingly remote. But does this mean our own future is set in stone, or can we read, most obviously from past experience, the routes best taken set against the ones to be avoided? Our freedom of choice will always be seriously limited, not only by environmental factors, but also our social and political formation. Looking into the past, into that critical moment on the cusp of the industrialising change in Britain, for instance, we can see with hindsight how the dominating socio-economic forces shaped and controlled the headlong rush into the carbon economy. Yet what is equally tantalising is the sweep of social movements from below, the plethora of dissenting voices, indeed, the revolutionary groundswell which might have delivered a very different country, a very different economy, to that which actually emerged.[1]

This is not to be diverted by counter-factual narratives; simply to remind ourselves that it is people who make history or, alternatively, acquiesce in what the more powerful, determined, aggressive, or occasionally more far-sighted make for them. What is significant about our own moment, however, is how well placed we are to review critically the whole sweep of human experience as never before. One might go further and suggest that, because we may well be standing

---

1   E. P. Thompson, *The Making of the English Working Class* (London: Penguin, 1963).

at the very apex of that experience, we are both summoned *and* liberated to reconsider it in this light. Part of the paradox of our present lies in the extent of knowledge historians, archaeologists and others have to enable them in this task, aided by the sophistication of the tools, techniques and laboratory processes to support them.[1] If this really is near-end time is not this equally the moment when students of the past need to come together to rethink the totality of what happened; why it took the course it did; how, where and when it went so wrong?

Without such insights, it is likely that humanity will be carried forward on inappropriate, increasingly authoritarian, if not lethal technocratic paths, without realising that there might have been other potentially safer, gentler, more socially just and people-empowering by-ways which might have been explored and developed for—as Chris Callow puts it—our surviving and thriving. And that is surely where the history comes in. As never before we need to dispense with 'the enormous condescension of posterity'[2] and learn instead from our predecessors how they adapted to and managed in conditions of plenty or scarcity, how they coped with adversity or worse, how they developed practical skills—and communal skill-sharing—for the good times and the bad, and sometimes even prospered. We cannot, and probably would not want, to go back to where they were. The fact that the vast majority of our ancestors lived without fossil fuels, and primarily from what they could grow, glean, scavenge, or hunt from their immediate environments, would have most of us—at least in the consumer-based West—reeling with incredulity, amazed applause or maybe repulsion. All the more reason why we need to understand how they did it. What was the nature of their social and cultural habitus which mentally equipped them to be resilient, purposeful and self-reliant? Was constraint built into their religious systems? In what ways did pre-industrial societies of the past, or the now entirely marginal indigenous communities of the present, see them-

---

1   See Ian Whyte, *World Without End? Environmental Disaster and the Collapse of Empires* (London and New York: I. B.Tauris, 2008), chapter 2, 'Environmental Systems and Processes'.

2   Thompson, *Making*, p. 13.

selves as custodians of their environments, practised in the virtues of restraint and with an eye to conserving the natural world around them for future generations? Where this did not happen, where societies fragmented, collapsed or died out, was this due to a weakness in their life-sustaining practices, or of their thought-systems, an economic or political overreach, a failure in their adaptability to new environmental conditions, including possibly climate change, or just bad luck?

Our desire to celebrate human resourcefulness has at all times to be tempered by the knowledge of disasters, self-inflicted or otherwise. It may indeed have been an initial revolutionary breakthrough in agriculture, on the back of favourable climate conditions, which began the spiral of violent inter-group competition for resources, the turn to war and imperial expansion, and with it the ancient seeds of drives to attain the unattainable. Ecological exhaustion leading to starvation, and epidemic infection leading to demographic collapse, have always stood in the wings as our nightmare scenarios just as have the fears of more pronounced natural calamity. Rescue!History was founded not to avoid these realities, but to confront them, just as it equally seeks to do with regard to our current planetary emergency. The purpose of our group, however, is not to fuel despair but, through reaching out to the past, to offer an alternative set of resources which may assist in the process of our restoration to the biosphere which nurtures and sustains us. This book is the result.

What does this book do?

Perhaps one should answer first by stating what it does not do. This is not a book which offers either a synoptic green history of the world, a history of climate change, or of an emerging scientific awareness of its anthropogenic dimension. There are some excellent studies on these themes and we encourage readers to investigate further.[1] By the same token, this is not a book with a single thesis, one geared

---

1   H. H. Lamb, *Climate, History and the Modern World* (London and New York: 1982); Tim Flannery, *The Weather Makers: The History and Future Impact of Climate Change* (London: Penguin, 2005); Mike Hulme, *Why We Disagree About Climate Change, Understanding Controversy, Inaction and Opportunity* (Cambridge: Cambridge University Press, 2009) as major examples.

towards any particular expert audience, or primarily angled at academic peers. Our essays are quite consciously intended as accessible to an enlightened lay readership. More immediately, the volume is directed to students who, in the light of present realities, seek new and different approaches to those on offer from a standard humanities fare.

The organisation of the book is loosely chronological, from prehistoric times to the present. More keenly, it is thematic, linking together essays in sections which explore different aspects of the relationship between the human past and a potential human end. All essays, but a final section more especially, cogitate on how we avoid that eventuality. To ourselves, we have described these essays as 'think pieces.' In other words, from a variety of perspectives, each of us is trying to work through where we, as a species, have come from, where we are now, and how knowledge of the past—or the present looked at through alternative prisms—can help overcome our contemporary crisis. We take it as an advantage that our backgrounds and interests are mixed: including approaches which begin from archaeology, literature, religion, psychology, sociology, philosophy of science, engineering and sustainable development, as well as from 'straight' history. Interestingly, though not by conscious design, there are no paid-up environmental historians or scientists among us. But we hope that this will give a freshness and diversity to our arguments, since one of the contentions of this book is that we all have to become environmentalists *and* historians now. Some of us do so from the beginning or middle of academic careers, while others are independent writers and researchers, each with a passionate interest in the human dimensions of climate change.

Overall, then, one could argue that all we are trying to do in these pages is to initiate a wider debate. Although currently this is largely confined to a narrow circle of specialists, our purpose is to find subject-matter and a form of common language which can help restore both past *and* future to everybody. Some of us do so by dealing with particular episodes, examples, or groups of people from the past; others by more consciously interrogating the writing of history or assumptions about it. Still others pose whether historical writing is sufficient to our purpose, as Peter Middleton does by asking whether novels might be a further way of forearming ourselves for the growing storm. Each essay thus can be treated as free-standing, but some also are better read in juxtaposition with others. In the section about Enlightenment and modernity, for instance, Nicholas Maxwell and Chris Shaw develop their analyses from quite different starting points. The former does not question the emergence of the modern scientific method but the consequences of its misapplication. The latter's argument is also in a critical sense about misapplication—specifically with regard to what constitutes dangerous limits to greenhouse gas concentrations in the atmosphere—but also as a launching pad for a much more wholesale assault on the outcomes of modernity. Whereas Maxwell thus sees a solution in a more holistic reappraisal of the Enlightenment design, Shaw would have us dig much deeper not simply into a pre-modern but a pre-agricultural past as the keenest way of confronting today's technological society.

There is tension enough here on top of quite distinct authorial registers. But Shaw's essay also begs the question what exactly can be learnt from our distant ancestors? In our first section on 'Deep History,' Kate Prendergast seeks to answer the question by proffering that human responses to climate change on the cusp of the Neolithic were never just about economics. On the contrary, if we want to genuinely understand our ancestors' behaviour we have to acknowledge their three-dimensionality, including not only an acute identification of changes in the natural world around them but a veneration which matched it. It was this building of the natural world into their cosmological world-view which, Prendergast argues, enabled prehistoric peoples to successfully adapt to a fast-changing climate. Implicitly, she also challenges the hubris of conventional wisdoms which dismiss, or relegate to a footnote, the spiritual dimension of human existence in favour of a narrow focus on an economic bottom-line. We have already noted Fulton and Roberts' proposition that traditional belief systems, whatever we make of them, were central to sustaining pre-modern communities' emotional as well as physical ability to ride out disaster. This is not to elide a further tension between religious injunction and economic imperatives. Tehmina Goskar's study of contemporary Parsis makes it abundantly clear how an ancient community which has ostensibly prospered in the modern world has become caught on the horns of a dilemma as to which is more important: affirmation of the wholeness of the human relationship with nature, or the entrepreneurial urge to materially succeed. Again, there is a strong implication that the blocking out of the former, in favour of the latter, is key to what gravely imperils us as an entire human community.

But then, the erasure of the past's inconvenient truths is arguably nothing new. In our second section, for instance, bleakly entitled 'Harbingers of the End,' the essay by Bryan Ward-Perkins reminds us of the degree to which ancient Rome assumed for itself an invulnerable permanence much as we do of our own globalised society. Like us, the Romans made huge assumptions about the military and economic basis upon which their society operated, rarely contemplating the possibility that its very complexity might also carry with it the seeds of breakdown. Undermine some of the central pillars of that society and collapse became irreversible, the consequence for the West being a dark ages from which it took centuries to recover. Leap to the further section on 'Surviving Catastrophe', and Mouhot's piece focusing on our fossil fuel dependency, and one cannot but make some marked contemporary parallels. As Mouhot argues, having fuel-powered machines to do the vast majority of our work means that we take for granted an energy supply just as in a not dissimilar way did slave-owning societies of not just earlier but also quite recent times. Even with a slowing down rather than complete elimination of an already precarious oil and gas supply, the Western-led global edifice would seize up a good deal faster than did that of Rome.

Mouhot's wider point about the hurt we inflict on other people, or the biosphere, through fossil-fuel usage has as its rejoinder the necessity to think through the consequences of our actions. But then how can a society genuinely sustain itself over the long-term without massive violence to either nature or fellow humans? By considering the example of Iceland, in other words an island—and a relatively recently occupied one at that—Callow argues that the potential for its medieval inhabitants' survival was not just a matter of engaging with its inherent ecological fragility, natural resource scarcity, or even quite dramatic variations in the climate over time. Equally important were power relations, the impact of land tenure and the way this fed both the best and worst of Icelandic farming practices. Callow thus identifies environmental threat, deforestation and the erosion of pasture, as a consequence of broader socio-political processes.

In the following 'Surviving Catastrophe' section, Roman Krznaric in his comparative analysis of pre-industrial Tokugawa Japan and a wartime USA between 1941 and 1945, develops a similar theme. Against the grain of traditional *laissez-faire* and big business opposition, the Roosevelt administration introduced both just and equitable price controls, and staple food rationing. Of course, this had nothing directly to do with environmental issues per se, but was a response to the needs of wartime resource allocation. Nevertheless, Krznaric's point is that the strong state can overcome the resistance of special interests where the common good dictates. Even more so in Japan; a calamitous collapse of forest cover through centuries of elite misuse was turned round in the seventeenth and eighteenth centuries in favour of an afforestation programme which literally saved Japan's wooden-structure civilisation. Again, strong leadership, in this case that of the authoritarian shogunate, was instrumental to this sustainability drive. This raises a further debate about whether imposed top-down solutions, even under emergency conditions, represent the most efficacious way out of danger. But then, as Krznaric points out, without grass-roots support for such policies, they are never likely to succeed: the key to Tokugawa success perhaps being Japan's ingrained culture of provision for the needs of future generations.

Jared Diamond's major contention in his *Collapse* is how, faced with the potentiality of disaster, societies can *choose* to change. The possibility of them being able to do so, however, may be dependent on several factors. In order to undergo transition they are likely to need either a social memory of what came before—though interrogated in such a way that they can purposefully implement a new

course founded on the valuable elements of the past experience—
or alternatively, model new scenarios for the future founded entirely
on present experience. A cultural milieu of both hope and fear may
have been valuable as a coping mechanism for recurrent pre-modern
calamities, but not necessarily sufficient to engender the sort of paradigm shift required for a society faced with total collapse. The climate
change novels considered by Middleton may provide a more ahistori-
cal premonition of the sort of apocalyptic world *we* might inherit as a
consequence of anthropogenic climate change, but without necessarily providing a catalyst for an effective response to its causes. All this,
of course, assumes that the social organism is coherent and united
in its willingness to embark on change. But why should we assume
people will be willingly led by leaders who insist on their own crisis
response? Why, by the same token, would we expect leaders to acquiesce to a people's will that was at odds with the state's own preservation instincts?

This all begs a further critical question: one of timing. Let us sup-
pose that a state, or states, are already far on the road to collapse.
In such an instance, a debate about change might seem fatuous. In
our penultimate section, ominously entitled 'Countdown to Self-
Annihilation', Rob Johnson reminds us of one arena, Central Asia,
where the signs of a possible 'Endgame' are already far advanced.
The region of the old Silk Road was once home to glorious civilisations which have come and gone, which perhaps offers some hope
that nothing need be ultimately irredeemable. Yet a combination of
exogenous geo-political and resource pressures on the region, combined with an environmental degradation of already massive proportions, suggests, to the contrary, that the situation may now be
irreversible. Will climate change be the last straw pushing Central
Asia over the edge? Above all, prospects hinge on the husbanding of
declining water supplies. If there is not enough water to meet human
and animal needs here—as in the Horn of Africa, another region on
the brink—then it will not be amelioration as the outlook, but rather a
landscape of endemic violence and mass flight. Whilst the hegemonic
West's attention is currently concentrated there ostensibly on account

of a perceived international terrorist threat, could Central Asia actually become one of the regions which will harbinger a more general water-related breakdown and population displacement as now repeatedly forecast?[1]

While we must focus our attention on how it is that some parts of the world have become both politically weak and environmentally stressed over recent history, it equally begs the question why others have become so strong. After all, while a Kazakhstan, a Bangladesh, or a Somalia, may be among the first mass casualties of global warming, the immediate anthropogenic capacity to destroy us all still resides with those states who have risen to compete for contemporary global hegemony. As Webb reminds us, it is the USA and post-USSR Russia, in the wake of the Cold War, who retain the quantities of nuclear weaponry for such a scenario. One of the ironies of our current situation may be that we have chosen to forget how dangerous those weapons remain (except when faced by the possibility of them falling into the hands of terrorists or so-called rogue states). Even putting aside the high possibility of conscious confrontation as, for instance, over dwindling oil resources, the very complexity and sophistication of the US and Russian early warning systems still pose a considerable risk of precipitating a nuclear missile exchange purely through computer error. Both sides still operate their weapons' systems on the basis of 'launch on warning'. As never before, insists Webb, the need for international education and cooperation are urgent if we are to draw back from still the most devastating and omnipresent potential for self-extermination present in our global system.

It is critical, therefore, to turn our attention to the historical trajectory which has brought us to this position. All the more so given that our final section aspires to 'Creating Conditions for Renewal'. Coope poses the problem of how a modern Western mindset has become desensitised to the natural world of which we are necessarily a part. He emphasises that this is a historical problem, the rise

---

1   See, most recently, Global Humanitarian Forum, 'Human Impact Report; Climate Change, The Anatomy of a Silent Crisis', May 2009, http://ghfgeneva.org/Portals/0/ pdfs/human_impact_report.pdf ; also Christian Aid, 'Life on the edge of climate change: the plight of pastoralists in Northern Kenya,' 2006, http://www.christianaid.org.uk/indepth.0611climatechange2/kenya_climate_change.pdf

of an Enlightenment-ordained scientism carrying with it the seeds of a psycho-cultural dysfunctionality which can only be cured by a 'renarrativisation' of history founded on a countervailing ecological-cum-ethical consciousness. Like Shaw, Coope challenges both the mantra of economic growth as well as obeisance to assumed modernist technocratic solutions to problems arising from it. The distinction between them is one of perspective: Shaw's approach is overtly green anarchist, Coope's, environmentalist but with an emphasis on the possibility of a psycho-therapeutic breakthrough to fundamental change. But there is another perspective in our final section, that of Biel, who offers a further, Marxist critique of contemporary dysfunction.

Biel's interpretation is all the more striking given that Marxism can be seen as a pronounced product of Enlightenment optimism, not least in its materialist reading of history as leading to a socially equitable, post-capitalist abundance for all humankind. This would seem to put it at some distance from most ecological thinking, with its emphasis on the planet's limited carrying capacity. The disparity is reflected, too, in the resistance of much residual leftist thinking to even consider the climate change challenge.[1] Biel, however, offers a searing analysis of the bankruptcy of capitalism, not as separate from, but entirely explanatory of the drive to planetary nemesis. Carbon emissions, thus, become indicative of the second law of thermodynamics towards entropy which can only be held in check by a social as much as ecological realignment in favour of diversity *and* sustainability.

Biel's analysis is at once profoundly depressing in his charting of the logic inherent in the hegemonic thrust towards planetary self-destruction, yet at the same time encouraging as to how humankind might begin a transitional process from capitalistic entropy to a socialist inspired eco-centrism. Moreover, Biel is not writing in the abstract. At the core of his vision are practical examples of both past and present permaculture, an enthusiasm he shares with an emerging

---

1   See Roman Krznaric, 'Does the Progressive Left really believe in climate change?', Climate Change Denial blog, 7 January 2008, http://climatedenial.org/2008/01/07/does-the-progressive-left-really-believe-in-climate-change/

Transition Towns movement.[1] Transition Towns represent one highly historically-attuned model for effective grass-roots action towards energy descent. On a broader scale, so does Aubrey Meyer's principle of Contraction and Convergence.[2] In seeking a route to an internationally negotiated reduction of carbon emissions to a scientifically-determined stable level founded on the principle of per capita equity, Meyer envisages a timeline in which the necessary global 'convergence' would be dependent on explicit rates of deep emissions ('contraction') made by the high carbon-emitting countries. In other words, Meyer, in considering humanity's predicament in its totality, implicitly highlights the historical imbalance between the powerful, industrialised West and the subordinate South. This, he argues, might only be comprehensively reconciled by a UN-adjudicated process in which the West's annually diminishing entitlement to pollute would be traded in favour of the poorest (lowest carbon-emitting) countries' right to develop: that is until carbon equity—'convergence'—is reached.

The problem is one of time: and we are running out of it, fast. The science is clear that without radical deceleration of greenhouse gas emissions we are set on course for planetary disaster.[3] Yet, for all the reams of information we now possess on climate change, the sort of social transformation necessary to meet the challenge hardly seems achievable on the basis of our current state of consciousness. To arrive there would seem to demand something else: 'some utopian leap, some human rebirth, from Mystery to renewed imaginative life.'[4] The words are that of social historian and activist, E.P. Thompson, not long before his death, writing of that great visionary, William Blake, who broke all the rules to imagine a new post-apoca-

1   Rob Hopkins, *The Transition Handbook, From oil dependency to local resilience* (Dartmouth, Devon: Green Books, 2008). Also http://www.transitiontowns.org
2   See Aubrey Meyer, 'The Case for Contraction and Convergence,' Cromwell and Levene, *Surviving Climate Change*, pp. 29–58.
3   See 'Climate Change: Global Risks', (revised) Synthesis Report of the International Alliance of Research Universities , July 2009, http://www.anu.edu.au/climatechange/wp-content/uploads/2009/07/synthesis_report_-_01072009.pdf for the most recent consensual assessment.
4   E. P. Thompson, *Witness against the Beast, William Blake and the Moral Law* (New York: The New Press, 1993), p. 193

lyptic age for humankind. Should we now feel enjoined to think with Blake, with Thompson, with Meyer and all the other modern—and ancient—prophets about our full *ethical* potential in the world? Such a possibility is embedded historically in all those great transforming movements of previous crisis times, not least Zoroastrianism as practised by the Parsis. It is there, too, in our ability to tell each other stories and of what we might achieve, as Middleton implies in our penultimate piece, if we could think through our full relationship to each other and the natural world.

The disjuncture between the way we have become materially grounded and what is actually required of us is also evident in the final work of Arnold Toynbee, the great historian of the *Oikumene*: 'the habitat of (hu)mankind':

> In the biosphere Man is a psychosomatic being, active within a world that is material and finite. On this plane of human activity, Man's objective, ever since he became conscious, has been to make himself master of his non-human environment, and in our day has come within sight of success in this endeavour – possibly to his own undoing. But Man's other home, the spiritual world, is also an integral part of total reality: it differs from the biosphere in being both non-material and infinite; and in his life in the spiritual world Man finds that his mission is to seek, not for a material mastery over his non-human environment, but for a spiritual mastery over himself.[1]

Will humanity heed Toynbee's prescient evaluation? Our dependency on the purveyors of 'business as usual', would suggest otherwise, whatever dystopian routes they ultimately may choose to follow. What is certain is that we in the West can no longer operate in the comfort zones of our insulated, commodity-rich and stable existences. In the distant past, the onset of danger meant escape to some other safer place, preferably far away from other humans. In more recent times, civilisational collapse plunged sedentary and nomad peoples alike into dark ages. In our own self-induced time of troubles, as environmental breakdown leads to human migrations

---

1 Arnold Toynbee, *Mankind and Mother Earth, A Narrative History of the World* (New York and Oxford: Oxford University Press, 1976), p. 18.

on an unimaginable scale, we will need to draw upon our deepest well of compassion, empathy and basic humanity if we are to avoid a crude descent into savagery. All the more reason why this is not the time to eschew the past but to recognise its great gift to us: the gift of human agency. We can be passive spectators at the self-inflicted demise of our species, or we can be, like the great social movements of history, true visionaries, who through our own actions may yet heal the world.

Part I: Deep History

---

1. Responding to Climate Change: Lessons from our Prehistoric Ancestors

Kate Prendergast

Introduction

What if we could speak to the people who lived in prehistory about their experiences of rapid and extreme changes in the earth's temperature and the effects on their survival strategies and beliefs? This question raises further ones. The first, extensively explored by archaeologists interested in the application of hermeneutics to archaeology, is how we might get prehistoric peoples to 'talk' to us at all when all we have are the remains of their material existence?[1] If we accept we *can* have a dialogue with prehistoric peoples by using this evidence—however ambiguous, open ended and multivalent—a second question arises: what might they say about how they responded to such changes in the earth's climate?

If we cannot rely on science alone as the medium for allowing our ancestors to talk but also need recourse to interpretative assumptions and values, we must acknowledge how far we may be 'putting words into their mouths'. But, the converse is equally true. The available evidence, and the interpretative methods we bring to bear on it, strongly suggests our ancestors have a great deal to 'say' and therefore to teach us, about how to cope with and respond to environmental change in a proactive and positive way.

If this is the case, the power of their voices is dependent on what we choose to hear, how we interpret it and what we do with it. At a

---

1 See for example, Julian Thomas, *Interpretive Archaeology: A Reader* (Leicester: Leicester University Press, 2000).

time when we must *live* with both climate change and our strategies to mitigate it, the response of our ancestors to significant changes in the earth's climate are highly relevant for shedding light on our contemporary social and political priorities.

This essay begins with an account of changes in the earth's climate between the end of the last glacial maximum, c.20,000BC to the onset of the interglacial period known as the Holocene around 9500BC, and their effects on human survival strategies and development. It then goes on to briefly explore interpretations of arguably the most important of these—the onset of agriculture in the Middle East. It concludes by suggesting how these interpretations may help to frame some of the issues at stake for us if we are to respond successfully, and sustainably, to climate change.

Climate change and human adaptations, c.20–9500BC

Throughout prehistory the earth's temperature was subject to massive changes during the protracted glacial and inter-glacial periods that characterise the earth's climate. Such climatic shifts are caused by the interplay between the angle of the earth's axis, changes in its angle and the shape of the earth's path as it orbits the sun. The combined effects of these processes cause the seasons, their severity and the timing of seasonal 'peaks' (the equinoxes and solstices).

These astronomical effects are subject to positive feedback within terrestrial ecology. During glacial periods cool summers in high latitudes prevent snow and ice melting. The eventual consequence is the build up of massive ice sheets. If the earth is covered with snow and ice more of the sun's energy is reflected into space, further cooling temperatures. Moreover, evidence suggests the amount of carbon dioxide in the atmosphere falls as ice sheets grow, further contributing to the cooling of the climate. During inter-glacial periods the opposite process occurs: rising temperatures release more carbon dioxide into the atmosphere, and ice-melt causes the oceans to store more of the sun's energy—leading to yet further temperature rises.

Such extreme climatic events were experienced by our ancestors in relatively recent phases of prehistory. The last glacial maximum occurred between 18–20,000 years ago.[1] Average temperatures in Europe are likely to have fallen to at least 10°C below present day levels. Glaciers expanded rapidly from mountain ranges, covering large areas of northern and central Europe in ice sheets. If the summers were not too different from ours, the winters would have been far colder and more prolonged.

But while archaic humans such as Neanderthals were forced to withdraw into niche environments when faced with the onset of extreme glacial conditions, modern humans had cultural skills such as language, collective logistical planning (for example, of large scale hunting expeditions), flexible and efficient tool kits and the capacity for symbolic representation (art and ritual).[2] As a result, they adapted to the glacial conditions—and prospered. Much of Europe would have resembled tundra and steppe: vast open landscapes, dominated by grasses and with little forest cover, over which huge herds of cold-adapted game such as reindeer, wild horse, steppe bison and woolly mammoth followed regular, predictable migration paths between summer and winter pastures. The exploitation of such animals formed the basis of the lives of these Upper Palaeolithic hunters and gatherers and enabled them to continue to develop their social and cultural presence in Europe, despite the harsh conditions they faced.

One example of the rich and complex cultural life of these groups are the 'Venus' figurines, found in western Europe and as far east as Siberia, which were produced between c.30–10,000 BC.[3] These figures include the extraordinary Venus of Willendorf—discovered at a Palaeolithic site in Austria, and the Venus of Laussel, carved on the wall of a cave in the Dordogne. Such objects testify to the social—and ritual—importance of women and female fertility, and their similar form, reproduced over time at sites hundreds and even thousands of miles apart, attests to the mobility and confidence of these people

1   Paul Mellars, 'The Upper Palaeolithic Revolution', in Barry Cunliffe, ed., *The Oxford Illustrated Prehistory of Europe* (Oxford: Oxford University Press, 1994), pp. 42–3.

2   Clive Gamble, *Timewalkers; the Prehistory of Global Colonization* (Cambridge MA: Harvard University Press, 1994).

3   Paul Bahn and Jean Vertut, *Journey Through The Ice Age* (London: Weidenfeld and Nicolson, 1997).

surviving on the edge of the glacial ice sheets.

This most recent period of repeated glaciation, the Pleistocene, is generally thought to have ended around 10,000 BC, when it gave way to the inter-glacial warm conditions of the Holocene, which continue to dominate the climate today.[1] But this is a somewhat arbitrary date, positioned roughly in the middle of a time lasting several thousand years, during which the earth experienced the dramatic changes associated with the end of glaciation.[2] Warm conditions appear to have dominated c.12–11,000 BC (the Bölling-Allerød). Glacial conditions briefly returned (the Younger Dryas), followed by the onset of the Preboreal of the early Holocene c.9500 BC.

The beginning of the Preboreal was a highly significant global climatic event: in some areas of the world, temperatures rose by at least 7°C within 50 years. Such warming happened with varying rapidity according to latitude, and the full effects of the shift to inter-glacial conditions occurred over several thousand years. However, people across the world were subject to huge environmental changes, often in a short time frame and had to adapt accordingly.

Between the last glacial maximum at around 18,000 BC to around 6000 BC, sea levels rose by about 130 metres. The rise was most pronounced from 12,000 BC, at the onset of the Holocene to the extent of some 35 metres. As a consequence, around 6500 BC, Britain was finally cut off from the continent.[3] However, rising sea levels were accompanied by the isostatic rising of the land, previously depressed by the weight of the ice. In some places in the far north, the effects were so dramatic it left shorelines over 250 metres above the present sea level.

Thus, these processes worked in opposite directions: while land rise liberated new areas to be exploited by flora and fauna, rising sea levels drowned huge existing territories and were responsible for cre-

---

1   Mellars, 'Upper Palaeolithic Revolution', p. 75.
2   Hilary Birks and Brigitta Ammann, 'Two terrestrial records of rapid climatic change during the glacial-Holocene transition (14,000–9,000 calendar years B.P.) from Europe', *Proceedings of the National Academy of Sciences of the United States of America,* 97 (2000), pp. 1390–94.
3   Steven Mithen, 'The Mesolithic Age', in Cunliffe, ed., *Oxford Illustrated Prehistory,* pp. 79-135.

ating the shoreline of the world today. Folk memories of these events may persist in the flood myths of many of the world's ancient mythological cycles.[1]

In the northern hemisphere, much of the open tundra became covered by woodlands.[2] Pollen cores show the succession in tree varieties that became established as the temperature in the Holocene rose and then stabilised. In northern Europe, the early post-glacial landscape was dominated by grasses, shrubs and cold tolerant tree species such as birch, aspen, willow and juniper. As temperatures increased, pine and hazel became dominant and were then followed by the broad-leaf species of oak, lime and elm.

Many of the animal species that had thrived in the glacial landscapes, including woolly rhino, mammoth, and giant deer, became extinct. Other species such as reindeer and elk migrated into far northerly latitudes to be replaced by red deer, roe deer, wild pig and aurochs. Northern oceans also became home to a far wider range of marine vertebrates and fish and freshwater habitats teemed with a rich variety of fish, mammals and birds.

Faced with the loss of their traditional prey, the hunter-gatherers of mainland Europe adopted a variety of strategies. Some groups were forced to push further north into Britain and Scandinavia. As the shoreline of the world today began to emerge, people began to exploit the newly available freshwater and coastal areas, while tending to abandon interior regions with their thick forest cover and fewer natural resources. There were some notable innovations during this period, including the first use of bows and arrows and, in southern Scandinavia, the independent invention of pottery. In some cases, such as at Lepenski Vir on the Danube, groups became sedentary. Overall, however, there was an abundant set of natural resources available to make viable the continuation of age-old hunting and gathering traditions, and for most groups, life continued much as it had before.

---

1   Alan Dundes, ed., *The Flood Myth* (Berkeley: University of California Press, 1988).
2   Mithen, 'Mesolithic Age', pp. 83–6.

Climate change and the beginnings of agriculture

Perhaps the most discussed human innovation, certainly at the onset of the Holocene, and perhaps of the entire prehistoric period, is the early, proto-development of agriculture. Agricultural techniques were developed independently in many parts of the world. However, it was the innovations that were adopted in the Fertile Crescent and the Levant (modern-day Syria, Jordan, Lebanon, Israel, Palestine, Turkey, Iraq and Iran) c.12–8000 BC that led to the eventual spread of the domestication of crops and animals across the Near and Middle East, north Africa, the Mediterranean and eastern and western Europe. The archaeological record in Mesopotamia and the Levant, across such a large timescale, is complex. There is no 'hard and fast' evidence for the ways in which hunter-gatherer groups responded to the environmental changes caused by the varying conditions of the Pleistocene-Holocene transition. Indeed, the relationship between climate change and social and economic innovations in this key area of the 'old world' remains hotly debated.[1] However few scholars doubt that climatic changes and their environmental impacts had a profound effect on the range of strategies employed in the Near and Middle East.

The sequences associated with the Natufian cultures of the Mediterranean Levant provide particular evidence for some extraordinary innovations that appear to be directly related to climate change. Natufian people were among the first hunter-gatherers to adopt a sedentary way of life, establishing large base camps with stone structures in the Mediterranean hills. This seems to have coincided with the warmer and wetter conditions of the Bölling-Allerød interstadial, when forests spread, the availability of fresh water increased and, most importantly perhaps, provided prime conditions

---

1   See for example, Ofer Bar-Yosef and Anna Belfer-Cohen, 'Facing environmental crisis. Societal and cultural changes at the transition from the Younger Dryas to the Holocene in the Levant', in R. T. J. Cappers and S. Bottema, eds, *The Dawn of Farming in the Near East. Studies in Early Near Eastern Production, Subsistence and Environment 6* (Berlin: ex oriente, 2000), pp. 55–66, and Natalie Munro, 'Small game, the younger dryas, and the transition to agriculture in the southern Levant', *Mitteilungen der Gesellschaft für Urgeschichte 12* (2003), pp. 47–71.

for wild cereal growth. With the onset of the much colder and more arid Younger Dryas, the retreat of exploitable habitats and marked fall in the distribution of wild cereal grasses appears to have forced the Natufians to return to more mobile practices in order to survive.[1]

The beginnings of agriculture occur at the transition between the Younger Dryas and the Holocene. This has led some archaeologists to speculate that cultivation began under the stresses engendered towards the end of the cold period. Others however, point to the relationship between rising temperatures and optimal conditions for cereal production to argue that it was the start of the Holocene that kick-started agriculture. Certainly there is no doubt that the shift to domesticated cereal production and animal husbandry was causally related to the changing climate, and it had a powerful effect on social organisation. Populations, even in the earliest Neolithic levels, increased with the sustenance provided by small-scale cultivation, settlements become much larger than in earlier Natufian phases, and more substantial. Some of these early farming settlements, such as Jericho on the West Bank and Catal Huyuk in Anatolia, are seen to be the forerunners of the first cities to emerge in the Fertile Crescent, around 4000 BC.

Agriculture, economics and social relationships

Perhaps the major reason why the origins of agriculture arouse so much interest is because they raise the issue of the long durée: of how far we can read back subsequent developments—such as urbanisation, surpluses and trade—into the earliest cultivation of cereals and domestication of animals. In the 1930s, Vere Gordon Childe used Marxist terminology to describe the beginnings of settlement and domesticated food production, famously coining the phrase 'the Neolithic Revolution.'[2] Childe argued that domestication represented a revolution in economic and technological practices in the classic Marxist sense of one form of economic production being superseded by another. However, Childe's Marxism was distinctly Whiggish

---

1   Munro, 'Small game', pp. 49–61.
2   Vere Gordon Childe, *Man Makes Himself* (London: Watts, 1936).

in kind. With little focus on 'class struggle,' he wanted to highlight the progressive, developmental attributes of this revolution, one that laid the foundations for food surpluses, urban development and trading networks that form the basis of our civilisation. In other words, Childe stressed the primacy of economics in determining social relationships, and saw (European) human history in terms of a steady path of progress and development.

Childe's views dominated prehistoric archaeology in the UK and elsewhere until they were challenged by the rise of the far more scientifically based 'processual' archaeology in the 1960s. However, as Michael Shanks and Christopher Tilley have so effectively demonstrated, much of the theoretical basis for processual archaeology was rooted in logical positivism: a theoretical experiment that was to have disastrous effects for many disciplines, not least for archaeology, since it all but removed the role of the human agent in its attempt to 'systematize' past behaviour according to strict laws.[1]

However, more nuanced critiques of Childe's interpretation have recently emerged. Julian Thomas, in particular, has urged that we cannot take for granted any continuity between our current forms of agriculture and landscape use and those of the early Neolithic.[2] Using this insight as a basis, Thomas has gone on to argue that whereas the reading of Marx employed by Childe assumed that societies are determined by economic production, Marx, in fact, identified an *interplay* between social relationships and subsistence practices. Moreover, the ways people interpret and understand the dynamics of this interplay frequently reside in the realm of social relationships rather than in a separate 'economic' sphere in which they are defined as human subjects.

Developing this line of thought, anthropologists such as Maurice Bloch and Marilyn Strathern have argued that many contemporary tribal societies do not recognise a distinct realm called 'the economy' but mediate production and exchange through social—and often cosmological—relationships, including those based on kinship,

---

1   Michael Shanks and Christopher Tilley, *Reconstructing Archaeology, Theory and Practice* (London: Routledge, 1987).
2   Julian Thomas, *Understanding the Neolithic* (London: Routledge, 1999), pp. 7–12.

gift giving and ritual.[1] For example, on the basis of her fieldwork in Papua New Guinea, Strathern argued that the crucial difference between 'gift exchange' and modern economies is that in gift societies relationships govern the production, exchange and consumption of goods whereas in modern economies production, exchange and consumption govern the way social relationships are understood. In other words, the idea that the economy is a separate sphere that determines personal identity and social relationships is a modern, Western one.[2]

Because Childe made this assumption, he failed to engage with the ways in which the transition to agriculture may have been understood in terms of relationships—between people, between people and animals, and between people and the natural world.

There is certainly strong material evidence to indicate that early agriculture was understood in terms of complex and dynamic relationships between people, animals and natural forces. At sites such as Catal Huyuk, small scale cultivation and husbandry was practiced in a landscape that was still largely wild. Moreover, the layout, decoration, material culture and evidence for ritual at the site indicates a society concerned, obsessed even with the interplay between the domestic and the wild. James Mellaart, the original excavator at Catal, discovered many female figurines, including a seated woman flanked by two lions.[3] Murals on the interior and exterior walls depict groups of hunting men, hunted animals and vultures swooping down on headless bodies. Ian Hodder, the current director of excavations at the site, interprets this evidence in terms of societies attempting to negotiate and come to terms with the domestication of what was still understood as a very 'wild' world.[4]

Similar themes are evident in the ways agriculture spread from

1   Jonathon Parry and Maurice Bloch, eds, *Money and the Morality of Exchange* (Cambridge: Cambridge University Press, 1989); Marilyn Strathern, *The Gender of the Gift* (Berkeley: University of California Press, 1988).

2   Anthony Giddens, *A Contemporary Critique of Historical Materialism, 1: Power, Property and the State* (London: Macmillan, 1981).

3   James Mellaart, Catal Huyuk, *A Neolithic Town in Anatolia* (London: Thames and Hudson, 1967).

4   Ian Hodder, *The Domestication of Europe* (Oxford: Blackwells, 1990), pp. 1–19.

its core area across southern and northern Europe. Across Europe, take up of agricultural practices by indigenous groups was slow and variable. As Julian Thomas, Richard Bradley and others have argued, this take up was not understood simply in terms of a transition from one form of economic subsistence to another.[1] Instead, such groups showed a similar concern as at Catal to interpret and understand 'domestication' in terms of the cosmological relationships that helped shape their understanding of the landscape and its use. In Britain for example, this included an emphasis on traditional pathways through the landscape, on the social and ritual exchange value of domesticated products such as cattle, on the veneration of natural features such as rocky outcrops and on the development of an elaborate megalithic culture.

Climate change and the beginnings of agriculture: lessons for today?

Thus, more recent interpretative approaches in both archaeology and anthropology do not support Childe's interpretation of domestication solely as an economic response to a changing climate. Instead, they point to how complex relationships governed the ways in which the transition to agriculture was mediated and understood. Indeed, evidence such as that at Catal Huyuk would indicate that these relationships were experienced within cosmological and ritual world views, in which the natural world—of changing temperatures and seasons, plants and animals—had significant power over human groups and their capacity to survive.

Such world views are arguably very different from those of our own contemporary societies, which have a greater tendency to define individuals and the relationships between them within specifically 'economic' spheres of activity. At the same time, the issue of the long durée cannot be completely abandoned either. The transition to agriculture was a remarkably successful adaptation to a changing climate. Once it had become established, settlements, cultivation and monu-

---

1   See for example, Richard Bradley, *The Significance of Monuments* (London: Routledge, 1998).

ments 'fixed' points in the landscape and within a few thousand years our practices on and over it had changed that landscape irrevocably.

The key question, however is what relevance does this interpretation of the onset of agriculture have in furthering our understanding of an anthropogenically causal responsibility for today's changing climate while also enabling us to both mitigate and, or adapt to it?

The modern Western view that economics defines our relationships supports the claim that the driving force behind contemporary climate change is a belief in the primacy of developmental economics. This sees the natural world largely in terms of the resources that can be extracted from it for human consumption.[1] This belief was not shared by our ancestors, who responded to a changing climate far more in terms of the veneration of the power of natural processes. Indeed, evidence for a 'mother goddess', for ritual contexts for exchange and the power of the wild landscape indicates societies looking back to their ancient hunter-gatherer traditions as much as forward to an increasingly cleared, 'tamed' and utilised landscape.

This difference of views may explain why our ancestors' responses to a changing climate were so successful, and—thus far—why our responses are so inadequate. Indeed, if the greatest threat facing small scale prehistoric groups was their closeness to the natural world, it also proved to be their biggest strength because they worked with nature rather than ignoring its power. In contrast, our greatest threat (in the Western world, at least) lies in our belief that our relationship to nature is purely economic and that we can be buffered from its worst effects by the wealth we have extracted from it. This is not likely to be a strength upon which we can draw to successfully mitigate and adapt to climate change, because, in reality, it will be almost impossible to protect either ourselves or our wealth from the kinds of environmental changes we may be subject to if temperatures rise beyond 2°C.

In this sense, the beliefs and practices of 'other' groups, whether of those who lived in prehistory or in the contemporary world, represent a highly valuable resource upon which we need to draw for guidance

---

1   See for example, George Monbiot, *Heat: How to Stop the Planet Burning* (London: Allen Lane, 2006).

about 'what to do' about climate change. Such beliefs—about the living qualities of nature—reveal a respect for its power to be both tamed and wild, to both give and take away. These, along with the practices of localised agriculture and the sustainable occupation of the landscape, are the ways of living, so powerfully expressed in the symbolism and ritual of the first farmers, which enabled prehistoric peoples to adapt to a fast-changing natural world. It is exactly the same values upon which our lives, like theirs, still depend.

Part II: Harbingers of the End

2. We'll cope, Mankind always has: The Fall of Rome and the Cost of Crisis

Bryan Ward-Perkins

The Romans and the Environment

The Roman period, and its end, offer sobering messages to the present day. They are sobering, above all, because the Roman example makes it quite clear (if this was ever in doubt) that the human urge to destroy the natural environment is very old—perhaps even embedded within our genetic makeup. It was only a lack of technology, and the comparatively small areas of the world that were then 'developed', that saved the planet from a dramatic environmental crisis some 2000 years earlier than the one we are now experiencing. An essential variable in our present crisis—the urge to destroy in the name of progress or profit—was very firmly in place.

This is clearly shown by evidence from three very different sites that have recently been investigated to shed light on the extent and impact of Roman mining and metal-working. The first is in the Jordanian pre-desert, the valley of the Wadi Faynan.[1] Here were rich veins of copper ore, already exploited in pre-Roman times but worked with particular intensity under the empire. These mines, like many in the Roman period, were at least partly dependent on convict labour, and acquired notoriety in Christian sources as one of the places where the faithful who had refused to bow to pagan persecution suffered and died. A recent extensive archaeological survey and

---

[1] Graeme Barker, David Gilbertson and David Mattingley, eds, *Archaeology and Desertification: The Wadi Faynan Landscape Survey, Southern Jordan* (Oxford: Oxbow Books, 2007).

analysis of the area has indeed confirmed the brutality and human cost of the place—some of the underground workings, for instance, have unnaturally small openings to the outside world, probably in order to hinder convict break-out.[1] But, more significant for our purposes, the recent research has also shown how the mining wrought extensive and long-lasting environmental damage. Palaeo-botanical studies have shown that copper smelting involved stripping the valley floor, and, almost certainly, the plateau above, of all combustible vegetation, thereby initiating a devastating process of desertification.[2] On top of this, the valley floor was also heavily polluted by large quantities of copper waste. In both instances—the desertification and the pollution—the damage has lasted until the present day. A survey of wild barley growing on the valley floor showed that plants growing nearest the site of ancient copper smelting produced only half the average number of seeds (14) as those growing a kilometre away (28).[3]

Right at the other end of the empire, in north-western Spain in the modern province of Léon, there is very different, but equally dramatic evidence of what the Romans could do, and chose to do, when the gains were high enough and where suitable technology existed. Here at a site known as Las Médulas, impressive enough to have been designated a UNESCO World Heritage site, is an extraordinary landscape of hills that look as if they have been half-eaten by giants. This was as a result of Roman goldmines, where the ore was extracted by a remarkable and highly damaging technique, the aptly named *ruina montium* ('the ruin of mountains').[4] Large quantities of water were brought to the site along an elaborate system of aqueducts, stored behind dams, and then used both to wash away overbur-

1   Barker, Gilbertson and Mattingley, *Archaeology*, p. 312.
2   Barker, Gilbertson and Mattingley, *Archaeology*, pp. 345–6 and 409. The impact of iron-age and Roman metal extraction is described as 'a sustained local ecological catastrophe whose consequences are still with us today'.
3   Barker, Gilbertson and Mattingley, *Archaeology*, pp. 86–9.
4   The term is derived from Pliny the Elder (writing in the first century A.D.), who describes the use of water for mining in Spain in some detail, and had probably witnessed it in action: Pliny, *Natural History*, XXXIII, xxi. See the H. Rackham translated, Loeb Classical Library edition (Cambridge MA. and London: Harvard University Press and William Heinemann, 1952) Vol. IX, pp. 51–61.

den and to flood galleries cut in the hillside, provoking the desired *ruina montium*. More water was then used to extract the gold from the collapsed soil and to evacuate the waste down into the valley below.[1] Without the aid of mechanical excavators or explosives, at Las Médulas whole hills were chewed up, and spewed out, by Roman mining operations.

The third location we are going to look at, the Greenland ice-cap, might at first sight seem an implausible place to find evidence of Roman metal extraction and metal working. But over the centuries, as snow has fallen over Greenland it has captured traces of atmospheric pollution, brought them to ground, and preserved them in a deep and cumulative layer-cake, which modern scientists have bored through, analysed and dated, thereby enabling them to document changing patterns of air pollution over the centuries. Strikingly, but unsurprisingly given the evidence from sites like Wadi Faynan and Las Médulas, the Roman period deposits, around 500 metres below the present surface, reveal a marked peak in lead and copper pollution, which then declined impressively and was not subsequently exceeded until the time of the Industrial Revolution.[2]

These three sites demonstrate conclusively that pollution and environmental damage are not new phenomena. However, fortunately for us, the Romans did not have access to the destructive powers of steam and of the internal combustion engine, and the only thing they could burn was wood—though Las Médulas shows that they could use water, their only source of mechanical power on land, to devastat-

---

1   Claude Domergue, 'L'eau dans les mines d'or romaines du Nord-Ouest de l'Espagne,' in Pierre Louis and F. and J. Métral, eds, *L'homme et l'eau en Méditerranée et au Proche Orient*, Vol. 3, L'eau dans les techniques (= Travaux de la Maison de l'Orient, 11, Lyon, 1986), pp. 109–19. F.-Javier Sanchez-Palencia, ed., *Las Médulas (León). Un paisaje cultural en la Asturia Augustana* (León: Instituto Léones de Cultura, 2000).

2   Sungmin Hong, Jean-Pierre Candelone, Clair C. Patterson and Claude F. Boutron, 'History of ancient copper smelting pollution during Roman and medieval times recorded in Greenland ice', *Science* 272 (1996), pp. 246-9; Sungmin Hong, Jean-Pierre Candelone, Clair C. Patterson and Claude F. Boutron, 'Greenland ice evidence of hemispheric lead pollution two millennia ago by Greek and Roman civilization', *Science* 265 (1994), pp. 1841-3. See also Barker, Gilbertson and Mattingley, *Archaeology*, p. 95, fig. 3.19.

ing effect.[1] Consequently, the damage the Romans were able to inflict on the environment was limited, not by a lack of will, but by a lack of technological capacity. It has been estimated, for instance, that, over the 800-year period of Greek and Roman civilization, on average an impressive half metric ton of lead fall-out was deposited every year over Greenland. However, in the sixty years between 1930 and 1990 (when lead pollution from petrol was at its height) the annual level may have been a full 100 times greater.[2] Sadly, thanks to our mastery of technology, we are in a different league to the Romans, all our own.

Collapse is Possible

What happened at the end of the Roman empire should also give us pause for thought, because it shows that disaster is possible. I discussed this in a book published in 2005, and even produced a foolhardy graph to illustrate, in the broadest possible brushstrokes, what happened to the sophisticated economy of the Roman period in five different regions of the empire when imperial power disintegrated in the fifth to seventh centuries.[3] My book has received some harsh criticism, some of it justified, over important details: for instance, that it exaggerates the extent of collapse in certain regions, that it fails to discuss decline before the end of Roman rule, and that it identifies too obviously with Roman upper-class lifestyles.[4] But the basic picture I outline—of extensive and almost universal economic decline in the post-Roman centuries—seems to be generally accepted, including

---

1 The remains of an aqueduct and mill were also identified in the Wadi Faynan, possibly to crush ore mechanically: Barker, Gilbertson and Mattingley, *Archaeology*, pp. 316–17.

2 Hong, Candelone, Patterson and Boutron, 'Greenland ice evidence'.

3 Bryan Ward-Perkins, *The Fall of Rome and the End of Civilization* (Oxford: Oxford University Press 2005), pp. 87–137, where most of what follows is fleshed out in more detail, with supporting references.

4 The most critical reviews, all by excellent scholars, have been the following: Garth Fowden in *Journal of Roman Archaeology* 19 (2006), pp. 706–8 ('grumpy', 'a veritable hymn to pots'); Guy Halsall in *Early Medieval Europe* 16 (2008), pp. 384–6 (a 'bracing and sometimes entertaining rant'); Walter Pohl in *English Historical Review* 124 (2009), pp. 109–11 (the author 'has fallen behind the state of the art').

the argument that in some parts of the empire the decline was precipitate and dramatic, in both its extent and speed.

In fifth-century Britain, within a few decades, whole industries disappeared. Some of these, like the craft of the mosaicist, were undeniably of marginal economic importance, and closely tied to rarefied elite markets, but others were much more basic and reached much lower down the social scale. The best documented of these, because its products survive so well in the soil, is the production of pottery. Third- and fourth-century Britain had a number of different production sites, producing good quality table-wares, shaped on the wheel, decorated with slip, and fired in kilns, which were sold over a wide geographical region and are found in the graves of wholly unremarkable people. In the early fifth century all these industries completely disappeared—west Britain was left with almost no ceramics at all, while the south-east of the island had to make do with very crude and friable pots, hand-shaped and poorly fired. Alongside the disappearance of specialised manufacturing, there are also other indicators of dramatic economic decline. The use of coinage as a medium of exchange, which had been widespread in Roman Britain (both in precious metals and in copper for small-change), virtually disappeared, and by A.D. 500 at the very latest there were no towns left that a fourth-century Roman would have recognised as urban. In my book, and again this seems to be widely accepted, I argue that fifth-century Britain relapsed to economic conditions even less developed than those of the immediately pre-Roman Iron Age (which had, for instance, the beginnings of pottery-industries, of native coinages, and of towns serving both political and trading functions).[1] Measured chronologically, the economy of fifth-century Britain regressed, very rapidly, by perhaps 500 years—the equivalent of dropping seventeenth-century Britain back into the twelfth century.

Other parts of the empire saw similarly precipitate economic decline: the Balkans at the end of the fourth and in the fifth centuries; and, more surprising (because here economic sophistication had been established since long before the Roman conquest), the Aegean world at the end of the sixth and in the early seventh century. In

---

1   Ward-Perkins, *Fall of Rome*, pp. 118–20.

the Aegean some economic sophistication continued—for instance, a degree of urban life in centres like Corinth, Athens, Smyrna and Ephesos, and some specialised production of pottery and other staple goods. But the overall picture is of huge change. Many of the great cities of Antiquity, like Perge and Side in Pamphylia, filled with classical monuments and Christian churches, were more-or-less abandoned, a state in which they remained until mass-tourism and archaeology once more populated them, though now only with day-trippers taking a break from their sun-loungers.

I do not think natural or man-made environmental degradation played a central role in these changes, because, as I have argued above, humans probably still lacked the technology needed to be truly destructive on a large scale. Warfare and insecurity were the most obvious drivers of change in the three areas where it was most sudden and most dramatic—Britain, the Balkans and the Aegean. But what is important for our purposes here, is to realise that complex economic structures, which contemporaries probably thought were as stable as we believed our own to be until 2008, can unravel disastrously, if faced with an overwhelming crisis. In the case of the post-Roman world, it was the break-up of the empire and the end of the *pax romana* that did this; in the twenty-first century something similar, or something different, could achieve the same—perhaps complete freefall in our banking and credit systems, or environmental breakdown and the human maelstrom that this could unleash.

The experience of the Roman world and, to a lesser extent our own experience in 2008-09, shows that economic sophistication is no protection against disaster. Indeed, as I explain in my book, in the case of the Roman empire it was precisely the economic complexity that preceded the crash that provoked the extraordinary scale of the subsequent downturn. Romans had got used to buying their high quality goods and services from specialised producers, sometimes working hundreds of miles away, and these producers, in turn, depended on large and diffuse markets to sustain their specialised production. When this complex web of economic interdependences began to unravel, as it did at the end of the Roman empire, the crash was much deeper and more prolonged than if all production had been small-scale and local. Our own, far greater degree of economic sophistication and complexity makes us immeasurably more vulnerable.

3. People, climate and landscape in medieval Iceland and beyond

Chris Callow

Introduction

The fragility of the modern Icelandic economy became tragically clear in 2008. For this small country what had seemed an economic miracle in the preceding decade turned abruptly to economic disaster as its indebted banks bore the brunt of a global financial collapse. In the short term this has brought one of the world's wealthiest countries to its knees. Where there had been economic growth, work opportunities for migrant labour and widespread wealth, there has been an exodus of a significant proportion of the foreign workforce, growing unemployment and an unprecedented need for social services. Sadly, this course of events says a lot about the restrictions on Iceland's ability to sustain its population both now and throughout its 1100-year history.

In the light of climate change projections, this is particularly significant not least as some experts have suggested that during the twenty-first century northern Europe will be overrun by people from further south as southern Europe and the Mediterranean region becomes too arid to support human life.[1] Superficially, Iceland might seem like one logical place of refuge. As global temperatures rise it could become an easier place in which to survive. Looking at Iceland's history however, might suggest a series of warning signs which we would ignore only at our peril.

What follows is an attempt to understand how successfully

---

1   Martin L. Parry, Osvaldo F. Canziani, Jean P. Palutikof, Paul J. van der Linden and Clair E. Hanson, eds, Climate Change 2007: *Impacts, Adaptation and Vulnerability. Contribution of Working Group II to the Fourth Assessment Report of the Intergovernmental Panel on Climate Change* (Cambridge: Cambridge University Press, 2007), p. 676.

Icelanders have coped with the restrictions their landscape and climate have imposed on them. I will also ask what lessons can be
learned from studying their attempts to adapt to what was once a
completely new and empty landscape; the effects of climatic change
and man's activities have made this an ever-changing environment.

Why did the Vikings colonise Iceland?

Iceland is an unusual place. It was first colonised as part of the Viking
expansion from Scandinavia in the ninth century but it still had less
than 100,000 people in 1900.[1] It is a country larger than Ireland, but
its climate, landscape, soils and natural resources pose significant
limits on human activities. Most human settlement has been confined to the country's coastal lowland because the interior is relatively mountainous, cold and otherwise inhospitable. Icelanders have
supported themselves primarily by raising sheep and cattle and by
exploiting the sea.

Historians and archaeologists have long been trying to understand
just why so many people left Scandinavia either to raid or settle other
places in the ninth and tenth centuries. We have very limited evidence on which to try to gauge what was probably a complex process. On the one hand it is easy to suggest a whole range of general
push and pull factors; on the other it is harder to understand exactly
why particular groups went at particular times from any one place to
another. Most experts would probably still see the Viking phenomenon as having overlapping, but slightly different causes according
to where 'the Vikings' came from, where they went to and whether
they only raided briefly or emigrated permanently (or both). Swedes,
Danes and Norwegians cannot always be separated, but there are still
some clear patterns.

Swedes mostly went east and raided, traded and settled in eastern Europe, exploiting connections with the Byzantine empire (effectively modern Greece and Turkey); they do not concern us here.
Many groups of Danes seem to have raided and traded in western

---

1   Gunnar Karlsson, *The History of Iceland* (Minneapolis: University of Minnesota
Press, 2000), p. 229.

Europe—following the cliché—before successfully taking political control in the British Isles and Normandy. In England, most notably, there was a military takeover of many regions, as well as a peasant migration, which has influenced language and culture in many ways.[1]

Iceland was different. It seems most likely that the country was settled by, at best, a moderately wealthy cross-section of Scandinavian society—despite the claims of later generations of medieval Icelanders that they had illustrious ancestors. The archaeological evidence from early Icelandic graves and settlements implies a very strong Norwegian influence from the beginning. The linguistic evidence also points to a strong Norwegian presence—Old Icelandic and Old Norwegian were virtually indistinguishable. Literary evidence and the geography of the North Atlantic both suggest that some of the colonists of this previously empty country had spent time in the British Isles before reaching Iceland. Recent (but preliminary) genetic studies of modern populations have pointed towards a very strong Irish component to the Icelandic gene pool, but Norwegians probably made up the majority of the population and the politically dominant group from the outset.[2]

Why, then, would Norwegians take the bold step of leaving the security of home for somewhere as far away as Iceland? Again, medieval Icelanders had a firm but probably exaggerated explanation: to escape the growing power of the Norwegian king who threatened the power of other regional overlords. Other, more mundane explanations were probably at the root of the migration and, in one way or another, they had some connection to climate. All the indications are that the period c.900 to c.1250 was a relatively mild one in northwestern Europe and, so, sometimes known as the Medieval Warm Period. While individuals may have had no awareness that this was the case, it was probably a fundamental reason why Iceland and the North Atlantic region seemed less hostile than it had seemed to earlier generations. Later Icelanders, for instance, made a point of retelling stories about 'the good old days' of the colonisation period when

---

1   Dawn Hadley, *The Vikings in England* (Manchester: Manchester University Press, 2007).

2   Agnar Helgason et al, 'Estimating Scandinavian and Gaelic ancestry in the male settlers of Iceland', *American Journal of Human Genetics,* 67 (2000), pp. 697–717.

cereal crops were grown, as they clearly could not be by the thirteenth and fourteenth centuries. It seems likely that the saga stories
depicted past realities just as they recorded the decline in woodland
which we can now measure using archaeology and other historical
material.

For people from Norway and the British Isles, the North Atlantic
may have seemed like a good place to settle, but it must still have
been a major effort for them to get there. They must have had a reason
to leave their homes behind. The conflict alluded to above, between
warring Scandinavian overlords, was probably a real one. Early
medieval politics always produced winners and losers and no doubt
some of those losers, equipped with the knowledge of somewhere
new and hospitable to live, and with serfs and slaves to build boats,
fight and farm, had the ability to get to Iceland. Not all Icelanders
may have had the illustrious ancestors that they would later claim,
but there were probably many moderately successful lords who left
Norway to go west.

Still, the indirect cause of this warfare may have had its roots
partly in the Medieval Warm Period. No historian would now claim
climate change as the *sole* underlying cause of the increase in population which western Europe witnessed in the Middle Ages—if that
were the case then we might expect an increased food supply, caused
by better growing conditions in a temperate region, to support more
people. Yet what is more likely to have happened was ever greater
incentive for lords and their military retinues to try to capture each
other's growing resources: in the face of such aggression people may
well have chosen to leave Scandinavia. It would be too simplistic to
argue just that population growth began everywhere to outstrip food
supplies. People may not have fought and moved because they were
on the verge of starvation but rather because life was getting less
comfortable. At some places at some times, then, it may have seemed
like it was worth moving to somewhere new because life would be
easier or better.

Of the potential destinations, Iceland was a difficult option because
it involved a long and dangerous sea crossing. Once there, of course,
it would have been worth it for the earliest settlers. Based on our cur-

rent evidence it is difficult to gauge accurately the social status of the first generations of settlers. Whatever their status in their homelands, the very earliest colonists seem to have divided the lowlands up into large estates and, quite soon, set up their own farms at locations which provided the maximum range of natural resources. Relative late-comers, arriving in the mid-tenth century perhaps, would have found a country already carved up into large estates owned by other people.[1] There was still plenty of room for those arriving later to be given a small farm in the lowlands, and plenty of space in the uplands for everyone's sheep to graze.

Iceland may not quite have been the promised land, even to ninth-century Norwegians in a hurry to live somewhere else, but the relatively mild climate of the time and its undisturbed landscape meant it still had things going for it. It had untouched birch woodlands, ungrazed lowland meadows, undug peat and unfished salmon and trout rivers. On top of these, the country had resources which to the modern, non-Icelander might seem unusual, but which were equally vital: vast numbers of sea birds and their eggs for food and down, seals and walruses for meat and skins, and seaweed for food, fuel or fodder for animals.

Faced with their new landscape, the problem for Iceland's Viking-Age colonists was to learn how the ecosystem worked. They had to make judgements about how to manage resources in an environment which looked very similar to the ones they had left behind, but which, ultimately, proved to react differently to the way they expected. Like us, their confidence about what they thought their environment could provide for them was entirely out of kilter with its actual capacity.

How well did Icelanders understand and manage their landscape?

The search for answers to this question has been one of the most exciting areas of new research in European archaeology in the last thirty years. Unfortunately the Viking colonisation of the North Atlantic has been relatively poorly studied in comparison with other

---

1   Orri Vésteinsson, 'Patterns of settlement in Iceland: a study in prehistory', *Saga-Book*, 25 (1998), pp. 1–29.

well-known European migrations. In recent decades, however, teams of archaeologists and environmental scientists have started to answer major questions about the human impact on Iceland's landscape and ecology.

The general picture is self-evident: man has had a damaging effect on the landscape. Any visitor to rural Iceland will have spotted signs of erosion and landslips which are the product of a loss of soil cover. But there the serious research questions begin. How much was this erosion a natural process and how much of it was down to overgrazing by sheep, goats or pigs? What was the impact of deforestation? What kinds of farming practices did the first colonists implement? To what extent did these practices change and why? Were they a response to early signs of erosion problems and how exactly did these begin? Has the process slowed down at any stage? Or was it accelerated, or perhaps decelerated, by particular climatic conditions? Of more immediate relevance, what are the implications today given that sheep farming is still a significant part of the Icelandic economy?

For many years our understanding of man's activities was limited to educated guesswork based on written sources. Sources such as sagas, annals, letters and tax registers are still referred to, but now with a greater appreciation of their limitations. And, since archaeological work first began, researchers' theories and questions have changed significantly. The 'old' view of the whole process has been neatly summarised in a recent research paper by Tom McGovern and colleagues:[1]

- The first colonists settled close to the coast and gradually settlement spread inland along river valleys to the uplands
- Those first colonists took large areas of land and gave out chunks of their estate to members of their entourage who became independent farmers
- The human impact on the ecosystem was 'immediate and severe'
- Native woodland was almost completely exhausted within

---

1   Thomas McGovern et al, 'Landscapes of Settlement in Northern Iceland: Historical Ecology of Human Impact and Climate Fluctuation on the Millennial Scale', *American Anthropologist*, 109 (2007), pp. 27–51, 30.

the first centuries of colonisation

- Common upland pasture was mismanaged so that eroded soils accumulated on lowland pastures
- Climatic cooling in the later middle ages compounded all the problems caused by man's damage to the fragile landscape
- The drive by Iceland's land-owning elite for increased revenue from those reduced to the position of tenant farmers drove those tenants to farm in an unsustainable way

Recent research has challenged some of this story and also shown that understanding the relationship between man, the landscape and the climate is more complex than we had once thought.

That Iceland's first colonists did not explore the country, or think about where they might settle, is the first idea which can be jettisoned. Archaeological and historical research has shown that inland regions were settled just as early as coastal ones. It looks as if settlers sought out what they thought were good natural resources, wherever they happened to be. Inland, around Lake Mývatn in the north east, people were permanently settled and making use of the lake's resources and the local woodland.[1] In the upper parts of the Borgarfjörður valley system in the west it looks as if the earliest, large farms clustered around good meadows for grazing cattle rather than simply being at the mouth of the estuary.[2]

Without the benefit of archaeological excavation on a vast scale, nor early contemporary historical evidence—the sagas were written much later than the early events they claim to depict—it is still hard to assess the nature of early political structures in Iceland. Yet it is also clear that historians' interpretations of the sagas have been affected by nationalistic Icelandic views from the nineteenth and early twentieth centuries. Claims for the independence of Icelandic farmers when the country was first colonised suited their cause when they were struggling for independence from Denmark, but now are seen as a misreading of the evidence. Current views tend towards seeing Iceland's tenurial pattern as one more akin to that found in

1   McGovern, 'Landscapes,' pp. 34–5.
2   Vésteinsson, 'Patterns of settlement'.

mainland Europe. In other words, Iceland had lords and tenants from the beginning; those 'independent' farmers and their farms were most likely legally dependent. The implications of this for landscape degradation are not always clear, but we might surmise that as land-management decision-making was made by relatively small, self-perpetuating elites it is likely to have had a more dramatic effect, for better or worse, than if it had been more decentralised.

The view that landscape degradation took place suddenly, almost as soon as Iceland was colonised, has also been challenged by recent research. The timing and scale of change seems to have varied from place to place, even at the level of individual settlements. For example, two farms close to Lake Mývatn in north-east Iceland seem to have witnessed completely contrary patterns of cultivation. At the first farm, Hofstaðir, careful management of local grasslands and woodlands has enabled the farm to survive to the present, continuously occupied. At the other, known as Sveigakot, the landscape was probably exhausted by the time it was abandoned not long after 1200.[1] Hofstaðir is more likely to have been run by an owner-occupier, Sveigakot by a tenant farmer, which may help to explain why they were apparently managed in different ways.

Patterns of deforestation now also look to have been more complex than was once thought, but the end result was still one of acute soil erosion. Recent research in the district of Eyjafallahreppur in the south of Iceland has shown that charcoal was produced at a wide range of locations and at different times. It looks as if the woodlands here were managed to some extent: coppiced birch trees were cut down in the spring each year, but at different periods, within the years 900 to 1300. Not all the birch woodland was exhausted immediately.[2] That said, the region still witnessed significant erosion during this period and the most likely cause was the removal of the birch woodlands.

What is missing from the picture above, but is intimately linked

---

1   Orri Vésteinsson, *Archaeological Investigations at Sveigakot 1998–2000*, FS134–00211. Unpublished archaeological site report, Reykjavík.
2   Mike Church et al, 'Charcoal production during the Norse and early medieval periods in Eyjafjallahreppur, Southern Iceland', *Radiocarbon*, 49 (2007), pp. 659–72.

to it, is that Iceland's population was heavily dependent on its live-stock. Occasional references in the written sources give the impression that thirteenth-century Icelanders understood that their fore-fathers had brought a wider range of animals with them than were reared in later centuries. The careful recording of animal bones, discovered scattered across archaeological sites and in rubbish heaps, has helped produce an ever more detailed picture of what is likely to have happened. In broad outline we can see that farming practices really did change so that a typically, fairly diverse colonist's farm evolved into one which depended mostly on sheep. Cattle, pigs and goats all declined in number—pigs and goats rapidly and almost completely—as sheep became an ever more important element in people's diet and wool products more important as an export. The speed and cause of this process is what is interesting for our understanding of man's relationship with the landscape and climate. It used to be assumed, for example, that people had allowed pigs and goats, renowned for their destructive effects, to destroy the native birch woodland. Instead, the archaeological evidence would now suggest that, in some parts of Iceland, pigs and goats disappeared before deforestation became severe. In other words, people may have been well aware of the damage that was being done and deliberately tried to change the nature of their herds to prevent deforestation. Unfortunately, this does not seem to have slowed down the inexorable landscape degradation wrought by human occupation.

Without doubt Iceland's colonists did understand that there were ways to try to improve the lowland pastures they used. As in many societies, farmers in the North Atlantic region were heavily dependent on manure as the key to sustaining soil fertility. For pastoralists in Iceland, the aim was to improve hay yields which in turn would allow them to provide better or bulkier feed for livestock over the long winter when there was little or no fodder. Recent research has tried to measure the impact of manuring, making use of computer models based on soil samples taken from hay-fields in north-east Iceland. This data suggests that the colonists, if they had added manure to their hay-fields, would have seen reasonable improvements in yields. However, only the next couple of generations of farmers after them could have made any further improvement.[1] This levelling-off of hay yields must go a long way to explaining the fact that eighteenth-century livestock levels look surprisingly similar to those from the earliest medieval figures. The environment's limitations seem to have been too powerful for Icelanders to overcome; it was only in the twentieth century that modern agrichemicals and large-scale drainage schemes were able to increase crop yields.

Climate and environmental restraints

Although recent research has emphasised the fact that medieval Icelanders *did* sometimes attempt to manage the landscape, it has also been possible to determine what they could not control. Climate variability may have been the key issue. Estimates of how much grazing was available to livestock, measured alongside known numbers of beasts owned, suggest that there probably never were so many sheep as to cause generalised overgrazing of the upland. Instead, the critical issue seems to have been the timing of the autumn sheep round-up, that is their removal from the uplands to the lowlands winter pasture. If the sheep were rounded up before temperatures started to drop significantly and grass growth had slowed, then all might be well. If they were allowed to graze for too long at the end of the season then this would have prevented sustainable vegetation growth, resulting in soil erosion and loss of the pasture altogether.[2] In this respect, climate really does appear to have been a significant factor. There seems every reason to believe that Iceland's medieval farmers were used to dealing with variations in temperature and rainfall, but the real problem may have been their lack of ability to determine longer-term changes in conditions. How could any of us in such a situation identify subtle changes in climate? A single bad year or couple of years

1   W. Paul Adderley, Ian A. Simpson & Orri Vésteinsson, 'Local-Scale Adaptations: A Modelled Assessment of Soil, Landscape, Microclimatic, and Management Factors in Norse Home-Field Productivities' *Geoarchaeology*, 23 (2008), pp. 500–27.
2   Ian A. Simpson et al, 'Crossing the thresholds: human ecology and historical patterns of landscape degradation', *Catena*, 42 (2001), pp. 175–92.

could be identified as such and, indeed, very dramatic environmental change was remembered, for example, the sagas' collective insistence on the disappearance of woodland. Yet if, decade by decade, people did not notice that the growing season in uninhabited uplands areas had reduced ever so slightly, then it could have had severe consequences on the landscape. Working out what was 'normal' became more and more difficult.[1]

Taking the whole of the period up to 1800, our proxy climate data is now good enough to suggest that there really were some substantial, short-term shifts in weather patterns. Key periods of change seem to have been from 980 to 1040 and 1425 to 1525.[2] These two time spans seem to have been periods where the weather was increasingly stormy. Such conditions would have made farming difficult for even the most astute pastoralist, given that accumulated knowledge would not have suggested to anyone that farming practices needed to change.

We can set alongside the significance of unpredictability the fact that more general climate cooling does not seem to have been sufficient on its own to cause natural vegetation change. The Medieval Warm Period has been mentioned above but we must not forget the other, better-known Little Ice Age which followed. When the former ended and the latter began is a matter of some debate—and it might be that the answer(s) depend a great deal on where we are talking about—but it certainly seems that there was generalised cooling in Iceland from c.1300 to c.1900, but with some decades which were notably milder.[3] Recognising these patterns, and having a variety of 'proxy' ways of measuring possible changes, has led to attempts to

---

1   This is a slightly different contention that dramatic changes provide a community with a collective understanding of the possibility of environmental change. For this argument see F. Hassan, 'Environmental Perception and Human Responses in History and Prehistory', in Roderick J. McIntosh, Joseph A. Tainter and Susan Keech McIntosh, eds, *The Way the Wind Blows. Climate, History and Human Action* (New York, 2000), pp. 131–4.

2   Andrew J. Dugmore et al, 'The Role of Climate in Settlement and Landscape Change in the North Atlantic Islands: An Assessment of Cumulative Deviations in High-Resolution Proxy Climate Records', *Human Ecology*, 35 (2007), pp. 169–78.

3   Astrid E.J. Ogilvie & Tinna Jónsson, '"Little Ice Age" research: a perspective from Iceland', *Climatic Change*, 48 (2001), pp. 9–52.

measure the possible impacts of temperature change on vegetation. Some of the most recent work is instructive because it suggests that the scale of change which took place during the Little Ice Age was not sufficient to alter vegetation patterns of its own accord.[1] This not only chimes in with the argument that it was grazing patterns that were the problem in the past, but also offers food for thought about future temperature rises. In the absence of humans, it is suggested that temperature drops of 2.5° celsius would have been required to make the same kind of impact on the southern Icelandic landscape as have been observed. We might speculate that it will take similarly significant rises in temperature, plus continued or improved stewardship of the landscape, to enable significant improvements in vegetation cover at erosion edges and/or agricultural productivity in the lowlands.[2]

Greenland, fish and the future

We need to put the stories told by historians and archaeologists of Iceland's past in some kind of perspective. The main fact that might strike anyone familiar with the Norse colonisation of the North Atlantic is simply that the continued occupation of Iceland can be viewed as something of a success; whereas the Norse occupation of Greenland ended before 1500. Part of the reason for the contrasting histories of Iceland and Greenland is their different environments and location: Greenland was harsher and more remote from the cultural origin of its north-western European colonists. It also seems that while Norse Greenlanders had the opportunity to learn from the pre-existing Inuit population about how to adapt to their environment, Iceland's medieval population managed to adapt only slowly. The latter was still a very gradual process and we must not forget that it must have come at the cost of many premature deaths and consid-

---

1   Andrew F. Casely & Andrew J. Dugmore, 'Good for glaciers, bad for people? Archaeologically relevant climate models developed from reconstructions of glacier mass balance', *Journal of Archaeological Science*, 34 (2007), pp. 1763–73.

2   For past policy on erosion management see A. Arnalds, 'Approaches to landcare – a century of soil conservation in Iceland', *Land Degradation and Development*, 16 (2005), pp. 113–25.

erable hardship—the kind of thing which is not written down either because it is unexceptional or unpalatable. Even by medieval western European standards, Iceland was a tough place in which to live.

It is perhaps surprising that, so far, fishing has hardly been mentioned. Since the Second World War Iceland has become an increasingly successful exporter of fish. This is nothing new in that we know that, by the fourteenth century, foreign fishing fleets were exploiting Icelandic waters. Some new research also suggests that sea-fishing was important well before this, perhaps even from the beginning of Iceland's colonisation.[1] Fish has certainly always supplemented people's diets and incomes in Iceland. One of the key issues, though, remains: how much it did so in the past and, given the global economic climate in 2009 and the availability of natural resources in and around Iceland, how much might it do so in the future? Despite the familiar association of Iceland and fishing, we really do not know how important it was to medieval Icelanders. Did they damage the landscape because it did not matter to them when they could depend on fishing more than we have realised. The ongoing archaeological research will give us a better sense of that. After all, we can see the changing effects of man and climate on the Icelandic landscape, but we need to understand more precisely why people farmed in the way that they did.

This poses questions for the future too. What directions should our conservation efforts take? Should we be prioritising fish or soil for the longer benefit of human survival in Iceland and the wider North Atlantic? Our understanding of human activities in Iceland over the longer term also matters for the future in other ways. Increasing temperatures in the North Atlantic could be a 'good' thing in a number of ways. Crop yields may go up: barley, hay, potatoes and other crops might all grow in places in which they struggled only to survive during the first centuries of colonisation. Iceland, as a result, could become more self-sufficient. At the same time, increased average temperatures will bring more crop diseases which can only be combated with increased use of agrichemicals which will have to be

---

1   Ragnar Edvardsson, 'Commercial and subsistence fishing in Vestfirðir', *Archaeologia Islandica*, 4 (2005), pp. 51–67.

imported. And those agrichemicals, in turn, are a product of an oil-based economy which is not only reaching its peak (and hence subsequent decline), but in terms of agricultural inputs are a major factor in carbon emissions. Considered in geographical isolation, climatic changes may or may not be a good thing for the upland landscapes discussed above; increased temperatures will only allow the significant regrowth of vegetation if rainfall continues to be sufficient and regular, and if grazing is properly managed. We do not know how the matrix of possible climatic and environmental changes will actually pan out.

Increased temperatures might also make Iceland a more attractive place for permanent and temporary migrants yet some thought must be given to sustainability in all senses of the word. How many people can Iceland really support when it will most likely have to manage its resources ever more carefully? In its pre-industrial past, when Iceland's population had no great expectations of a high standard of living, when the population was below 100,000, and when Iceland was less dependent on communication with the wider world, this was not an issue. The deliberate increase of both fish exports and tourism have been ways to maintain economic growth in the past, but these depend, respectively, on one resource which is vulnerable to exhaustion, and another which is finite. In more recent decades Iceland has exploited its ability to generate electricity from geothermal or hydroelectric sources. The continued viability of these home-grown energy sources depends on a globalised economy and at the expense—where hydroelectric dams are built—of the landscape which provides food and tourist income. Thus, there are multiple resources which Iceland's population has exploited in the past and, in these newer energy sources, more into which it might yet tap. These activities have all been dependent on a changing physical and economic climate; human society will have to continue to respond to them rapidly if Iceland is to remain a place where humanity not only survives but thrives.

4. The Wrath of God: explanations of crisis and natural disaster in pre-modern Europe

Elaine Fulton and Penny Roberts

Historians have identified the fourteenth to seventeenth centuries as a period of crisis—demographic, socio-economic, cultural and political—not only in Europe but across the globe. Dramatic fluctuations in population, repeated pandemics, persistent subsistence crises, and increasing civil unrest, were exacerbated by significant changes in climate, as well as generating spiritual uncertainty. The period witnessed the Little Ice Age at its height, and the inhabitants of Europe experienced a palpable drop in temperature and an increase in floods and severe storms that held serious implications for the preservation of harvests. Combined with a world in which other natural phenomena such as earth tremors and fire caused by lightning strikes could cause sudden, massive destruction in a matter of minutes, and it becomes clear why so much of pre-modern church liturgy, preaching and early news pamphlets were devoted to explaining the harsher side of God's creation. An increasing climate of fear and intolerance also emerged, accompanying an overwhelming sense of vulnerability and uncertainty. Millenarianism, the belief in the imminent end of the world and the advent of the Last Days, was behind the emergence of groups such as the Flagellants and the Fifth Monarchists. Interrogation of the reactions to the crises which authorities and people faced in the pre-modern era can give us insights into the human capacity for resilience and recovery. However, whilst the psychological response needs to be placed in its proper historical context, it reflects a universal, if unpalatable, exacerbation of resultant anxiety and prejudice. Both prior to, and in the wake of, the Reformation, a clear pattern of blame emerged: of the people for not being fervent enough in their devotions, and of the religious and sometimes ethnic 'other' for having angered God by their very existence. It demonstrates humanity's continued need for non-scientific explanations of natural disasters, and highlights the 'blame game' that often accompanies such events. The conclusions of historians may also allow us to speculate upon the necessity of a very different response in our age if we are to succeed in dealing with an unprecedented crisis caused by accelerated human activity of quite a different sort to that of pre-modern times.

The impact of climate change was as significant a feature of life in pre-modern Europe as it is today; perhaps more so in view of the dependence of the vast majority of the population on agriculture for both subsistence and livelihood. In the early fourteenth century, famine in northern Europe accompanied a noticeable drop in temperature and the effect of a succession of harsh winters and wet summers on grain crops. The population of Europe, which is estimated to have peaked at around 65 million by the end of the thirteenth century, was already malnourished due to over-cultivation of the land. As the temperature dropped, so higher ground froze and was unable to be cultivated, exacerbating an already crisis situation which in many ways was relieved by the devastating impact of the Black Death which killed approximately one third of the population of Europe between 1348 and 1351. Population growth would continue to be depressed by recurrent visitations of plague, only regaining its momentum by 1500. Nevertheless, the effects of climate change which had contributed to the demographic decline would continue into the sixteenth and seventeenth centuries, and would need to be interpreted and dealt with by successive generations.

In particular, those who inhabited western and central Europe in the latter decades of the sixteenth and in the early decades of the seventeenth centuries would experience the peak of the Little Ice Age. Historical climatologists such as Christian Pfister have noted that, having enjoyed a warm phase between 1530 and 1564, Europeans found themselves faced with a climatic deterioration that set in quickly and fiercely around 1565, with what Pfister calls 'cumulative cold sequences' for the years 1565–74, 1583–89 and 1623–28.[1] The

---

1   Wolfgang Behringer, 'Weather, Hunger and Fear: Origins of the European Witch Hunts in Climate, Society and Mentality', *German History*, 13:1 (1995), pp. 1–27: p. 8 citing Christian Pfister, *Klimageschichte der Schweiz 1525–1860* (Bern: Haupt, 1988), pp. 118–27. See also Christian Pfister, 'Climatic Extremes, Recurrent Crises

people of early modern Europe would certainly have been aware of the novelty and significance of their situation as they experienced the impact of this climate change. For example, the freezing of the largest Alpine lake, Lake Constance, once in 1563 and again in 1572–73 for a full sixty days, is known to have aroused the curiosity of contemporaries. There is also anecdotal evidence that suggests that Elizabeth I liked to take a daily constitutional on the River Thames when it froze over during her reign. Yet the main effects of the Little Ice Age were undoubtedly extremely serious in their impact. Thanks to the work of Pfister, we are particularly knowledgeable about the impact of this period of climate change on sixteenth- and seventeenth-century Switzerland. Here, Alpine glaciers and the mountain snowline began a steady and discernible advance toward the valley populations. Most notorious were the so-called 'years without summer' of 1587 and 1628. In the former, snow fell in the Swiss lowlands in June and July, and the valleys were yet again covered with snow by mid-September; in the latter, one village in the Bernese Oberland experienced snowfall every month of that year. By the mid-1560s, the climate was also becoming increasingly damp, with the year 1588 being estimated the wettest of the century.

The results of this climate change were occasionally dramatic, but were rarely less than devastating for the populations of early modern Europe. The drama came in the form of a major increase in the number of severe storms and cases of flooding, such as that which killed an estimated 3,000 people in the Low Countries on the night of 1 November 1570, an event later known as the All Saints' Flood.[1] Indeed, it has been calculated that on the Flemish coast, the number of severe storms soared by 400 per cent in the latter half of the sixteenth century.[2] Slower to make an impact, but more widespread and lasting

---

and Witch Hunts: Strategies of European Societies in Coping with Exogenous Shocks in the Late Sixteenth and Early Seventeenth Centuries', *The Medieval History Journal*, 10 (2007), pp. 33–73.

1 Raingard Esser, 'Fear of water and floods in the Low Countries', in William G. Naphy and Penny Roberts, eds, *Fear in Early Modern Society* (Manchester: Manchester University Press, 1997), pp. 62–77.

2 Christian Pfister and Rudolf Brázdil, 'Climatic Variability in Sixteenth Century Europe and its Social Dimension: A Synthesis', *Climatic Change*, 43 (1999), p. 31.

in its effects, was the significance of such climatic deterioration for the supply of food. Year on year of cold, wet weather, combined with soil exhaustion, led to drastically lower, later harvest yields as crops rotted in the fields. Livestock also suffered, and the results were food shortages, a high level of price inflation, and ultimately famine and disease on a massive scale. By the 1580s, inflation in the southern German territories was at such a height that it led to a clear decline in the standard of living; inflationary problems continued well into the 1590s, and as Wolfgang Behringer has noted, 'hunger was the mark of inflationary crisis—its dreadful symbol'.[1] Under such circumstances, disease could thrive virtually unchecked, and the miseries of the late sixteenth century were compounded by two major plague epidemics in 1585–88 and 1592–93, and a major famine in Central Europe in the 1570s, which 'must have profoundly shocked this relatively affluent society'.[2] Add to such conditions the ongoing, sometimes violent confessional conflicts and spiritual uncertainties associated with the religious Reformations of the period, and the spectre of the military rise of the Ottoman Turks, regarded as the infidel, and we see a people gripped by fears in many ways not so different from those that dominate today.

What was markedly different, however, was the way in which climate change and its disastrous effects were interpreted in early modern Europe. There were certainly attempts at an early form of what we might call 'scientific' analysis of environmental patterns: there still survive, for example, at least thirty-two 'weather diaries', covering between them climatic observations from across much of central Europe for the period 1481–1613. Yet to the pre-modern mind, any patterns to be found in the workings of the physical world were just that. God and God alone was the prime mover of nature, and it was His hand that ultimately directed the path of all creation. As Johann Neubeck, Bishop of Vienna, expressed it in a sermon of 1591:

> Nature is an instrument and tool of God, and is therefore a secondary cause; God is *causa prima*. Nature is the servant of God,

---

1   Behringer, 'Weather, Hunger and Fear',pp. 13–14.
2   Behringer, p. 9

but God is the Lord and Master, who regulates and orders the effects and deeds of nature according to His will, for He is the Father and Lord of His house.[1]

Such thoughts were cross-confessional: in 1578 the Lutheran alma-nac-writer Matthaeus Bader wrote in similar fashion how '... God, the Almighty Lord, is not bound to secondary causes, so that every-thing must occur according to nature and not otherwise. Rather, he is a free agent ... who works with and without nature'.[2] God would therefore, in His mercy, often allow man the luxury of familiar sea-sons and a natural world that was usually fairly predictable in its temperature, elements and supply of bounty for human sustenance. Sometimes, however, He would choose to alter the physical envi-ronment in order to communicate His message to uncomprehending man, through natural disasters such as earthquakes and floods, natural wonders such as the appearance of comets or 'monstrous' births and, of course, through the advent of unusual climatic conditions with all their attendant side-effects. The early modern world was thus, as has been described by Robert Scribner, a 'moralised universe', and God's message, as interpreted by the main thinkers—including clerics—of the day, was always the same: repent, for the end is nigh.[3]

To the early modern mind, there could be no doubt that the world

1 Johann Caspar Neubeck, *Zwo catholische Predigen. Gehalten zu Wienn in Österreich, in offentlichen versamblungen zum gemeinen Gebett, wider die Schröckliche Erdtbidem, so sich Anno 1590. den 15. September und nachmals vil-feltig erzeigt haben...* (Vienna: Nassinger, 1591). Neubeck's sermon as cited here was concerning a recent earthquake in Vienna, but his expression of God's author-ity over nature is also relevant for early modern interpretations of other unexpected environmental shifts, such as the deterioration in climate.

2 Cited in C. Scott Dixon, 'Popular Astrology and Lutheran Propaganda in Reformation Germany', *History*, 84:3 (1999), p. 415.

3 Robert Scribner, 'Reformation and Desacralisation: From Sacramental World to Moralised Universe', in Po-Chia Hsia and R.W. Scribner eds, *Problems in the Historical Anthropology of Early Modern Europe* (Wiesbaden: Harrassowitz, 1997), pp. 75–92. For helpful comments on the limited significance of confes-sional differences on this subject in the early modern period, see Dixon, 'Popular Astrology', esp. pp. 415–16. In particular, Dixon notes that although Lutheranism rejected the notion of the material world as a 'repository of the sacred', the Lutheran Reformation 'did not desacralize or disenchant the natural world, though this has often been claimed'.

would end, and soon; outbreaks of war, disease and famine, as well as unusual natural phenomena only confirmed that the final cataclysm was approaching ever more quickly. Holy Writ seemed crystal clear on the subject: the New Testament records Jesus himself as having said that in the end times,

> You will hear of wars and rumours of wars, but see to it that you are not alarmed. Such things must happen, but the end is still to come. Nation will rise against nation, and kingdom against kingdom. There will be famines and earthquakes in various places. All these are the beginnings of the birth-pains.[1]

The Book of Revelation also promised that the earth itself would be diverted from its usual composition at the end of time, at the opening of the sixth seal:

> There was a great earthquake. The sun turned black like sackcloth made of goat hair, the whole moon turned blood red, and the stars in the sky fell to earth ... the sky receded like a scroll, rolling up, and every mountain and island was removed from its place.[2]

Successive waves of millenarianism swept across pre-modern Europe at times of particular crisis, and were exemplified by different groups who felt duty-bound to warn the wider community of the need for repentance, or indeed enacted this out physically as in the case of the Flagellants in the wake of the Black Death.[3] A more disturbing aspect of such movements was the violence done to others, notably the Jews, whose conversion was believed to be a necessary prerequisite for the Second Coming that would precede the Last Judgement. By the sixteenth and seventeenth centuries, ideologically radical groups were more concerned with preparing themselves and their communities for the Last Days, most notably the Anabaptists at

---

1   Matthew 24: 5–8 (New International Version).
2   Revelation 6: 12–13 (NIV). See too Revelation 8: 1–5, especially verse five on the opening of the seventh seal: after an angel flings a golden censer to the earth, 'there came peals of thunder, rumblings, flashes of lightning and an earthquake'.
3   Norman Cohn, *The Pursuit of the Millennium: Revolutionary Millenarians and Mystical Anarchists of the Middle Ages* (London: Pimlico, 1993 edn), esp. pp. 127–8, 131–9.

Münster, Germany in 1535, the Mennonites in central Europe, and the Fifth Monarchists in interregnum England. Even more mainstream theologians interpreted the dramatic political, religious, economic and environmental shifts of late sixteenth-century Europe as clear signs that the end of time was come at last, and astrology was employed widely, including by members of the clergy, to pinpoint more precisely the date of the earth's final death throes.

As Scott Dixon has noted, as the sixteenth century wore on, popular prognostications grew ever more bleak, with particular weight being placed on the significance of the year 1588. As one Lutheran pastor wrote in a doom-laden work published in 1587:

> in 1588 there will follow horrible, frightening, hitherto unheard of things ... it is certain, that a great change will affect the entire world. Firstly, there will be frightful storms, earthquakes, and floods, destroying the crops and causing misfortune. Secondly, following from this, there will be inflation, famine and pestilence[1]

Right across Europe, expectations that 1588 would be the age of death of the anno domini world grew. Yet this year, just as other years that had been the subject of similar fearful predictions, came and went with its fair share of drama—in this case, the Spanish Armada—but no apocalypse. Undeterred, the prophets of doom kept up with their predictions: the world would end in 1600, then in 1604, and then in 1623. But in many ways it did not matter that the anticipated end did not come as predicted; such eschatological inaccuracies could easily be explained away as a miscalculation on the part of the relevant astrologer, or, more likely, as a sign of God's continued mercy for those living on the earth. The astrological prediction for 1524 that it would be the year of a great flood, despite the fact that the summer turned out to be unusually dry leaving communities susceptible to conflagration rather than to deluge, did not deter future prophecies. It was primarily a moral message that was at the heart of early modern interpretations of climate change and all the disaster that it carried in its wake: war, famine, disease, disaster and the up-ending of the natural world were a divine clarion call for true repentance on the part of

---

1   Cited in Dixon, 'Popular Astrology', p. 410.

sinful man.

For almanac-writers making use of the thriving printing presses, and for clerics preaching to their parishioners, Holy Scripture was again replete with texts with which to persuade their anxious audiences that the ever-increasing horrors of early modern life were a sign of God's wrath and call to repentance. After all, had not God sent the Ten Plagues to Egypt as a mark of His judgement? And were not the fire that destroyed Sodom and the flood from which God saved Noah and his family also marks of divine wrath? As one Lutheran pastor summarised it in 1573:

> God has been provoked to reveal to us through natural and super-natural means, in water, on earth, air, in the fiery elements, even in the starry firmament, his wrath, mercy, and works of wonder, that our adamantine hearts, poisoned by the Devil's tempting counsel, might relent, turn from evil, and come to rights.[1]

Similar sentiments were also expressed in English pulpits: according to a sermon preached by Welsh clergyman Hugh Roberts in Sussex in 1598:

> everie plague, everie calamitie, sudden death, burning with fire, murther, strange sicknesses, famine, everie flood of waters, ruine of buildines, unseasonable weather: everie one of these and of the like adversities, as oft as they happen in the world, are a sermon to repentance to all that see them, or heare therof ... a memento to every one of us to looke to our selves, and to call to remembrance our owne sins, knowing that the same God that will take vengeance of everie sinne, and transgression of men, & that he will strike with a more heavie hand, if his warning, and example of his justice be not regarded.[2]

For a German almanac-writer in 1578, it was however even possible that 'oftimes the prayer of a truly pious man can stave off or at least ease future misfortune'.[3] Across Europe, then, the printing presses churned out endless accounts of tragedy that rarely ended

---

1   Cited in Dixon, 'Popular Astrology', p. 411.
2   Cited in Alexandra Walsham, *Providence in Early Modern England* (Oxford: Oxford University Press, 1999), p. 116.
3   Cited in Dixon, 'Popular Astrology', p. 415.

with any punch-line other than that of the need to repent with speed and sincerity, in the hope that God would spare man further pain. From devastating floods in Norfolk, Somerset and Gloucestershire in 1607, to an earthquake in Münster in 1612 and the Neapolitan province of Calabria in 1638, 'millions of varieties of transgressions' were noted as the cause.[1] In short, to cite Alexandra Walsham, in the early modern period no-one 'could pass up the opportunity afforded by a major conflagration, blizzard, drought, inundation, or epidemic to deliver a thundering diatribe on the doctrine of divine judgements'.[2]

In early modern Europe, then, hostile environmental change and subsequent subsistence crises were read as signs of the wrath of God at work in the end times of the world. And in many ways, the response was in some ways as unhelpful and unedifying as modern reactions to catastrophe, where angry apportionment of blame is the first and sometimes only, paralysing action. In the search for scapegoats, early modern Europeans did not have to look far. As Behringer has argued, there is a 'striking correlation' between the peak of European witchcraft persecutions, roughly between 1560 and 1630, and the years of the height of the Little Ice Age. Whereas in previous centuries, heretics, Jews and lepers were singled out and accused of deliberately attacking and destabilising Christian society, the sixteenth and seventeenth centuries provided a new target. Witches in this period were widely regarded as having weather-making powers, as the author of one anonymous German pamphlet from 1590 makes clear:

> So many kinds of magic and demonic apparitions are gaining the upper hand in our time that nearly every city, market and village in all Germany, not to mention other peoples and nations, is filled with vermin and servants of the devil who destroy the fruits of the fields, which the lord allows to grow with his blessing, with unusual thunder, lightening, showers, hail, storm winds, frost, flooding, mice, worms and many other things ... causing them to rot in the fields, and also increase   the   shortage   of   human subsistence by spoiling livestock, cows, calves, horses, sheep, and others, using all their power, not just against the fruit of the

1   Walsham, *Providence*, p. 122.
2   Walsham, *Providence*, p. 116.

fields and livestock, but yes, not even sparing kinsfolk and close
blood-relatives, who are killed in great numbers.[1]

For a community suffering year on year of poor harvests as a result
of difficult climatic conditions, what better than to find a malevo-
lent force outside of themselves to blame, isolate, persecute and ultimately kill. Across Europe, therefore, so-called 'witchcrazes' grew,
gaining particular force in Germany, Switzerland, Austria, England
and Scotland, and resulting in the executions of an estimated 10,000
victims, the majority of whom were women who had committed no
crime greater than failing to 'fit' satisfactorily into the life of their
local parish and community. Such was the ferocity of these purges, in
the German Duchy of Westphalia and the archbishopric of Cologne
up to 2,000 people were burned as witches in the years after 1626.
That such a level of persecution took place under the aegis of the
Archbishop of Cologne, Ferdinand of Bavaria (1579–1650), suggests that sometimes even the ecclesiastical leaders of the day found
it easier to blame others for environmental crises than to take the
advice of their own sermons and look to remedy their own behaviour.
Elsewhere in Europe, other scapegoats were found for the misfor-
tunes that befell communities, including Alpine plague-spreaders and
vagrant arsonists who were accused of setting fire to towns in France,
England and Germany.[2]

There remain, however, some positive messages to be taken from
the response of the people of sixteenth- and seventeenth-century
Europe to the multiple crises they faced. For one, 'society was not
impotent in the face of [fear], as some historians have tended to por-
tray in the past. There was much that could be done to assuage fear;
people were not paralysed by it'.[3] To return to a case already mentioned, that of the All Saints' Flood that devastated the Low Countries
in 1570, this did result in some cases of finger-pointing across the
area's deep confessional divide, with Catholic Spanish writers imply-

---

1   Behringer, 'Weather, Hunger and Fear', pp. 9–10.
2   William G. Naphy, *Plagues, Poisons and Potions: Plague-Spreading Conspiracies
in the Western Alps, c. 1530–1640* (Manchester: Manchester University Press,
2002); Johannes Dillinger, 'Terrorists and Witches: Popular Ideas of Evil in the
Early Modern Period', *History of European Ideas*, 30 (2004), pp. 167–182.
3   'Introduction', in Naphy and Roberts (ed.), *Fear in Early Modern Society*, p. 6.

ing God's judgement on the Calvinist Dutch, and the Calvinist Dutch suggesting that it was in fact the Catholic Spaniards who were the chief targets of divine wrath. Yet behind the scenes, something else was happening: in a retrospective account of the history of the dike written in 1644, Martin Boxhorn attributed the flood damage of 1570 not to the wrath of God at all, but rather to the mismanagement of the ruling Spanish who had diverted resources away from dike-building and repair to fight costly wars. According to Boxhorn,

> the remedy against this mismanagement is community action in the form of common financial contribution and the willingness to fulfil one's responsibility towards the community. Every coastal inhabitant should be expected to help with the necessary repair and maintenance works at the dike.[1]

This help was to include not only intense and communal physical labour, but the willingness to pay contributions to defensive works through taxes that would be set and spent locally. In the area around Leiden in 1575, it was even decided that such was the need to prioritise dike repair in that year, that the region could not pay its annual contribution to the salaries of academics at the university. Such brutal pragmatism and willingness to learn quickly the lessons that the environment was teaching, has been described by leading analyst of historical disasters, Franz Mauelshagen, as 'a landscape of coping' in which 'dike law will be interpreted as the most obvious expression of a "hydrographic society" that has emerged from co-operation, communal organisation, and conflict'.[2]

In early modern European cities, similar pragmatism and communal co-operation can be seen in steps taken to prevent and reduce the damage caused by fire, another chief terror of the day that was also connected to the hand of God as conflagrations were frequently the result of lightning strikes. Whilst arson was often suspected, and foreigners or those of another faith often blamed, practical measures were taken to safeguard against the risk. Householders and workers in the building trade were made responsible for fire-fighting provi-

---

1   See Esser, 'Fear of water'.
2   Franz Mauelshagen, 'Flood Disasters and Political Culture at the German North Sea Coast: A Long-term perspective', in *Historical Social Research*, 32 (2007), p. 133.

sion, and money was raised on a regional or even national basis to relieve the victims. Thus, following the Great Fire which devastated London in 1666, rumours abounded of the involvement of the French and the Dutch, as well as organised criminal gangs, whilst its aftermath led to a major project of urban planning and renewal. Therefore, a combination of suspicion and practicality, fear and pragmatism ultimately characterised pre-modern responses to disaster and crisis much as they do today.

Keith Thomas points out that the period after the peak of the Little Ice Age also saw the emergence of the insurance industry which, as Daniel Defoe noted in 1697, made it possible 'for all the contingencies of life [to] be fenced against ... thieves, floods by land, storms by sea, losses of all sorts, and death itself'.[1] Yet whilst such responses to disaster, environmental and otherwise, may be seen as 'self-help', none of this is to imply a wholly secular response to crisis. The local church, whatever its confessional hue, remained at the centre of the early modern community, often playing a pivotal role in the publication and announcement of practical measures against fire, flood, and the series of other catastrophes that seemed to be visiting their parishioners with alarming frequency. Post-disaster, it was again the church that was a key centre of aid for those left destitute. Even the church liturgy associated with the amelioration of environmental disaster, such as days of prayer and abstinence in Reformed Europe and special masses and processions in Catholic Europe—which to some modern minds may seem at best futile and at worst a dangerous distraction—did much not only to bring genuine comfort to the participants, but to draw the entire community together at the very moment when cohesion and common purpose were critical for survival. The early modern understanding of environmental change and crisis may have been rather different from that which dominates today, and led on dark occasions to the scapegoating of the socially vulnerable, but also demonstrates a pragmatism, directness of action and communal spirit that we could do worse than to emulate in the twenty-first century. Whilst the problems and their impact may now be more global

---

1   Cited in Keith Thomas, *Religion and the Decline of Magic* (London: Penguin, 1973), p. 782.

in scale, and some of the responses to them will have to be equally collective, it is perhaps first at the level of the local community that some of the solutions will need to be developed. Regaining this sense of community may be one of the greatest challenges we face in dealing with a global crisis. Climate change requires major adjustments in the use of dwindling resources and, therefore, in lifestyle. Our premodern ancestors were much better attuned than we are to making such practical adjustments: in approaches to cultivation, resource-management and distribution, in harnessing natural sources of power, handling daily economies, and even family planning. Their collective, although sometimes exclusive, response to crisis suggests too that, if old certainties are swept away, there will be positive human resources on which we can draw whilst striving to avoid the more negative aspects of a climate of fear.

Part III: The Debate about the Enlightenment and Modernity

5. The Urgent Need for an Academic Revolution

Nicholas Maxwell

Two great problems of learning confront humanity: first, learning about the nature of the universe and about ourselves as a part of the universe, and second, learning how to live wisely—learning how to make progress towards as good a world as possible.

The first problem was solved, in essence, in the seventeenth century, with the creation of modern science. A *method* was discovered for progressively improving knowledge and understanding of the natural world, the famous empirical method of science. There is, of course, much that we still do not know and understand, three or four centuries after the birth of modern science. Nevertheless, during this time, science has immensely increased our knowledge and understanding, at an ever accelerating rate. And with this unprecedented increase in scientific knowledge and understanding has come a cascade of technological discoveries and developments which have transformed the human condition.

But the second great problem of learning has not yet been solved. And this puts us in a situation of unprecedented danger. Indeed, all our current global problems can be traced back, in one way or another, to this source. Global warming, the lethal character of modern war and terrorism, stockpiling of modern armaments, pollution of sea, air and earth, vast inequalities of wealth and power round the globe, rapid increase in population, destruction of tropical rain forests and rapid extinction of species, and even the AIDS epidemic: all these crises have been made possible by modern science and technology.

Solving the first great problem of learning enormously increases our power to act, via the increase of scientific knowledge and technological know-how. But without wisdom—without a solution to the second problem of learning—our immensely increased power to act may have good consequences, but will as often as not have all sorts of harmful consequences as well, whether intended or not. Even the AIDS epidemic would not have occurred without modern methods of travel, made possible by modern technology. As long as humanity's power to act was limited, lack of wisdom did not matter too much: we lacked the means to inflict too much damage on ourselves or on the planet. But with the immense increase in our powers to act that we have achieved in the last century or so, our powers to destroy have become unprecedented and terrifying: global wisdom has become, not a luxury, but a necessity. Solving the second great problem of learning, now that we have solved the first one, has become our most urgent priority.

But how can we solve this second great problem, the problem of learning to live wisely, and create a better world? Can it be solved at all? We can at least improve our ability to solve the second problem. But in order to do this, there is one vital step that we need to take. *We need to learn from our solution to the first problem how to solve the second.* That is, *we need to learn from scientific progress how to make better social progress towards a wiser world.*

The Enlightenment

Indeed, this is not a new idea, but is the basis of the eighteenth century French Enlightenment: to learn from scientific progress how to make social progress towards world enlightenment.[1]

Unfortunately, in developing and implementing this profoundly important idea, the *philosophes* of the Enlightenment blundered. They botched the job. They developed the idea in a seriously defective form, and it is this immensely influential, defective version of the idea, inherited from the eighteenth century that is built into the institutions of inquiry that we possess today. Our current traditions

---

1   Peter Gay, *The Enlightenment: An Interpretation* (2 vols, London: Wildwood House, 1973).

and institutions of learning, when judged from the standpoint of helping us learn how to become more enlightened, are defective and irrational in a wholesale and structural way, and it is this which, in the long term, sabotages our efforts to create a wiser world, and prevents us from avoiding the kind of horrors we have been exposed to during the twentieth century.[1]

The *philosophes* of the eighteenth century—Voltaire, Diderot, Condorcet and the rest—assumed, understandably enough, that the proper way to implement the Enlightenment idea was to develop social science alongside natural science. Francis Bacon had already stressed the importance of improving knowledge of the natural world in order to achieve social progress. The *philosophes* generalised this, holding that it is just as important to improve knowledge of the social world. Thus they set about creating the social sciences: history, anthropology, political economy, psychology, sociology.

This had an immense impact. Throughout the nineteenth century the diverse social sciences were developed, often by non-academics, in accordance with the Enlightenment idea.[2] Gradually, universities took notice of these developments until, by the mid-twentieth century, all the diverse branches of the social sciences, as conceived of by the Enlightenment, were built into the institutional structure of universities as recognized academic disciplines.

But, from the standpoint of creating a kind of inquiry designed to help humanity learn how to live wisely, all this amounts to is a series of monumental blunders. In order to implement properly the basic Enlightenment idea of learning from scientific progress how to achieve social progress towards a wise world, it is essential to get the following three things right.

1. The progress-achieving methods of science need to be correctly identified.
2. These methods need to be correctly generalised so that

---

1   Nicholas Maxwell, *From Knowledge to Wisdom: A Revolution for Science and the Humanities* (London: Pentire Press, 2007, second edition).

2   Raymond Aron, *Main Currents in Sociological Thought*, vol. 2 (London: Penguin, 1970); F. A. Hayek, *The Counter-Revolution of Science* (Indianapolis: Liberty Press 1979); J. Farganis, ed., *Readings in Social Theory*, Introduction (New York: McGraw-Hill, 1993).

they become fruitfully applicable to any worthwhile, problematic human endeavour, whatever the aims may be, and not just applicable to the scientific endeavour of improving knowledge.

3. The correctly generalized progress-achieving methods then need to be exploited correctly in the great human endeavour of trying to make social progress towards an enlightened, wise world.

Unfortunately, the Enlightenment got all three points wrong—the third point disastrously so. That the *philosophes* made these blunders in the eighteenth century is forgivable; what is unforgivable is that these blunders still remain unrecognized and uncorrected today, over two centuries later. Instead of correcting them, we have allowed our institutions of learning to be shaped by them as they have developed throughout the nineteenth and twentieth centuries, so that now the blunders are an all-pervasive feature of our world.

First Blunder: Scientific Method

The *first* blunder concerns the nature of the progress-achieving methods of science. Scientists and philosophers of science today make the assumption, inherited from the Enlightenment, that science makes progress because, in science, theories are assessed impartially on the basis of evidence alone, *no permanent assumption being made about the nature of the universe independent of evidence.* But this orthodox, standard empiricist conception of science is untenable, as the following simple argument demonstrates. Physics only ever accepts theories that are (more or less) *unified,* even though endlessly many empirically more successful disunified rivals can always be concocted. Such a theory, T (Newtonian theory, quantum theory, general relativity or the standard model), almost always faces some empirical difficulties, and is thus, on the face of it, refuted (by phenomena A). There are phenomena, B, which come within the scope of the theory but which cannot be predicted because the equations of the theory cannot (as yet) be solved. And there are other phenomena (C) that fall outside the scope of the theory altogether. We can now artificially concoct a disunified, 'patchwork quilt' rival, T*, which asserts that everything occurs as T predicts except for phenomena A, B and C: here T* asserts, in a grossly ad hoc way, that the phenomena occur in accordance with empirically established laws, L_A, L_B and L_C.

Even though T* is more successful empirically than T, it and all analogous rival theories are, quite correctly, ignored by physics because they are all horribly disunified. They postulate different laws for different phenomena, and are simply assumed to be false. But this means physics makes a big, implicit assumption about the universe: that all such 'patchwork quilt' theories are false.

If physicists only ever accepted theories that postulate atoms even though empirically more successful rival theories are available that postulate other entities such as fields, it would surely be quite clear: physicists implicitly assume that the universe is such that all theories that postulate entities other than atoms are false. Just the same holds in connection with unified theories. That physicists only ever accept unified theories even though empirically more successful rival theories are available that are disunified means that physicists implicitly assume that the universe is such that all disunified theories are false.

The orthodox standard empiricist view is, in other words, untenable.[1] Physics makes a big implicit assumption about the nature of the universe, upheld independently of empirical considerations—even, in a certain sense, in violation of such considerations: the universe is physically comprehensible, in the sense that it possesses some kind of underlying dynamic unity, to the extent at least that it is such that all disunified physical theories are false. This is a secure tenet of scientific knowledge, to the extent that empirically successful theories that clash with it are not even considered for acceptance.[2]

At once it is clear that science is confronted by a fundamental dilemma. In order to proceed at all science must assume, even if only implicitly, that the universe is comprehensible in some way, to some extent at least (since otherwise science would be overwhelmed by

---

1   Nicholas Maxwell, *The Comprehensibility of the Universe* (New York and Oxford: Oxford University Press, 1998), chapter 2.

2   See Maxwell, *From Knowledge*, 2nd edition, chapter 14; also Maxwell, *Comprehensibility*, chapter 2.

endlessly many empirically successful, disunified, non-explanatory theories). But it is just here, concerning the ultimate nature of the universe, that we are most ignorant, and most likely to get things entirely wrong. Science both must, and cannot, assume knowledge about the ultimate nature of the universe.

The solution to this dilemma is to construe science as making a hierarchy of assumptions concerning the comprehensibility and knowability of the universe, less and less being assumed as one goes up the hierarchy. At the top of the hierarchy no more is assumed than that the universe is such that some knowledge can be acquired. This assumption is legitimately a permanent item of knowledge since, if false, knowledge cannot be acquired whatever is assumed. Lower down in the hierarchy, those assumptions are adopted which seem to lead to the greatest growth of empirical knowledge. These assumptions are revised in the light of the empirical success and failure of the scientific research programmes to which they give rise.

This hierarchical view, in stark contrast to the current orthodox conception of science, inherited from the Enlightenment, is the key to the success of modern science. The basic aim of science of discovering how, and to what extent, the universe is physically comprehensible is profoundly problematic; because of this, it is essential that we try to improve the aim, and associated methods, as we proceed, in the light of apparent scientific success and failure. In order to do this in the best possible way we need to represent our aim at a number of levels, from the specific and problematic, low down in the hierarchy, to the highly unspecific and unproblematic, high up in the hierarchy, thus creating a framework of relatively unproblematic, fixed aims and methods within which much more specific and problematic aims and methods of science may be progressively improved in the light of apparent empirical success and failure. The result is that, as we improve our knowledge about the world we are able to improve our knowledge about how to improve knowledge, the methodological key to the rapid progress of modern science: see diagram 1.

The adoption and explicit implementation of this hierarchical view by the scientific community as the official, orthodox conception of science would correct the first blunder of the Enlightenment.

Second Blunder: Rationality

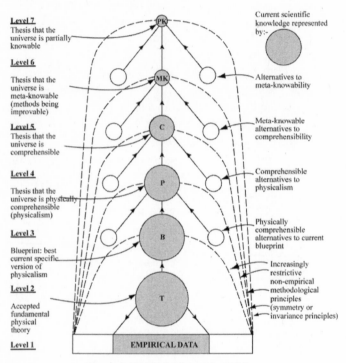

Diagram 1: Hierarchical Conception of Science

The *second* blunder arises in connection with generalizing the progress-achieving methods of science. The task, here, is to generalize correctly the progress-achieving methods of science to arrive at a conception of progress-achieving rationality, fruitfully applicable to any problematic, worthwhile human endeavour (science being just a special case).

Needless to say, having failed to specify the methods of science properly, scientists and philosophers have also failed to arrive at the proper generalization of these methods. What we need to do in order to correct this second blunder is to take the above hierarchical conception of the progress-achieving methods of science as our starting point, and generalize that.

It is not just in science that aims are problematic; this is the case in life too, either because different aims conflict, or because what we believe to be desirable and realizable lacks one or other of these features, or both. Above all, the aim of creating a wiser world is inherently and profoundly problematic. Quite generally, then, and not just in science, whenever we pursue a problematic aim we need to represent the aim as a hierarchy of aims, from the specific and problematic at the bottom of the hierarchy, to the general and unproblematic at the top. In this way we provide ourselves with a framework within which we may improve more or less specific and problematic aims and methods as we proceed, learning from success and failure in practice what it is that is both of most value and realisable. Such a hierarchical conception of rationality is the proper generalisation of the hierarchical conception of science.

Third Blunder: Social Inquiry and the Humanities

So much for the second blunder, and how it is to be put right. We come now to the *third* blunder. This concerns, not *what* the methods of science are, but *to what* they should be applied, when appropriately generalized.

This is by far the most serious of the three blunders made by the Enlightenment. The basic Enlightenment idea, after all, is to learn from our solution to the first great problem of learning how to solve the second problem—to learn, that is, from scientific progress how to make social progress towards an enlightened world. Putting this idea into practice involves getting appropriately generalized progress-achieving methods of science *into social life itself*! It involves getting progress-achieving methods into our institutions and ways of life, into government, industry, agriculture, commerce, international relations, the media, the arts, education. But in sharp contrast to all this, the Enlightenment sought to apply (misconstrued) generalized scientific method, not to social *life*, but merely to social *science*! Instead of helping humanity learn how to become wiser by rational means, the Enlightenment sought merely to help social scientists improve knowledge of social phenomena. The outcome is that today academic inquiry devotes itself to acquiring knowledge of natural and social phenomena, but does not attempt to help humanity learn how to live more wisely. This is the blunder that is at the root of our current failure to have solved the second great problem of learning. It is at the root of *the* crisis of our times: possessing science without wisdom.

Social scientists today, like natural scientists, do of course seek to apply the knowledge they acquire to help solve social problems. That is, indeed, the traditional Enlightenment idea: first, acquire knowledge, then apply it to help promote social progress. But such a procedure is quite different from what emerges as a result of correcting the three blunders of the traditional Enlightenment. This involves applying, not knowledge, but the generalised, progress-achieving meta-methodology of natural science, to personal and institutional life. It means that social inquiry is social *methodology* and not, in the first instance at least, social *science* concerned to acquire (and apply) *knowledge* of social phenomena to social life. The outcome of correcting the three blunders I have indicated would not necessarily be to enhance the contribution of social scientists towards solving social problems. Rather, it would transform the whole way in which social inquiry would set about this task.[1]

In order to correct this third, monumental and disastrous blunder, we need, as a first step, to bring about a revolution in the nature of academic inquiry, beginning with social inquiry and the humanities. Properly implemented, the Enlightenment idea of learning from scientific progress how to achieve social progress towards an enlightened world would involve developing social inquiry, not as social *science*, but as social *methodology,* or social *philosophy*. A basic task would be to intrude into personal and social life, and into other institutions besides that of science—into government, industry, agriculture, commerce, the media, law, education, international relations—hierarchical, progress-achieving methods (designed to improve problematic aims) arrived at by generalizing the methods of science. A basic task for academic inquiry as a whole would be to help human-

---

1   See Maxwell, *From Knowledge*, chapters. 2–7, especially chapter 7. Also Nicholas Maxwell, *Is Science Neurotic?* (London: Imperial College Press, 2004), chapters 3 and 4.

ity learn how to resolve its conflicts and problems of living in more just, cooperatively rational ways than at present. This task would be intellectually more fundamental than the scientific task of acquiring knowledge. Social inquiry would be intellectually more fundamental than physics. Academia would be a kind of people's civil service, doing openly for the public what actual civil services are supposed to do in secret for governments. Academia would have just sufficient power (but no more) to retain its independence from government, industry, the press, public opinion, and other centres of power and influence in the social world. It would seek to learn from, educate, and argue with the great social world beyond, but would not dictate. Academic thought would be pursued as a specialised, subordinate part of what is really important and fundamental: guiding individual, social and institutional actions and life. The fundamental intellectual and humanitarian aim of inquiry would be to help humanity acquire wisdom—wisdom being the capacity to realize (apprehend and create) what is of value in life, for oneself and others, wisdom thus including knowledge and technological know-how but much else besides.[1]

What is at issue, here, is not, of course, merely that academic inquiry should become more 'socially relevant' or less isolated from the social world. It is, rather, that a central task of academia should be to help humanity towards progress-achieving meta-methods exploited so successfully by natural science. One outcome of bringing into social and institutional life this kind of aim-evolving, hierarchical methodology as generalised from science, is that it becomes possible for us to develop and assess rival philosophies of life as a part of social life, somewhat as theories are developed and assessed within science. Such a hierarchical methodology provides a framework within which competing views about what our aims and methods in life should be—competing religious, political and moral views—may be cooperatively assessed and tested against broadly agreed, unspecific aims (high up in the hierarchy of aims) and the experience of personal and social life. There is the possibility of cooperatively

---

1   Maxwell, *From Knowledge*, 2nd edition, p. 79.

and progressively improving *such philosophies of life* (views about what is of value in life and how it is to be achieved) much as *theories* are cooperatively and progressively improved in science. In science, ideally, theories are critically assessed with respect to each other, with respect to metaphysical ideas concerning the comprehensibility of the universe, and with respect to *experience* (observational and experimental results). In a somewhat analogous way, diverse philosophies of life may be critically assessed with respect to each other, with respect to relatively uncontroversial, agreed ideas about aims and what is of value, and with respect to *experience*—what we do, achieve, fail to achieve, enjoy and suffer—so that they offer greater help with the realisation of what is of value in life. This hierarchical methodology is especially relevant to the task of resolving conflicts about aims and ideals, as it helps disentangle agreement (high up in the hierarchy) and disagreement (more likely to be low down in the hierarchy): see diagram 2.

The whole idea, as I have stressed above, is that, whatever we are doing, our aims at some level are almost bound to be problematic, because unrealisable, undesirable, or both, and thus it is vital that we seek to improve aims as we act. The dire consequences of a general failure to appreciate that aims are all too likely to be problematic, and thus in need of sustained articulation, criticism and improvement, are all too apparent in our world. For decades it was assumed that agricultural, industrial and economic growth is good, without awareness of the negative aspects of these aims: destruction of natural habitats and extinction of species, depletion of irreplaceable natural resources and global warming. Nations set out to increase their security by building up armies and armaments, thereby provoking neighbouring nations to do likewise, the net result being an increase in international tension and an undermining of security. Banks gamble in pursuit of profits, and fail to consider the dire consequences when house prices and shares take a tumble. There is a desperately urgent need to build hierarchical meta-methodologies analogous to those depicted in diagrams 1 and 2 into our financial, commercial, industrial, agricultural and political institutions. So far, social scientists, victims of the three blunders indicated above, have not even seen the need to do this.

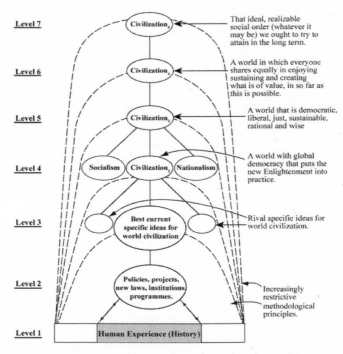

Diagram 2: Implementing Generalization of Hierarchical Conception of Scientific Method in Pursuit of Civilization

Wisdom-inquiry, because of its greater rigour, has intellectual standards that are, in important respects, different from those of knowledge-inquiry. Whereas knowledge-inquiry demands that emotions and desires, values, human ideals and aspirations, philosophies of life are excluded from the intellectual domain of inquiry, wisdom-inquiry requires that they are included. In order to discover what is of value in life it is essential that we attend to our feelings and desires. But not everything we desire is desirable, and not everything that feels good is good. Feelings, desires and values need to be subjected to critical scrutiny. And feelings, desires and values must not be permitted to influence judgements of factual truth and falsity. Wisdom-inquiry embodies a synthesis of traditional rationalism and romanticism. It includes elements from both, and it improves on both. It incorporates romantic ideals of integrity, having to do with motivational and emotional honesty, honesty about desires and aims; and at the same time it incorporates traditional rationalist ideals of integrity, having to do with respect for objective fact, knowledge, and valid argument. Traditional rationalism takes its inspiration from science and method; romanticism takes its inspiration from art, from imagination, and from passion. Wisdom-inquiry holds art to have a fundamental rational role in inquiry, in revealing what is of value, and unmasking false values; but science, too, is of fundamental importance. What we need, for wisdom, is an interplay of sceptical rationality and emotion, an interplay of mind and heart, so that we may develop mindful hearts and heartfelt minds.[1] It is time we healed the great rift in our culture, so graphically depicted by C. P. Snow.[2]

Conclusion

Humanity is in deep trouble. We urgently need to learn how to make progress towards a wiser, more civilised world, geared towards living in more cooperatively rational ways than at present, in which impending disaster may be avoided or mitigated and in which humanity may be able to reach its full individual and social potential. This in turn requires that we possess traditions and institutions of learning rationally designed—*well designed*—to help us achieve this end. It is just this that we do not have them at present. What we have instead is natural science and, more broadly, inquiry devoted to acquiring knowledge. Judged from the standpoint of helping us create a better world, knowledge-inquiry of this type is dangerously and damagingly irrational. We need to bring about a major intellectual and institutional revolution in the aims and methods of inquiry, from knowledge-inquiry to wisdom-inquiry. Almost every branch and aspect of academic inquiry needs to change.

---

1   See Nicholas Maxwell, *What's Wrong With Science?* (Frome: Bran's Head Books, 1976), especially p. 5, see also Maxwell, *From Knowledge*, chapter 5, for a sustained discussion of the point that rationality needs to include emotion and desire.

2   C. P. Snow, *The Two Cultures: And a Second Look* (Cambridge: Cambridge University Press, 1986)

A basic intellectual task of academic inquiry would be to articulate our problems of living (personal, social and global) and propose and critically assess possible solutions, possible actions. This would be the task of social inquiry and the humanities. Tackling problems of knowledge would be secondary. Social inquiry would be at the heart of the academic enterprise, intellectually more fundamental than natural science. On a rather more long-term basis, social inquiry would be concerned to help humanity build hierarchical methods of problem-solving into the fabric of social and political life so that we may gradually acquire the capacity to resolve our conflicts and problems of living in more cooperatively rational ways than at present. Natural science would change to include three domains of discussion: evidence, theory, and aims—the latter including discussion of metaphysics, values and politics. Academia would actively seek to educate the public by means of discussion and debate, and would not just study the public.[1]

This revolution—intellectual, institutional and cultural—if it ever comes about, would be comparable in its long-term impact to that of the Renaissance, the scientific revolution, or the Enlightenment. The outcome would be traditions and institutions of learning rationally designed to help us acquire wisdom. There are a few scattered signs that this intellectual revolution, from knowledge to wisdom, is already under way. It will need, however, much wider cooperative support— from scientists, scholars, students, research councils, university administrators, vice chancellors, teachers, the media and the general public— if it is to become anything more than what it is at present, a fragmentary and often impotent movement of protest and opposition, often at odds with itself, exercising little influence on the main body of academic work. I can hardly imagine any more important work for anyone associated with academia than, in teaching, learning and research, to help promote this revolution.

---

1   For an indication of just how important, and how appalling public education is in both the USA and UK, one need only consider the fact that both George Bush and Tony Blair were re-elected after the disastrous 'war on terrorism' and the Iraq war. See Nicholas Maxwell, 'The Disastrous War against Terrorism: Violence versus Enlightenment', in Albert W. Merkidze, ed., *Terrorism Issues: Threat Assessment, Consequences and Prevention* (New York: Nova Science Publishers, 2007), pp.111–133, for further discussion.

6. Dangerous Limits: Climate Change and Modernity

Christopher Shaw

Introduction

Current state, corporate and NGO responses to climate change are predicated on normative assumptions about the existence of a two degree centigrade 'dangerous limit' to anthropogenic warming of the climate. This essay argues that the primary purpose of constructing climate change as a phenomenon with a dangerous limit is not to protect people from danger but to legitimate the processes and institutions of modernity. This happens for two reasons. Firstly, by means of the two degree limit, climate change is constructed as a quantifiable problem and thus amenable to management through the application of industrial technologies. Secondly, the two degree limit makes climate change a problem for the future which allows humanity to continue with 'business as usual' whilst the search for a techno-fix continues. The two degree limit fails to protect people from danger because emerging climate science research indicates that dangerous anthropogenic interference with the climate has already begun. Consequently, I propose, it is now time to imagine—or more exactly *re*-imagine—alternative futures.

Limitless modernity

Modernity, for the purposes of this essay, is defined as the sum of the meanings, values and structures necessary for the reproduction of what Ellul has described as the technological society.[1] I argue this process of reproduction is fuelled by an ideology which refuses to countenance limits. Space travel acts as a powerful symbol for this

---

1   Jaques Ellul, *The Technological Society* (London: Jonathan Cape, 1965).

ideology; the apogee of science, technology and human organization which allows humanity to break free from the limited and bounded confines of Earth into the infinite and boundless universe. Not only does the space programme remind us that there are no limits to human endeavour, but it also articulates a positive vision of the globalised world which is so key to modernity—one small step for man, one giant leap for mankind. The symbolic discourse of space travel also acts to reproduce and legitimate a much more pressing and socially embedded doctrine of limitlessness, namely limitless economic growth. The relentless drive to increase material wealth 'implies and requires a doctrine of general human limitlessness; *all* are entitled to pursue without limit whatever they conceive as desirable'.[1] Such limitlessness requires a lot of energy, the sort of energy that only fossil fuels can provide. It is because limitless growth requires limitless energy that I identify climate change as a problem of modernity.

Questions about whether or not there is such a thing as modernity and—if it does exist—whether it should be considered good or bad, have exercised the minds of concerned citizens for more than two hundred years. There is not the scope in this essay to do justice to those debates. Nonetheless, the argument that I am making does require further exploration of the relationship between limitlessness, modernity and instrumental rationality. These themes are explored in the following discussion of the theoretical framework used to guide the ideas presented in this essay.

Green critical theory and modernity

Green critical theory (or green theory) encompasses a range of well established critiques of the technological society.[2] The norms and paradigms which legitimate modernity are identified by green theory as historically specific and epiphenomenal products of par-

---

1   Wendell Berry, 'Faustian Economics: Hell hath no limits,' *Harpers Magazine*, May 2008, p. 36.
2   Significant authors in this debate include Murray Bookchin, John Zerzan, Jaques Ellul, Christopher Manes, Paul Shepard and Peter Kropotkin. Many of these authors espouse views closely aligned with the ideas of green anarchism, or primitivism, which argue that the adoption of agriculture was a tragedy for humanity.

ticular economic and social relations. Explanation of these relations requires recognition of the fact that there is always a reality more real and therefore more important than isolated facts and tendencies, namely the reality of the total process, the totality of social development.[1] The perspective offered by green theory requires us to stand apart from this totality, in order the better to understand it. This often means making comparisons with previous non-industrial societies. This essay is predicated on those same analytical precepts.

Jacques Ellul and Erich Fromm, amongst others, trace the development of the social relations of most relevance to my argument to the breakdown of medieval society.[2] The collective nature of medieval society was, in these accounts, superseded by the atomisation of human relationships, which Ellul identifies as a necessary precursor to the development of industrial society.[3] This atomisation was inevitable following the loss of the support and sense of belonging provided by medieval social and religious structures[4] and was replaced with a developing sense of the self as an individual. Fromm and Ellul both see this individualism as offering a freedom from the ties of community and tradition. But, they argue, this freedom left people feeling isolated, afraid and in need of support and a sense of belonging. There was nowhere left to turn for this support but the newly emerging nation state. Consequently, the nation state becomes a type of secular God, the giver of laws, close at hand yet remote, with powers of life and death.[5] But the state-god is unable to help us answer what Bill McKibben has identified as the key question asked by the citizens of this new world, namely 'Is my life amounting to something'?[6] Absent a Christian God sitting in judgement as to whether or not one's life has been well lived, and how do we give our lives meaning? I propose that the gospel of material progress confers modernity with this otherwise absent sense of purpose, making

---

1   Harvey Lee, *Basics in Critical Social Research* (London: Unwin Hyman 1990).
2   Erich Fromm, *The Fear of Freedom* (London: Routledge, 2001); Jaques Ellul, *The New Demons* (New York: Seabury Press, 1975).
3   Ellul, *Technological Society*, p. 54.
4   Fromm, *Fear*, esp. pp. 33–53.
5   Ellul, *New Demons*, p. 81.
6   Bill McKibben, 'Posthuman,' *Harpers Magazine*, April 2003, p.15.

it both a moral imperative and humanity's 'necessary and inevitable destiny.'[1]

As a result, time is no longer understood as a circular phenomenon—the typical perception of non-industrial societies—but is instead 'linear and irreversible, as expressed through the infinite accumulation of knowledge.'[2] Wealth and knowledge are both forms of capital and it is this marking of time through the accumulation of these two forms of capital which generates a kind of philosophical force, pushing us ever 'forward' and blocking the path behind us. The sum of these forces, narratives and promises foreclose any sense of being able to 'go back' and we are instead 'imperilled to chase after the tomorrow which is always better than today.'[3] Being unable to escape the problems of modernity by returning to the past, we have no choice but to develop our antidotes from the poison. Thus, no matter how great the threats, we can only look to the structures and discourses of modernity for a solution.

Critical treatments of science

Green theory assumes that critique of oppressive structures involves a critique of the scientific knowledge which sustains them. Science's promise of understanding and control requires that all problems be quantified, any problems not amenable to quantification being consequently ignored. With this control comes the opportunity for profit and power. John Nef, in his analysis of the cultural foundations of industrial civilisation, argues that the dominance of number, ushered in with Newton's quantitative epistemology, is a prerequisite for the development of trade and commerce.[4] It is apparent then, that from the off, science, technology, and the dominance of number have been

---

1   Gustavo Esteva, cited in Andrea Zhouri, 'Global-Local Amazon Politics: Conflicting Paradigms in the Rainforest Campaign', *Theory, Culture and Society*, 21:2 (2004), p. 85.
2   Guy Debord, *Society of the Spectacle* (London: Rebel Press, 1983), p. 13.
3   Zygmut Bauman, cited in Peter Beilharz, *The Bauman Reader* (Chichester: Wiley Blackwell 2001), p. 219.
4   John U. Nef, *Cultural Foundations of Industrial Civilisation* (Cambridge: Cambridge University Press, 1956).

vital aspects in the development of bourgeoisie sensibility. However, the victory of science and instrumental reason was far from assured upon its first appearance. Paul Feyerberand explains that in the seventeenth, eighteenth and nineteenth centuries science competed with other views and ideologies and its methods and achievements were subject to an ongoing and widespread critical debate.[1] However, whatever the initial barriers faced by the scientific mindset, its dominance today is now complete and it faces no cultural resistance. The notion of science as a progressive force is not self-evident and the message requires constant repetition and defending. No holds are barred in the maintenance of this ideal of science because without continual technological innovation economic progress would cease. Today, science is argued by green theorists to exist primarily to provide both profits for industry and the technologies of control and discipline necessary for the reproduction of existing power relations.

The notion alluded to above—that in modernity all problems can be made to seem questions of technological adjustment—is the product of a world view dominated by instrumental reason.[2] Instrumental reason serves to justify living with the constraints of a society built around the needs of industrial technology. Ellul was concerned to analyse exactly what social changes were required to give the machine primacy in our lives and how our assent to such a situation was achieved. He used the concept of technique to answer questions such as: how has society been affected by our internalisation of the machine's requirements? How has our understanding of the world been shaped by the need to accommodate the products of science? He understood technique as the process whereby the machine is integrated into society, in the process creating the kind of society the machine needs. Thus, in the technological society technique becomes the centre of society; civilisation is created for technique by technique and is exclusively technique. In this world the human is reduced to the status of a device for recording effects and results effected by techniques. Freedom is reduced to choosing the tech-

---

1   Paul Feyerabend, *Science in a Free Society* (London: Verso 1978), p.74.
2   Vincent Geohagen, *Reason and Theory: The Social Theory of Herbert Marcuse* (London: Pluto Press, 1981), p. 71.

nique which gives the maximum efficiency: 'do nothing to change the social order is the maxim of technical society.'[1] Ellul's ideas of technique and efficiency support the thesis that modernity relies on limitlessness because there is never any end to the improvements in efficiency; nor is there any end to the areas of existence which can be made more efficient. As I will seek to demonstrate, this perspective is of profound relevance to the climate change debate.

Science offers the promise of ceaseless improvement, with no end goal in sight. A limitless future without horizons. There is no magic number for economic growth, no amount of wealth which marks the point at which we stop. There is no agreed lifespan upon which we are agreed as sufficient, no set number of diseases to cure after which we say, enough is enough: the suffering of animals in experiments is at an end. This quest for growth has become synonymous with rationality. The terms instrumental reason and instrumental rationality are used interchangeably and both refer to the idea that only that which can be quantified is to be worthy of consideration. Max Weber compared instrumental rationality to value rationality. Value rationality concerns itself with choosing the ends to which our efforts are directed, and for Weber was properly the domain of ethics, morality and politics.[2] Because there is no 'rational' way of choosing between one value and another, ultimately our dominant values are defined by those actors who possess the most power. Instrumental rationality, on the other hand, is concerned only with the most efficient means of achieving a subjectively ordered list of ends or desires and assumes 'one can master all things by calculation.'[3]

Considering climate change options within this typology, any attempt to resolve the problem by reconsidering the sort of world we want to live in is irrational, by dint of the fact that such considerations are beyond the calculus of instrumental rationality. The only rational response is to find the most (cost-) efficient means of reproducing the current social order. Such a constrained response to climate change only appears reasonable because instrumental rational-

---

1   Ellul, Technological Society, p. 417.
2   Nicholas Xenos, *Scarcity and Modernity* (London: Routledge, 1989), p. 77.
3   ibid., p.79.

ity has come to dominate over all other considerations about human activity. Consequently, climate change is—as with the Stern report—reduced to a cost-benefit analysis; the cost, in terms of GDP, of avoiding dangerous climate change as opposed to the costs as measured by GDP, of doing nothing.[1] Whether a future measured by GDP is a good or bad thing—being beyond the means of our reasoning—becomes simply irrelevant.

In summary, there is a significant body of literature which argues that modernity should be understood as a period of human history which has two characteristics of particular relevance to our further discussion. Firstly, modernity asks us to believe in a world without limits, which in turn assumes limitless human potential. Secondly, in modernity science is the ultimate form of knowledge but this knowledge is only concerned with the quantifiable elements of the world. All problems can be understood and resolved through the application of number. Into this party gatecrashes the spectre of climate change and the insistent cry that we recognise a limit which undermines the dreams of modernity—a limit to the capacity of the atmosphere to carry the carbon dioxide being emitted by industrial processes. In response, policy makers have come back with a limit of their own in order to guide our understanding of climate change and the range of appropriate responses—the two degree dangerous limit. It is to a critical discussion of this dangerous limit that I now turn.

The two degree dangerous limit

> If I had to pick out one piece of misinformation that is doing the most damage it would be this statement: 'This is safe, this is a safe level'.[2]

Dominant discourses from policy, media and NGO communities

---

1 Sir Nicholas Stern, The Stern Report, 2006, http://www.hmtreasury.gov.uk/independent_reviews/stern_review_economics_climate_change/sternreview_index.cfm

2 Lee Ketelsen, cited in Mary O'Brien; 'Science in the service of good: The precautionary principle and positive goals' in Joel Tickner, ed., *Environmental Science and Preventative Public Policy*, (London: Island Press, 2003), p. 379.

leave no doubt that climate change is best understood as a quantitative phenomenon—global measurements charting the rise of atmospheric carbon dioxide concentrations; deciding on a dangerous limit to warming; online personal carbon footprint calculators—all assure us that climate change is amenable to management through the application of industrial technologies. Such attempts to quantify a dangerous limit to climate change, as we have already suggested, derive from the dominance of instrumental reason. In accepting the legitimacy of instrumental reason we should accordingly recognise that empirical measurements provide valid information for guiding our actions. Empirical measurements reveal that, *ceteris paribus*, climate will change in line with variations in the amount of carbon dioxide in the atmosphere. At a global scale it is assumed that increases in atmospheric concentrations of carbon dioxide will lead to increases in temperatures at the surface of the earth large enough to have harmful impacts on the biosphere.

Yet, after thirty years of dealing with climate change as a technical problem such concentrations are rising at over twice the rate of increase during the 1990s.[1] Therefore, there is no empirical evidence for the belief that dangerous climate change can be avoided within the paradigm of technological society and its attendant epistemology of instrumental reason. Which means, in the absence of any alternative, that we are required to continue relying on a religious belief in a technology, as of yet unseen, to provide the means for our salvation. Yet we continue to treat climate change as a technical problem for political and ideological reasons—framing the climate change question in predominantly scientific, technical and quantitative terms'.[2] However, given the inability of a quantitative framing of climate change to provide any meaningful response to the crisis we must ask: 'Who has constructed [this technological understanding of climate change] and what interests does it serve to protect and pro-

---

1   'Sharp rise in CO2 levels recorded', 14 March 2006 http://news.bbc.co.uk/1/hi/sci/tech/4803460.stm

2   I am indebted to Jerome Ravetz for his 'Post-Normal Science in the context of transitions towards Sustainability' paper prepared for the International Workshop Series, Workshop No. 1, 'Transitions to sustainable development: complexity, co-evolution and governance.' Personal communication, 2 July 2007.

mote? What and who has been silenced by this discourse'?[1]

I would argue that constructing climate change as a phenomenon with a dangerous limit serves to open up a 'possibility space'[2] for the development of technological, market-based solutions geared towards the reproduction and legitimisation of modernity. These technological responses describe a future of ecological modernisation; a world in which we can enjoy the benefits of industrial activity but avoid the environmental downsides. EU climate change policy, in being defined by the end point target of two degree centigrade 'dangerous limit' to anthropogenic warming is an example of such ecological modernisation. Constructing climate change in this way makes the problem appear not just manageable, but manageable by application of the scientific toolkit of our ecological modernity.

In other words, though this quantification of climate change gives the air of neutrality, truth and objectivity its definition as a phenomenon with a dangerous limit owes more to values and power relations than 'objective' science. Discussion of the two degree limit first appeared in print over thirty years ago.[3] My PhD thesis provides a full account of how this discourse has been reproduced and legitimated across various epistemic communities over this period, leading up to the formalization of the dangerous limit concept in the EU's Energy and Climate Strategy.[4] The full two degree timeline is long

---

1   Helen Smith, 'Disrupting the global discourse of climate change: the case of indigenous voices,' in Mary E. Pettenger, ed., *The Social Construction of Climate Change: Power, Knowledge, Norms, Discourses* (Aldershot: Ashgate Publishing, 2007), p.150.

2   Torsten Hägerstrand, 'Decentralisation and Radio Broadcasting: On the "Possibility Space" of a Communication', *European Journal of Communication*, 1 (1986), pp. 7–26.

3   Work by the economist W. D. Nordhaus, from 1979, is cited as the first systematic treatment of two degrees as a 'reasonable' limit set against the maximum warming experienced within the range of long- term natural variations over the last 10,000 years. See Michael Oppenheimer and Annie Petsonk, 'Article 2 of the UNFCCC: Historical Origins, Recent Interpretations', *Climatic Change*, 73: 3 (2005),p.197.

4   See Europa press release, 'Limiting Global Climate Change to 2 degrees Celsius,' 10 January 2007. http://www.europa.eu/rapid/pressReleasesAction.do?reference=ME MO/07/16&format=HTML&aged=0&language=EN&gui Language=en. The legislation requires the EU to cut greenhouse gases by at least 20 per cent from their 1990 levels by 2020. Also Chris Shaw, 'An acceptable risk? The management of

and complex and I can do little more here than briefly highlight what I have identified as three key events in this process.[1]

The development of the two degree limit

1. The 'dangerous limits' ball got rolling in a serious manner with the United Nations Framework Convention on Climate Change in 1992 calling for the 'stabilization of greenhouse gas concentrations in the atmosphere at a level that would prevent dangerous anthropogenic interference with the climate system'.[2] The Convention made no attempt to define what constitutes a dangerous limit, seeing such definitions as beyond the role of science. Consequently the EU, keen to take the process forward, commissioned the German Advisory Council on Global Change (WBGU) to investigate the matter further.

2. The WBGU published three reports (WBGU 1995, 1997, 2003). The original 1995 report concluded that two degrees centigrade of warming represents an 'acceptable' limit on the basis of two principles: (a) safeguarding creation and (b) avoidance of unreasonable costs.[3] The authors arrived at the two degrees number by first looking at the highest average global temperature over the last 10,000 years—which is calculated as 16.1 degrees centigrade—then adding a further 0.5 degrees because apparently modern humans are more adaptable than our hunter-gatherer forebears. These calculations lead to a maximum allowed warming of 1.3 degrees centigrade relative

---

climate change,' forthcoming, University of Sussex PhD.

1   Interested readers are referred to accounts by Oppenheimer & Petsonk, 'Article 2 of the UNFCCC,' pp.195–226; Shardul Agrawala, 'Early science–policy interactions in climate change: lessons from the Advisory Group on Greenhouse Gases', *Global Environmental Change* 9:2 (1999), pp.157–169; Peter Newell, *Climate for Change: Non-state Actors and the Global Politics of the Greenhouse* (Cambridge: Cambridge University Press 2000); Tim Flannery, *The Weather Makers* (London: Penguin, 2005); Spencer Weart, *The Discovery of Global Warming* (Cambridge MA: Harvard University Press, 2003) and Sonja Boehmer-Christiansen, 'Climate protection policy: the limits of scientific advice,' *Global Environmental Change* 4:2 (1994), pp.140–59.

2   UNFCCC, 1992, Article 2.

3   Statement on the occasion of the First Conference of the Parties to the Framework Convention on Climate Change in Berlin, March 1995, p 7. http://www.wbgu.de/wbgu_sn1995_engl.pdf.

to 1995, which approximates to 2 degrees relative to pre-industrial times.[1]

3. The WBGU reconfirmed these assumptions in their subsequent two reports. Their analysis and recommendations have been operationalised in the EU's Climate and Energy Strategy Paper which lays out the legislation requiring member states to cut carbon dioxide emissions to levels which will prevent a breaching of the two degree centigrade limit.[2]

The deficiency of the EU's decision making process[3] is evident from the fact that even as the ink dries on its Strategy Paper, it is becoming clear that not only is there next to no possibility of staying under the two degree centigrade limit[4] but that such a limit, anyway, is in excess of anything that might reasonably be considered dangerous.[5] How could our Enlightenment-based institutions, peopled by rational people, have got it so wrong? Perhaps, because the primary object of the exercise is not to prevent anthropogenic forcing of the climate but to keep the modernity show on the road. From this per-

---

1   'First Conference of the Parties', p. 13.

2   Europa, 'Limiting Global Climate Change.'

3   Richard Tol, 'Europe's long-term climate target: A critical evaluation', *Energy Policy* 35 (2007), pp.426–27, describes the methodology as 'sloppy' and 'inaccurate'.

4   See comments of Vicky Pope, manager of the Met Office Hadley Centre's climate change research programme, 'World likely to pass dangerous warming limits-study,' *Reuters*, 10 September 2007.

5   Rajendra Pachauri, head of the Intergovernmental Panel on Climate Change (IPCC), told a Reuters Environment Summit in 2007, 'People are actually questioning if the 2 degrees centigrade benchmark that has been set is safe enough... There are some responsible voices that are raising this question. I expect that this will multiply.', *Reuters* 2 October, 2007. John P. Holdren, president of the American Association for the Advancement of Science, believes we have already passed the 'danger' threshold. See 'A New Middle Stance Emerges in Debate over Climate'. *New York Times*, 2 January 2007. James Hansen has added his voice to those calling for a reassessment of what amount of warming might be considered dangerous, claiming that 1 degree of warming is likely to be too much http://www.grist.org/news/maindish/2007/05/15/hansen/ Hansen's recent pronouncements have led to the establishment of a new campaign group, www.350.org <http://www.350.org>, which seeks to raise awareness of the maximum safe level of atmospheric CO2 concentrations. Current atmospheric levels of CO2 are approximately 385ppm, and rising at 2ppm per year.

spective the two degree figure provides a discursive resource through which Western elites can have their cake and eat it, in the process effectively condemning the global South to a future of ever increasing uncertainty and risk.[1]

One consequence of allowing the climate debate to become dominated by an end-point warming target is that we can always change the numbers, raising the bar to three degrees, four degrees, or whatever is needed to leave the elephant in the room (modernity) undisturbed.[2] But if we are to give any credence to the 'ultra-conservative' warnings from the climate science community then we must surely accept that the situation is very serious if not, indeed, terminal.[3] In such circumstances should not *everything* be up for discussion? Is modernity an evolutionary triumph so joyous and life affirming that it is better to die than to try imagining a future without it?

Lessons from the Stone Age

We have seen that climate change imposes upon us a consciousness of limits which threatens to expose modernity's mythology of limitlessness. Ecological modernisation, in constructing climate change as a process with a distinct, quantifiable dangerous limit, seeks to articulate a compromise position between these two points. The promise of a two degree limit is that we can buy ourselves enough time to find a way to maintain the limitlessness of modernity without breaching the limits of the ecosphere's ability to absorb the carbon dioxide being

---

1   As one prominent climate scientist told me: 'most of us are aware that this is going to kill people elsewhere in the world but they are a long way away, they're poor and they're generally black and we don't care…it's a socially politically constructed number it's not a scientifically derived number.'

2   For instance, Sir David King considers 3 degrees of warming the only politically feasible target. 'Chief scientists warns bigger rise in world's temperature will put 400 million at risk, *Independent*, 15 April 2006. See also 'Climate change: Prepare for global temperature rise of 4C, warns top scientist', *Guardian* 13 August 2008, for comments from Defra's chief scientific adviser. See also John Vidal, 'What will happen if Britain becomes 3C warmer?' *Guardian*, 8 May 2006.

3   For example, Peter Barrett, director of Victoria University's Antarctic Research Centre, claimed to be speaking for a 'huge community of scientists' in describing the potential for climate change to end human existence within 100 years, *Times of India*, 20 November 2004.

generated by the reproduction of modernity. That promise, however, has been broken; the science clearly indicates that dangerous anthropogenic interference with the climate has already begun.[1]

So where now for the dangerous limits discourse? Those who perceive this current juncture in human history to be at a crisis are, in effect, 'trying now to deal with the failure of scientists, technicians and politicians to think up a suitable version of human continuance.'[2] Dan Hind proposes that another form of the Enlightenment other than modernity is required, and that anarchism is the true heir to Enlightenment ideals. For Hind, the Enlightenment inheritance means that we should be willing to pursue lines of enquiry associated with previously discarded schools of thought, and be willing to focus on the facts, no matter how uncomfortable that may make us feel. In other words, we must seek to confront our settled convictions and never forget that enlightenment is knowledge in the service of liberation. This also happen to mean recognising that the dominant institutions of modernity—the state and corporations—are the true enemy of reason.[3] In opposition to what such institutions would have us believe about the human condition—that we are vicious brutes whose only hope is to surrender up our freedoms to the safekeeping of our masters—we might perhaps be better served by turning our attention to those authors who argue that our natural condition is one of an egalitarian individualism, a state of affairs posited by the anthropologist, Hugh Brody, as the hunter-gatherer's greatest gift and lesson to modern humanity.[4] This egalitarian individualism could also be described as the essence of anarchy.

But what sort of anarchy? One of the leading lights of the Left, Noam Chomsky, has decried green anarchism because, in abandoning civilisation it would lead to starvation for millions of people or, put more prosaically—as he himself is unable to grow food—it fails

1   See Daniel Harvey, 'Dangerous anthropogenic interference, dangerous climatic change, and harmful climatic change: non-trivial distinctions with significant policy implications', *Climatic Change*, 82 (2007), pp. 1–25.

2   Berry, 'Faustian Economics', p. 39.

3   Dan Hind, *The Threat to Reason* (London: Verso, 2007).

4   Hugh Brody, *The Other Side of Eden* (London: Faber and Faber, 2002), p. 308.

to be a viable option.[1] However, put the matter the other way round and it is difficult to understand how anarchism, defined by the free association of individuals, could support an industrial society. Must anarchy not, by definition, mean a green anarchy?

Of course, the idea of looking outside of modernity, or even to the grass-roots for a solution to the climate problem remains a matter of profound distaste for most professional and academic elites—including social scientists—who see in a growing distrust for science 'the arrival of a new dark age.' 'Too hot a radicalism,' for instance, might 'fan popular widespread doubts about science into sheer destruction.'[2] Clearly, the process of destroying the world is best left to the experts.

Though climate change is in essence a political problem, many self-appointed guardians of our future continue to present it as one of technique, rendering the opinions of the scientifically illiterate invalid, and, thus, turning political choices again into technical options.[3] Back in the 1960's Herbert Marcuse saw the consequences of such reasoning as leading to the extinction of critical thought and action. We look to technological rationality for the answers to all our problems and forget the historically transcendent concepts which allow us to understand 'what is so really terrible about this well-ordered and affluent society.'[4]

The climate change debate is premised on the assumption that any move away from the comforts and conveniences of modernity will mean pain. But if, as many expert commentators believe, it could spell the end for industrial civilisation anyway, is it not worth investigating this taboo without the fetters of a technophilia-inscribed discourse of modernity? I am not going to argue that we should, or could return to a hunter-gatherer lifestyle but instead ask that if we are to follow the injunction of green critical theory to stand outside of soci-

1   Noam Chomsky, 'Questions about Anarchism –1 of 5' http://www.youtube.com:80/watch?v=nO2e0DrnYg4.
2   Immanuel Wallerstein, 'Social science and contemporary society: the vanishing guarantees of rationality,' *International Sociology*, 11:1 (1996), p. 10.
3   Paul Anderson, 'What risks are eclipsed when risk is defined by corporatism?' *Theory, Culture and Society*, 21:6 (2004) p. 154.
4   Cited in Vincent Geohagen, *Reason and Eros: The Social Theory of Herbert Marcuse* (London: Pluto Press, 1981), p. 65.

ety in order to interrogate it, then we should stand in exactly that place which has defined humanity for the vast majority of its existence. From that perspective—of our hunter-gatherer forebears—we might better understand our current position for what it is: an aberration, rather than one point on a teleological pilgrimage to humanity's true destiny.

Hunter-gatherers certainly didn't rush into a life of agriculture. On the other hand, once a sedentary lifestyle became the global norm, their marginalisation, then destruction, took on a relentless quality. In colonial Africa, for instance, bushmen were legally defined as vermin who could be shot at will.[1] (Bushmen and cavemen: the terms tell us so much. Are modern humans to be reduced to the status of 'housemen', or 'car men'?) The extermination of hunter-gatherers was justified using imagery that is with us still today; they were primitive beasts, a reminder of our shameful natural history. Who doesn't still recoil at the thought of the imbecilic Neanderthals, digging around in the dirt for grubs, spending every hour in fear of their lives, waiting for evolution to deliver the intelligence needed to free them from this misery?

Green anarchists such as John Zerzan argue that such myths have an important role to play in modernity, reminding us all us where we would be without the rule of bosses, priests and kings.[2] Zerzan has called for a more disencumbered approach to the recent anthropological literature, a literature which asks us to reconsider whether our stagnant prehistory wasn't actually an idyllic life fit for purpose. The sort of research Zerzan has in mind indicates that during the majority of the last three million years, up to the Holocene and the development of agriculture, for the majority of humanity '...the landscape would have been a true Garden of Eden, with beautiful freshwater lakes, beautiful shorelines and forests along the rivers. There would have been open spaces allowing early humans to exist easily, with water and lots of resources.'[3] The people who inhabited this landscape were not retarded; the symbolic use of colours, for instance, suggests an

---

1   John Seymour, *The Ultimate Heresy* (Hereford: Green Books, 1986), p.13.

2   John Zerzan, *Future Primitive* (New York: Autonomedia, 1994), p.13.

3   Mark Maslin and Beth Christensen, 'Tectonics, orbital forcing, global climate change, and human evolution in Africa: introduction to the African paleoclimate,' *Journal of Human Evolution* 53: 5 (2007), pp. 443–64.

abstract thinking going back at least 200,000 years.[1] Thomas Wynn is another who, picking up on Piaget's ideas on the development of intelligence, claims that stone tools from a further 100,000 years ago suggest an intelligence equal to that of modern humans.[2] As for our Neanderthal cousins, we are now having to reconceptualise the archetype of barbaric ignorance and accept that Neanderthals were in fact 'intelligent and emotionally complex people'.[3]

All this begs the question: if everything was so great, what could have forced that initial move to a settled lifestyle? If the move to farming was the single most important event in the human experience yet, at the same time, a change that occurred after an unimaginably long hunter-gatherer existence, one is tempted to propose that an external forcing mechanism must have been at play. Some anthropologists and archaeologists claim that population pressures caused the shift to agriculture, perhaps in combination with climate change. Again, recent research is shedding some interesting light on these questions. Investigations from the University of East Anglia in 2006 conclude that civilisation arose from environmental catastrophes 5–10,000 years ago:

> We find similar evidence (from around the world) for increasing aridity ... and the emergence of urban centres where people have been forced to congregate by a drying environment. Such changes were accompanied by a decrease in life expectancy, and increases in social inequality, hierarchy, organised violence and warfare.[4]

Understanding the shift to agriculture as a defensive move forced upon humanity in response to an unprecedented global crisis, rather

---

1   L. Barham, 'Modern is as modern does? Technological trends and thresholds in the south-central African record,' in P. Mellars, et al., eds, *Rethinking the Human Revolution: New Behavioural and Biological Perspectives on the Origin and Dispersal of Modern Humans* (Cambridge: McDonald Institute for Archaeological Research, 2007), pp. 165–76.

2   Thomas Wynn, 'Intelligence of fossil man,' 1 September 1997. http://www.asa3.org/archive/asa/199709/0037.html

3   'Early Humanoids 'Intelligent And Emotionally Complex,' *Sunday Times*, 1 June 2005.

4   Nicholas Brooks, 'Climate Change, Drought and Pastoralism in the Sahel', (Discussion Note for World Initiative on Sustainable Pastoralism, (WISP/IUCN 2006).

than an evolutionary leap forward, might help provide a more enlightened and reasoned grounding for discussions about humanity's options for the future, allowing us to see beyond the limits of modernity. Thus, while Hobbes famously argued that the modern state delivered us from the nasty, brutish and short life of the savage, Derek Jensen has proposed to the contrary that violence is endemic to modernity. He claims civilisation is based on a particular hierarchy of violence—violence done by those higher up the hierarchy to those lower down is nearly always invisible and unnoticed (though when noticed fully rationalised) while, conversely, violence done by those lower down to those above is unthinkable, and on the rare occasions it occurs regarded with shock, horror and fetishisation of the victims.[1]

By the same token, modern discourses of medical progress, as if this was modernity's greatest gift to humanity, also suggest similar blockages of vision. It has been forcibly argued that the primary motive force in human actions can be understood in terms of death anxiety, or death denial.[2] In modernity, death anxiety is addressed through self-assertion, in which individuals affirms their specialness, importance and power. Yet it seems as if modernity's provision of the opportunity to enjoy these attributes offers little solace for those gripped by death anxiety. How else can we explain the ongoing obsession with medical advance? Though there have been increases in life expectancy during the twentieth century this has been accompanied by an exponential rise in population which has played a large part in the current ecological crisis. In addition, issues of life expectancy are seldom dealt with honestly—an extra 20 years of life doesn't limit the infinity of death by any amount whatsoever. Additionally, what improvements in health have been achieved appear to owe little to modernity's rule of technique—'the health of man is determined essentially by his behaviour, his food and the nature of the world around him, and is only marginally influenced by personal medical care.'[3] By compari-

---

1   Derek Jensen, *Endgame: The Problem of Civilisation,* vol 1 (New York: Seven Stories Press, 2008).

2   Michael Zimmerman, *Contesting Earth's Future, Radical Ecology and Postmodernity* (Berkeley: University of California Press, 1994), p. 54.

3   Thomas McKeown, cited in Steven Shapin, 'Possessed by the Idols,' *London Review of Books* 28: 23 (30 November 2006), p. 32.

son, *immortality* in pre-modern societies was achieved through self-effacement and the collective life: which existed before and continued beyond the life of the individual.

Perhaps for the majority of people debates such as this are meaningless; nothing is going to change and it is a sign of immaturity to keep raging against the world. Whilst it may be possible to find a psychological explanation for each and every view point, such explanations do not take us very far. If the anarchist suffers from a 'killing the father' syndrome, one can charge that the industrialist suffers from a 'killing the mother' impulse. Instead, what is required, but currently lacking, is a democratic discussion of alternatives to the bankrupt vision offered by the industrial processes and institutions which characterise modernity.

Conclusion

I have sought to argue that climate change is a problem of modernity and, if Ellul's analysis is correct, it cannot be reformed. It would follow from these assumptions that a solution to climate change requires an end to modernity. Yet, currently, such an aspiration is unthinkable, and so we live with the myth of a 'dangerous limit' to climate change which forestalls the need to face up to the inherent tension between it and modernity.

However, there may be a route out of this logjam. Firstly, we must argue that alternatives to modernity are not only possible but also desirable. This chapter has tried to signpost the ways in which we might viably make such an argument. The second part of the process is to change the way we talk about climate change. Instead of talking about 'dangerous limits', we need to talk about 'acceptable limits' to climate change. Such a rewording makes a range of considerations relevant, rather than the notion inherent in 'dangerous limits' that if it doesn't kill us then it's acceptable. In addition, by thinking about what is acceptable we bring the ideas about alternative patterns of social organisation into the mix rather than continuing to believe we can avoid 'bad' (i.e. dangerous) climate change without the need for any significant change in our lives. Unfortunately, we do not currently have the social structures and institutions which would support such a debate. However, as change is upon us, whether we like it or not, perhaps we should strive to ensure whatever path humanity takes is at least the result of a discussion held by all those living and in which a true plurality of viewpoints and aspirations are treated equally. We need to choose between a future that holds the potential for human flourishing or resign ourselves to profound ecological and social change of a much darker nature courtesy of an overheated atmosphere. Is that any kind of choice at all?

Part IV: Coming to Terms with a Recent Historical Legacy

7. Five Lessons for the Climate Crisis: What the History of Resource Scarcity in the United States and Japan can teach us

Roman Krznaric

Introduction

Climate change is often described as a global challenge without historical precedent. Never before has there been a problem that is so potentially destructive to humanity, so irreversible or so borderless. The temptation, therefore, is to look to the future for solutions (such as new technologies) rather than to look to the past. How could one draw lessons from the past if there are no comparable crises, if climate change is unique?

However, if we think about climate change not as a scientific or ecological problem, but as one of responding to acute resource scarcity that requires massive social adjustment, then history does become relevant. Why is climate change about scarcity? Because only a limited amount of carbon dioxide (and other greenhouse gases) can be safely emitted into the atmosphere. Current emission levels need to be drastically reduced and new ways of allocating the right to emit carbon dioxide urgently need to be drawn up. Of course, carbon dioxide is not scarce in the same way that food is scarce during a famine, since there continues to be large amounts of fossil fuels available for producing it. The point is that reducing carbon dioxide emissions to levels that avoid two degrees Celsius of global warming requires treating it *as if it were scarce*.

The historical parallel is that human societies have, at various points, faced imminent collapse or breakdown due to overuse or scarcity of resources, yet managed to adjust and avoid destruction or impoverishment. Two of the most pertinent examples are the response to forest depletion in pre-industrial Japan during the Tokugawa period (1600–1868), and the introduction of extensive rationing and price controls in the United States during World War II. Both these instances of social change have been subject to comprehensive scholarship but there has been no in-depth analysis of how they can inform policies for tackling climate change.[1]

The purpose of this essay is, therefore, to present two case studies of responses to acute resource scarcity and then to highlight the lessons they provide for confronting the climate crisis. My hope is that an historical perspective will help us to step back and look at the big picture of global warming, and be a reminder that major policy shifts are possible even when they conflict with prevailing economic ideology or political orthodoxy.

For each case study I will examine the context in which scarcity arose, the processes and policies through which the problem was tackled, the degree of success of the response, and finally the underlying reasons for the success of the response (in addition to explanations for aspects of failure). I will leave discussing the lessons we can draw until the conclusion.

Rationing and Price Controls in the United States during World War II

Context

Commentators on the climate crisis often invoke the system of war-

---

1   I have discussed them further in Roman Krznaric, 'Food Coupons and Bald Mountains: What the History of Resource Scarcity Can Teach Us About Tackling Climate Change', Occasional Paper 2007/63, Human Development Report Office (New York: United Nations Development Programme, 2007).

time rationing in Britain—rather than the USA—as an example of how it is possible to deal successfully with resource scarcity. They argue that the extensive system of controls on everyday items such as tea, cheese, meat and petrol imposed from 1940 up until the early 1950s demonstrates that it is possible for governments to shift consumption patterns on a national scale—and that, by analogy, it is therefore possible to ration carbon emissions today or to otherwise reduce our consumption of goods and services with a high carbon footprint. Indeed, between 1938 and 1943, consumption as a share of net national expenditure in Britain fell from 87 per cent to 55 per cent, and by 1942, rationed and price-controlled foods constituted over 50 per cent of total food expenditure.[1]

Critics counter that the analogy is a poor one, primarily because today climate change does not present a danger equivalent to the imminent invasion of British soil by Germany in the Second World War, or the immediate prospect of severe food shortages. That is, the fear and sense of crisis that drove extensive rationing does not exist in the present. This is certainly true for the majority of countries (exceptions include Tuvalu, which is already disappearing due to rising sea-levels), and one of the reasons why it is more appropriate to examine rationing and price controls in the USA: the United States managed to impose severe restrictions on consumption even though there was no immediate threat of invasion and food supplies were not under severe pressure. Moreover, in the 1940s, the USA had a more developed consumer culture than Britain and more powerful business interests to contend with, making it more like contemporary economies attempting to confront global warming. So how was it possible that, in the world's greatest centre of industrial capitalism, the most fundamental element of a capitalist economy—prices freely determined by the market—was largely suspended?[2]

---

1   Ina Zweiger-Bargielowska, *Austerity in Britain: Rationing, Controls and Consumption, 1939–1955* (Oxford: Oxford University Press, 2000), p. 31.

2   Rationing and price controls have a long history, going back to 301 CE when the Emperor Diocletian issued an edict fixing maximum prices for around 900 goods throughout the Roman Empire. See Humphrey Michell, 'The Edict of Diocletian: A Study of Price Fixing in the Roman Empire', *Canadian Journal of Economics and Political Science*, 13:1 (1947), pp. 1–12.

Despite the fact that US soldiers were dying for their country along-side their British counterparts, after the US entered the war in 1941 following Pearl Harbour, the situation on the American home front was markedly different. While Britain was in an era of austerity, the US was experiencing a wartime economic boom: civilian consumption increased 22 per cent during the war. According to the economist John Kenneth Galbraith, head of the government's price control system at the Office of Price Administration (OPA), the sacrifices US consumers had to make were relatively mild: 'Never in the long history of human combat have so many talked so much about sacrifice with so little deprivation as in the United States during World War II.'[1]

Nevertheless, US citizens were subject to rationing and retailers were faced with a comprehensive system of price controls throughout most of the war. It is remarkable that so many aspects of the price mechanism were placed under government control in a country with such a strong free market heritage and ideology, and that the system worked as effectively as it did.

Why were rationing and price controls introduced? One reason is that there was—as in Britain—a need to shift raw materials to wartime production and to divert food supplies to troops abroad; that is, scarce resources had to be allocated more effectively and efficiently. A second reason differed from the British case: instead of policymakers being motivated by the fear of food and other consumer-item shortages, the greater fear was inflation resulting from a full-employment war-production economy. In 1940 and 1941, writes Galbraith, fear of inflation reached 'paranoia' levels in government circles.[2] Third, there was a desire amongst some members of the administration to consolidate the ethos of government intervention in the economy and Keynsian demand management that had been established in the New Deal period in the 1930s, and to ensure the equitable distribution of scarce goods.[3]

---

1   John Kenneth Galbraith, *A Life in Our Times: Memoirs* (London: André Deutsch, 1981), p. 172.
2   Galbraith, *A Life*, p. 127.
3   Meg Jacobs, "How About Some Meat?': The Office of Price Administration, Consumption Politics, and State Building from the Bottom Up, 1941-46', The *Journal of American History*, December (1947), pp. 910–941, p.911; Paul M.

How did the system develop?

Unlike Britain, the US had not undertaken significant preparations for wartime rationing and price controls. However, once the US entered the war, the OPA (which operated from 1941 to 1946) played a major role in economic life and eventually had over 60,000 paid staff and some quarter of a million volunteers.[1] The OPA, like Britain's Ministry of Food, wished to impose a system of cheap prices and equitably distributed goods during the war. Yet it was more difficult for the OPA to act with undisputed authority, partly because the war was more distant and less directly threatening than in Britain. The OPA was thus forced to be more political, building coalitions with unions, consumer groups and other organisations in opposition to industry, and having continually to lobby Congress to be given new powers.

The fear of inflation was strong, and in January 1942 Congress gave the OPA the authority to enforce rationing, rent control and price control. In April 1942 President Roosevelt announced the General Maximum Price Regulation ('General Max'), which instructed sellers of goods to take as the ceiling the price that had been charged in March for the same or similar item. This method of price control left much to the discretion of the seller. Another problem was that agricultural products had been exempted from General Max, a situation that was reversed by the Economic Stabilization Act of October 1942. The system was given a major boost by Roosevelt's 'Hold the Line' order of April 1943, which introduced standardized dollar-and-cents prices for a whole range of consumer items, allowing shoppers to check prices against an official list. By 1944 the OPA affected 3 million businesses, issued regulations controlling 8 million prices,

---

O'Leary, 'Wartime Rationing and Governmental Organization', *American Political Science Review*, 39: 6 (1945), pp. 1089–1106, p. 1089; Amy Bentley, *Eating for Victory: Food Rationing and the Politics of Domesticity*, (Urbana and Chicago: University of Illinois Press, 1998), pp. 14–15.

1   Jacobs, 'How about some meat', p. 911; Geofrey Mills and Hugh Rockoff, 'Compliance with Price Controls in the United States and the United Kingdom During World War II', *Journal of Economic History*, 47:1 (1987), pp. 197–213, p. 209.

and stabilised rents for 14 million dwellings (affecting 45 million tenants).

The OPA was also responsible for rationing food and other items to 30 million shoppers through a mixture of points and ration stamps. Within 16 months after Pearl Harbour there were 13 major rationing programmes in operation, covering products such as tyres, cars, petrol, sugar, coffee, meat, processed foods, fat and cheese. By the end of the war rationing accounted for around one-third of the value of consumer goods purchased (compared to about half in Britain).[1]

Whereas the post-war Labour government in Britain pushed for the continuation of rationing and price controls, by 1946 US Congressmen (especially those representing ranchers, textiles and wheat) were doing their best to deprive the OPA of its powers. The meat packers put their market domination into practice, cutting slaughtering by 80 per cent, which led to the so-called 'meat famine' (highly problematic in a country where eating meat had great cultural importance).[2] Under such pressures the administration was forced to dismantle the OPA and reinstate the price mechanism, despite continuing inflationary pressures.

How successful was the system?

Although scholars tend to emphasise the failures, it is clear that OPA policies played a major role in keeping inflation down during the war. Consumer prices rose less than 2 per cent between 1943 and 1945, and total food costs, constituting a third of the average family budget, actually fell 4 per cent.[3] The mobilisation of hundreds of thousands of volunteers to enforce the system (see below) demonstrated a widespread support for price controls amongst consumers. As Galbraith points out, however, not all the credit for keeping inflation down should go to rationing and price controls, as taxation and compulsory savings also played an important part in dampening demand.[4]

There were serious problems with the system and it is clear that

---

1   Mills and Rockoff, 'Compliance', p. 209.
2   Jacobs, 'How about some meat', pp. 939–940; Bentley, Eating for Victory, p. 94.
3   'How about some meat', p. 918.
4   Galbraith, *A Life*, p. 130.

there was more evasive and illegal activity in the US than Britain.[1] Amongst the difficulties with General Max were that retailers often charged exorbitant under-the-counter prices, sold shoddy merchandise at regular prices or simply closed down and reopened with new higher prices to avoid the General Max price ceilings.[2] It is estimated that in mid-1944 as much as 40 per cent of meat was being sold on the black market.[3] Selling or trading coupons by consumers was technically illegal but rarely prosecuted.

More generally, trade association and business leaders mounted fierce opposition to the OPA, in stark contrast with British business's largely accepting attitude to wartime economic necessities. The opposition of the meat packing lobby (a virtual cartel) has already been mentioned above. The OPA attempted to introduce textile rationing, but opposition from industry forced it to abandon the idea.[4] In 1941 the head of the OPA suggested limits on car production as it was draining enormous resources that were required for the war effort. Industry representatives, unsurprisingly, attacked the idea viciously.[5] Nevertheless, it was still possible to force all plants to cease production of passenger cars, and commuting by car was limited by petrol rationing (most car owners were allocated three gallons per week).[6]

What accounts for the accomplishments?

To the extent that rationing and price controls were successful, three explanatory factors need to be highlighted.

The first is voluntary action. Shoppers—especially women—became invigilators of the price control system. Hundreds of thousands of women took 'The Home Front Pledge', publicly swearing an oath to 'Pay no more than Ceiling Prices' and to 'Pay your points in full'. Over 250,000 volunteers worked with 5,525 local War Price and Rationing boards, regularly checking neighbourhood prices to

---

1   Mills and Rockoff, 'Compliance', p. 197.
2   Jacobs, 'How about some meat', p. 917.
3   O'Leary, 'Wartime Rationing', p. 1103.
4   Mills and Rockoff, 'Compliance', p. 208.
5   Galbraith, *A Life*, p. 150.
6   http://en.wikipedia.org/wiki/Homefront-United_States-World_War_II.

ensure that local retailers were not cheating the system.[1] Here the OPA was drawing on a long tradition of US civic participation and a growing culture of consumer rights. By 1945, 7 per cent of all women shoppers (around 2.1 million people) claimed to have reported a price violation. An historian of the system emphasises, 'For one of the few moments in history, and certainly the only time at the government's initiation, the possibility of an organized, broad-based, cross-class consumer movement existed'.[2]

A second factor was home production of food. Like Britain, there was a mass government campaign for people to grow their own vegetables in their gardens or on allotments, in what were known as 'Victory Gardens'. By 1943, 20 million households (around three-fifths of the population) were producing more than 40 per cent of the vegetables Americans consumed. Amongst the incentives were that Victory Gardeners were granted 300 miles of extra petrol rations. As in Britain, 'wartime victory gardening and canning functioned as community builders'.[3]

A final explanation of US rationing success concerns the structure of industry. The highly oligopolistic structure of major US industrial sectors—such as steel, aluminium, oil, chemicals and pharmaceutical—made it easier to impose price controls. As Galbraith says, 'It is far easier to deal with a handful of large firms that with a plethora of small ones'.[4]

Overall, it is easy to be critical of the system of rationing and price controls in the US due to the extent of the black market and strong opposition from some business sectors, such as the meat industry. Yet it remains extraordinary that the government was able to intervene so extensively in the economy. Few people today remember—or would even believe—that the US government was able to force its car producers to stop making passenger vehicles, or to control prices for so many items on supermarket shelves.

---

1   Jacobs, 'How about some meat', p. 921.
2   'How about some meat', p. 924.
3   Bentley, *Eating for Victory*, pp. 114–115.
4   Galbraith, *A Life*, p. 173. See also John Kenneth Galbraith, *A Theory of Price Control* (Cambridge MA: Harvard University Press, 1952), p. 67, reprinted extract in Hugh Rockoff, ed., *Price Controls*, (Aldershot: Edward Elgar Publishing, 1992).

Responses to Forest Depletion in Tokugawa Japan

Context

Japan today should be an impoverished, slum-ridden, peasant society subsisting on an eroded moonscape, rather than a wealthy, dynamic and highly industrialized society living on a luxuriant, green archipelago.[1]

It seems hard to believe this apocalyptic vision of the environmental historian, Conrad Totman. Yet for centuries Japan seemed 'bent on accomplishing its own destruction' through ravaging its woodlands, leaving bald mountainsides where there had once been dense forests.[2] Pre-industrial Japan was a wooden-structured civilisation as dependent on timber as we are today on oil. In order to meet its huge appetite for timber, the old-growth forests of the three main islands (especially in the Kinai Basin, encompassing Kyoto and Osaka) were largely cut down or otherwise depleted, particularly between 1570 and 1670. Natural re-growth and scattered efforts of re-planting were unable to keep pace with demand. By the eighteenth century, during the Tokugawa shogunal regime, this destruction of the forests had led to severe resource scarcity that raised the prospect of economic and social collapse.

How was the impending environmental catastrophe averted? How is it that today Japan is a 'green archipelago', 80 per cent of which is covered with forested mountains, rather than a 'slum-ridden, peasant society'? The short answer concerns an innovative system of woodland management that primarily benefited future generations.

It is important to understand how Japanese society was organised at the time of the threat. The Tokugawa *bakufu* (shogunate) was a

---

1 Conrad Totman, *The Green Archipelago: Forestry in Pre-Industrial Japan*, (Athens: Ohio University Press, 1989), p. 171.

2 Totman, *The Green Archipelago*, p. 25; Conrad Totman, *The Origins of Japan's Modern Forests: The Case of Akita*, (Honolulu: University of Hawaii Press, 1985), p. xiii. The following material draws substantially but not exclusively on Totman's studies, which have recently received public attention through their discussion in Jared Diamond, *Collapse: How Societies Choose to Fail or Survive* (London: Penguin, 2005), pp. 294–306.

military dictatorship based in Edo (today's Tokyo), which directly administered one-quarter of Japan. The remainder was ruled by around 250 subordinate barons or *daimyo*, each in charge of their own government or *han*. The bureaucracies of both the *bakufu* and *han* were staffed by samurai. Of the country's 30 million population in the eighteenth century, some 85 per cent lived in rural areas, the vast majority being peasants. A peculiarity of the Tokugawa regime is that it enacted a policy of economic and cultural isolation from foreign influences and effectively became an autarky, engaging in almost no foreign trade that could help relieve its resource scarcity.[1]

What caused such extensive forest depletion in the seventeenth century? First was the vast construction boom instigated by the elite, which required a surge in logging and the wholesale destruction of forests to build thousands of wooden castles, mansions, palaces, temples and shrines. Unlike in Europe during the same period, there was little use of alternative materials such as stone, bricks or mortar.[2] Governments in particular were continually requisitioning lumber for these monumental building projects, many of which were designed to enhance the status of major regime officials and leaders. Second, cities and towns were growing at a fast pace, leading to greater demand for housing construction timber (almost every element of a Japanese home being made from wood) and also for wood for fuel (firewood and charcoal). By 1800 the population of Edo, at 1 million, was greater than that of Paris or London. General population growth exacerbated the demand for timber.[3] A third factor was the expansion of agricultural land for food production at the cost of forests. Finally, agricultural development required large amounts of natural fertilizer because of the intensely farmed poor soil, and much of this fertilizer (e.g. scrub brush and leaf fall) was sourced from woodland.[4]

1 Fernand Braudel, *The Structures of Everyday Life: The Limits of the Possible*, Volume 1 of Civilization and Capitalism 15th-18th Century (London: Collins/ Fontana Press, 1981), p. 156.
2 Totman, *The Green Archipelago*, p. 79; Braudel, *Structures*, pp. 266–282.
3 The evidence suggests that population growth levelled off in the latter part of the Tokugawa period. See, for example, Susan B. Hanley and Kozo Yamamura, *Economic and Demographic Changes in Preindustrial Japan 1600–1868* (Princeton: Princeton University Press, 1977).
4 Totman, *The Green Archipelago*, p. 175; Conrad Totman, *A History of Japan*

Deforestation was not only problematic because of the potential constraints it placed on urban development and agricultural production (through the scarcity of fertilizer). Governments were dependent on timber as a source of income, selling it from their own lands or raising taxes from commercial logging. Villagers were dependent on woodland for their everyday livelihood. And forests also played a vital role in preventing erosion and flooding of Japan's ecologically fragile lowlands. These forests, it should be noted, were not 'owned' but rather subject to a complex system of overlapping use rights. Some were effectively controlled by governments and ruling lords (*ohayashi*), some by villagers who sourced timber for their daily needs, but in practice most forests were used by both rulers and commoners.[1]

How did the responses to forest depletion develop?

The responses to the timber crisis developed in two stages. First was the introduction of a 'negative' regime of regulations to limit timber extraction. This was followed by a far more successful 'positive' regime of producing trees, which saw the initiation of plantation forestry from around the 1760s.

A negative regime of ad hoc woodland management was gradually introduced between 1630 and 1720 as a response to forest depletion and the increasing competition for forest resources between government, merchants and villagers. Awareness of timber scarcity in the islands was possibly spurred on by the Meiriki fire, which swept through the city of Edo in 1657, killing around 100,000 people and destroying thousands of mansions and dwellings. It is estimated that reconstructing only half the houses of commoners would have required logging some 2,500 hectares of prime forest.[2]

Policies pursued by both the *bakufu* and *daimyo* governments included: decrees closing forests to logging to allow for regenera-

(Oxford: Blackwell, 2005, second edition), p. 255; Totman, *Origins*, pp. 7–12.

1   Iwamoto, Junichi, 'The Development of Japanese Forestry' in Yoshiya Iwai, ed., *Forestry and the Forest Industry in Japan*, (Georgetown: University of British Colombia Press, 2002).

2   Totman, *The Green Archipelago*, p. 68.

tion; placing limits on the amount of timber that could be extracted from government-controlled lands; and limiting the felling of trees over a certain size or of a particular species. At the local level, limits were placed on the gathering of fuelwood and organic fertiliser on both household and communal land. In addition to these supply-side controls were a series of demand-side regulations to limit wood consumption, which amounted to a system of rationing. Edicts were introduced specifying the type, size and number of pieces of wood that could be used to construct or repair bridges, dykes, dams, and boats. The size of new buildings was also regulated, and peasants were forbidden from using certain precious woods when building their homes (though the rich were allowed to use scarce timbers for their own houses).

Although this negative regime constituted an elaborate system of administrative controls and legal sanctions, it was poorly enforced and had little effect on regenerating Japan's increasingly scarce woodlands. Government continued to demand lumber and villagers flaunted the rules on tree felling. Overall the main role of the negative regime was that it 'bought time' until the introduction of plantation forestry.[1]

The real saviour of Japan's forests was the development of a positive regime of afforestation during the eighteenth century, which has continued into the present. Like the negative regime, it was a slowly evolving and often localised response to a long-term problem that only became consolidated and relatively systematic from around 1760. There were three main elements to its development.

First was the emergence of new forms of silviculture knowledge from the seventeenth century, often in the form of manuals or treatises on how to plant trees and maintain forests to maximise timber yields (e.g. new methods of propagation and tree aftercare). This arboreal knowledge helped foster a basic conservation ethic in pre-industrial Japan. It was also a necessary part of the establishment of successful plantation forestry for it transformed it into a potentially profitable enterprise.

Second was the widespread planting of new forests, rather than

---

1   *The Green Archipelago*, p. 115.

just the protection of old ones or reliance on natural regeneration. This was undertaken primarily by governments but also by village communities and entrepreneurs in the timber trade who could reap the yield of their investment after several decades. In the region of Hida, for example, the *bakufu* forests had been largely stripped of timber by the 1740s. From then on officials ordered villagers to plant new trees and by the 1850s they were being paid to set out around 100,000 seedlings per year. Entrepreneurial tree planting developed more slowly and commercial forestry did not become common until the mid-nineteenth century.[1]

A third element in the establishment of successful plantation forestry was changes in landholding arrangements. As noted above, most woodland had been open to multiple users for centuries, making for a complex regulatory environment. A new system gradually emerged where forests were designated as having a single or primary user. One example was the practice of *wariyama*, in which lord's forest or village common land was divided amongst householders in a village, helping to clarify use rights and reduce disputes. Rental forests became more common, often in the form of *nekiyama*, in which a villager planted a site and sold the timber in advance to a merchant. The villager nurtured the trees and when the trees were harvested after several decades, the villager could replant and re-lease the land.

By the mid-nineteenth century long-term forest stability had been achieved across the archipelago, a revolution of sorts that had involved government, villagers and entrepreneurs in a mosaic of practices that contributed to the development of plantation forestry.

Why was afforestation successful?

There are several underlying factors explaining the successful development of plantation forestry in pre-industrial Japan, which was fundamental in preventing an ecological catastrophe that could have brought about severe economic and social breakdown.

The authoritarian political system permitted new woodland management systems to be introduced without significant opposition (just

---

1   Totman, *The Green Archipelago*, pp. 166–67.

as the effectively authoritarian government that existed in Britain during World War II could introduce rationing without substantive resistance). Much plantation forestry took place as a consequence of decrees by the Tokugawa shogunate and regional barons, who realised that their long-term survival and financial solvency depended on maintaining and developing forests. Frequently the result of such top-down policies deprived villagers of their customary use rights. Governments, furthermore, were able to draft in cheap or forced (corvée) peasant labour to undertake the arduous task of planting. [1]

There was also significant grass-roots action by local communities. It was often village communities who put in place new regulations and use-rights to help adjudicate between those disputing over access to scarce forest resources. Villages planted forests on communal lands or limited lumbering to ensure an inheritance for all their future members, not just for their own families. Additionally, they planted woods to protect their lands from erosion and flooding. [2]

A third factor concerned the changing economics of the timber industry. Plantation forestry was an extremely long-term, costly and risky investment. There was usually around fifty years between planting and harvesting the timber, large amounts of labour were required for planting and aftercare, and trees could easily be lost in severe weather or through disease. Plantation forestry expanded when it became financially viable or profitable for governments, entrepreneurs and villagers to make such a substantial investment. A new investment climate emerged due to the scarcity of timber (which pushed up its price), improved silviculture knowledge and the shift from multiple to single-use forests. All this depended on Japanese society continuing to rely on timber as one of the central resources of everyday life as well as on ever-increasing demand due to rising urban population. [3]

One of the puzzles of forest recovery in pre-industrial Japan was why anybody would be interested in planting trees that could only be harvested after fifty years, when those who had instigated the plant-

---

1   Totman, *The Green Archipelago*, p. 148.
2   Iwamoto, 'The Development of Japanese Forestry', p. 5; Totman, *The Green Archipelago*, p. 43.
3   Totman, *The Green Archipelago*, pp. 113, 130–131, 147–148.

ing might well be dead. An answer lies in the great concern for the well-being of future family generations in traditional Japanese culture (which partly has Confucian roots), in addition to the principle of heredity that shaped political authority.[1] Shoguns and barons envisaged their descendents surviving as rulers into future generations, and plantation forestry became a means of ensuring their patrimony. This held for entrepreneurs and villagers as much as for political leaders: 'a basic assumption on which villagers commonly planned the future was that ideally one's heir would inherit one's estate'.[2] Such cultural attitudes created a long-term vision which encouraged them to invest in plantations and engage in long-term contracts that would ultimately benefit the family lineage rather than themselves.

In sum, a conjunction of top-down and bottom-up policies, and producer responses to the changing timber marketplace, all set against a cultural background of respect for the well-being of future generations, helped ensure that today's Japan is not the denuded lunar landscape it could so easily have become.

Five lessons for the Climate Crisis

It would be unwise to draw too many specific lessons for tackling climate change from the evidence of only two historical examples. The contemporary world is very different from wartime America, let alone the era of the Japanese shoguns. Moreover, social change can take place in many more ways than these cases illustrate.[3] Yet history remains one of the best sources for thinking about the climate crisis, since it reminds us of what has—and has not—been possible in human societies. I see five lessons for policymakers confronting global warming.

---

1   See the discussions in Linda G. Martin, 'Changing Intergenerational Family Relations in East Asia, *Annals of the American Academy of Political and Social Science*, 510 (1990), pp. 102–114, p. 105; Anita D. Bhappu, 'The Japanese Family: An Institutional Logic for Japanese Corporate Networks and Japanese Management', *The Academy of Management Review*, 25: 2 (2000), pp. 409–415, pp. 410–412.

2   Totman, *The Green Archipelago*, p. 185.

3   For an analysis of paradigms of change in over a dozen academic disciplines, see Roman Krznaric, 'How Change Happens: Interdisciplinary Perspectives for Human Development' (Oxford: Oxfam Research Reports, 2007).

1. Radical policy is politically possible

The first lesson is that it is feasible rather than unrealistic for governments to introduce radical legislation. The case studies show how
political leaders can initiate far-reaching, successful reforms to tackle
resource scarcity, and change patterns of consumption, production
and distribution. Despite concerted opposition from powerful business interests, the United States suspended the free market in core
economic sectors, and in Japan fundamental shifts in the supply of,
and demand for, timber resulted from regulation by the shogunate
and regional barons. It is rare to see such radical policies today, as
most governments are more interested in gradual change, in compro-
mising, in following the path of least resistance. But politicians and
the public should never underestimate what is possible. Admittedly,
the US rationing and price controls were a temporary measure lasting
only a few years, whereas today we need more long-term legislation.
Yet millions of consumers were able to get used to the system—just
as London's car drivers have become accustomed to paying to drive
in the city centre in recent years. In light of these examples, radical
policies to tackle climate change no longer appear so unrealistic.

However, it is important to recognise that in the case studies, the
problem of scarcity was largely contained and confronted within
national borders. Japan's policy of isolationism meant it did not look
to import timber from abroad to resolve its difficulties, while consumption and scarcity in the United States were hardly affected, for
instance, by its trade patterns with Latin American nations. In both
cases policy responses could be effective at the national level without the need for international cooperation or action. Climate change,
however, is an inherently cross-border problem requiring international collective action to achieve significant carbon reductions. This
inevitably adds a barrier to radical policy change.

2. Top-down solutions are essential

Japan dealt successfully with scarcity partly because there was a military dictatorship which meant that comprehensive policies could

be instigated without significant opposition. Similarly, the US government introduced rationing and price controls in a context of wartime exceptionalism which, though not amounting to government by decree, certainly permitted more radical policies than would have been possible in peacetime. Governments had the power and will to make change happen. In today's representative democracies, it is more difficult for political leaders to impose their priorities or vision. They must be sensitive to the desires of the electorate, wealthy party funders, big business interests and the media. They therefore often lack the resolve to push through the unpopular policies that are needed to tackle climate change, such as massive tax hikes on oil-based fuel. Confronting resource scarcity will require top-down solutions, so ruling parties need to find political authority without being lured into political authoritarianism. That is, they must display strength without slipping into dictatorship.

3. Grass-roots action makes a difference

While a top-down approach is vital, it is important to recognise that local initiative is also required, as demonstrated by Japan's village forestry schemes, and America's price-checkers and Victory Gardeners. Similarly, tackling climate change cannot succeed only through a series of national laws and international agreements. History needs to be made from below. Our efforts to create a more sustainable world must be fuelled not only by renewable energy but by a new culture of local activism, cooperation and education that encourages those with high-carbon lifestyles to reduce their footprint. We need to build on grass-roots low-carbon initiatives such as the Britain's Transition Towns movement and the Climate Outreach and Information Network (COIN).

4. Black markets will emerge

We must face up to the inevitability that black markets and other forms of corruption will emerge in schemes to ration greenhouse gas emissions. Extensive black markets existed in the US during World

War II, and illegal timber trading and use also took place in Japan. The lesson from the past is that both individuals and companies will be tempted to bend the rules of any rationing system that is imposed by governments, whether it be individual carbon allocations, or collective initiatives like the European Union's Emissions Trading Scheme. This is not to say that we should complacently accept corrupt practices, but that mechanisms must be put in place to limit the damage that it does to the successful operation of the scheme.

5. Empathy for future generations must be generated

A primary explanation for why Japan solved its woodland depletion problems was because it had a deeply ingrained culture of concern for future family generations. The country's elites were able to envisage their descendants in political power: a long-term vision of hereditary rule that facilitated afforestation schemes which would reap benefits only after decades. This attitude to future family generations existed throughout society and helped bolster change at the village level. In contrast, contemporary Western culture lacks this kind of long-term thinking. Politicians can barely see beyond the next election, and most citizens are subsumed in a culture of immediacy in which they desire the instant gratification of consumption and entertainment. While people care about the lives of their own children, there is not the same cultural concern with future generations as existed in Tokugawa Japan. Yet this is precisely what is needed to make us act today to tackle climate change, since the most disastrous impacts for Western societies—such as floods, droughts and food shortages—are likely to hit towards the end of, or after, our own lifetimes. The question is, therefore, how can we instigate a cultural shift based on generating empathy for future generations?

Of course, we must not ignore the fact that we are also extraordinarily insensitive to the plight of people in developing countries who are being affected by global warming today in the form of droughts, floods and other extreme weather events.

Ultimately, therefore, confronting the climate crisis requires new ways of imagining the lives of strangers—distant both through time and across space—and of stepping into their shoes and seeing the world from their perspectives. As I have suggested elsewhere, this will require an educational revolution not only in our schools, but in our workplaces, communities and everyday relationships, so that we all develop our powers of empathy.[1]

---

1   I have discussed this issue in Roman Krznaric, 'Empathy and Climate Change: Proposals for a Revolution of Human Relationships,' in Stefan Skrimshire, ed., *Future Ethics: Climate Change and Apocalyptic Imagination* (London: Continuum, forthcoming), and Roman Krznaric, 'You Are Therefore I Am: How Empathy Education Can Create Social Change' (Oxford: Oxfam Research Reports, 2008).

8. 'We are All Slave Owners now': Fossil Fuels, Energy Consumption and the Legacy of Slave Abolition

Jean-Francois Mouhot[1]

It is well-known that we often tend to 'see the speck in other people's eye but fail to notice the beam in our own'. Slavery, for example, is often approached with the underlying assumption that modern civilisation is now morally much superior to those barbaric slave owners' societies. Yet, before jumping too quickly to the conclusion that Europeans or Americans who owned slaves in the eighteenth or nineteenth century were incomprehensible barbarians, we should pause for a moment. If we look at current attitudes towards fossil fuels and climate change, on the one hand, and the behaviour of slave owners, on the other, there are more similarities than one might immediately perceive. I have previously argued[2] that slavery and its abolition are related in various causal ways to industrialisation, which triggered our large scale burning of coal and oil. The purpose of this piece, however, is to propose that there are many linkages between slave owning societies and our own.

It is a feature of human history that whenever societies have had the possibility to find someone *or something* else to work for them for free, or for a small financial cost, they have almost always taken advantage of it, whatever the moral cost, and with subsequent rationalising efforts the inevitable corollary. The way this operates, irrespective of gender, class, religion or ethnicity, is amply demonstrated by the fact that there were a number of slaveholders in the American

1   I am grateful to Pierre H. Boulle, Francesca Carnevalli, Cécile Folschweiller, Martin Forster, John R. McNeill, Caroline Mullen, for their comments on an earlier version of this chapter.
2   Jean-Francois Mouhot, 'Free the Planet', *History Today*, 58 (2008), p.42. A broader discussion of this theme, 'Past connections and present similarities in slave ownership and fossil fuel usage', has been submitted to *Climatic Change*.

South who had themselves been slaves. If slavery reminds us of 'our (slave and slave-owners alike) shared humanity, not only our triumphal possibilities but also our profound limitation',[1] the same could be said of fossil fuel usage. Even if Western countries are on average high greenhouse gases emitters, it is worth noting that amongst the ten highest emitting countries *per capita*, seven are not found in the West, but in the tiny oil-producing nations of the Persian Gulf, and some of the small countries in the West Indies.[2]

Thus, both slave owners and the average inhabitant of developed countries relied and still rely on the work of an external 'source of energy' to live in the way they felt, or feel, is their due. In the first case, labour came from slaves; in the other, 'work' – in the sense physicists use the word – is mostly provided by energy of the fossil fuel variety. As Marc Davidson recently put it: 'today the United States is as dependent on fossil fuels for its patterns of consumption and production as its South was on slavery in the mid-nineteenth century'.[3] Drawing on an earlier comparison,[4] Davidson convincingly argues that there are three types of similarities between slavery and the use of fossil fuels: vested interests in the electorate; transfer of costs to third parties and resistance to social change. Yet it is possible to go further and find even more resemblances.

New studies have shown that 'in the 1990s the average global citizen [...] deployed about twenty 'energy slaves', meaning twenty

---

1   David Brion Davis, *Inhuman Bondage. The Rise and Fall of Slavery in the New World* (Oxford: Oxford University Press, 2006).

2   G. Marland, T.A. Boden, and R. J. Andres, 'National CO2 Emissions from Fossil-Fuel Burning, Cement Manufacture, and Gas Flaring: 1751–2004', Carbon Dioxide Information Analysis Center, Oak Ridge National Laboratory, Oak Ridge, Tennessee, 2007; http://cdiac.ornl.gov/trends/emis/top2004.cap). The high figures for oil-producing countries are not due to gas flaring. 'CO2 emissions from gas flaring [...] now account for less than 1 per cent of total emissions' of Saudi Arabia (idem, 'Global, Regional, and National CO2 Emissions', *Trends: A Compendium of Data on Global Change,* Carbon Dioxide Information Analysis Center, 2007; http://cdiac.ornl.gov/trends/emis/tre_sau.htm).

3   Marc D. Davidson, 'Parallels in Reactionary Argumentation in the US Congressional Debates on the Abolition of Slavery and the Kyoto Protocol', *Climatic Change*, 86 (2008), pp. 67–82.

4   David Orr, '2020: A Proposal', *Conservation Biology*, 14 (2000), pp.338–41.

human equivalents working 24 hours a day, 365 days a year'.[1] That is, if we wanted to do without any petroleum, coal, natural gas, or electricity, we would need to employ several dozen persons, or more, working full-time for us. 'Who had the possibility, only a century ago, to afford the equivalent of several tens of servants to get fed, washed, transported, diverted, and so on, with the sole product of one's work?', asks Jean-Marc Jancovici.[2] This astoundingly high figure come from the fact that a single litre of petrol contains the equivalent of about 9 kWh of energy, while the output of an average human being is about 3 kWh in the course of a 40-hour working week.[3] Consider how many people would be needed, and for how long, to push an average car weighing 1 ton for 15 miles. A reasonably efficient car can do this with just one litre of gasoline or diesel and at a much greater speed. Compared to the cost of the level of labour offered by fossil fuels, we pay little for our oil. It is no wonder that people in the nineteenth and twentieth century enthusiastically adopted new energies and technologies, or that the majority of us want to continue to enjoy the numerous positive aspects of fuel-pow-

1   John Robert McNeill, *Something New under the Sun: An Environmental History of the Twentieth-Century* (London: Allen Lane, 2000), p.15. See also James Howard Kunstler, *The Long Emergency: Surviving the Converging Catastrophes of the Twenty-First Century* (London: Atlantic, 2006), p. 31, who argues that 'fossil fuels provide for each person in an industrialized country the equivalent of having hundreds of slaves constantly at his or her disposal', or Richard Heinberg, *The Party's Over: Oil, War and the Fate of Industrial Societies* (Gabriola Island: New Society Publishers, 2003), pp.30–31: If we were to add together the power of all the fuel-fed machines that we rely on to light and heat our homes, transport us, and otherwise keep us in the style to which we have become accustomed, and then compare that total with the amount of power that can be generated by the human body, we would find that each American has the equivalent of over 150 'energy slaves' working for us twenty-four hours a day'. All in all, I have come across over ten authors making similar claims, even though the figures vary widely. Recently, Colin Campbell told the BBC: 'Today's energy supply is equivalent, in energy terms, to 22 billion slaves working round the clock - we are basically working with this enormous stock of slaves working for us in the form of oil' (*Natural World*; 'A Farm for the Future', broadcast BBC2, 20 February 2009).

2   Jean-Marc Jancovici, and Alain Grandjean, *Le Plein, s'il vous plaît! La solution au problème de l'énergie* (Paris: Seuil, 2006).

3   Richard Douthwaite, 'Sharing out the Rations', *The Irish Times*, 13 January 2007; comparable figures are provided in Jancovici and Grandjean.

ered machines.

The idea that black slaves have been replaced with 'black gold' is also conveyed in a 60-second television advert produced by the Competitive Enterprise Institute, shown in the USA in 2006. Over the picture of a black woman at work, and then a tractor ploughing a field, an off-camera voice claims: 'The fuels that produce CO2 have freed us from a world of back breaking labour'. The picture of the black woman brings to mind the work of slaves. Whether on purpose or not, the image suggests that the 'backbreaking labour' referred to is the work of slaves and that slavery was abolished because a replacement (fossil fuels) was found.

Besides the similarities between the convenience brought to us by fossil fuel- powered machines and the convenient life slaves brought to slave owners, one can draw a parallel between the harm caused to human beings by slavery and the harm caused by the current large-scale burning of fossil fuels. Some might argue that it is not possible to compare pain triggered by the use of slaves and pain caused by the use of oil, gas or coal, as in the latter case we are dealing with inanimate objects that obviously cannot suffer. However, when we burn oil or gas above what the eco-system can absorb, we are causing pain and suffering to other human beings. The reports from the Intergovernmental Panel on Climate Change (IPCC) make it clear that the release of carbon dioxide is already causing harm and is expected to produce much more in the future, by increasing droughts and flooding, threatening crop yields and displacing large numbers of people. The future looks grim for the world, whether the IPCC looks at freshwater resources and their management, ecosystems, food or health.[1]

> By mid-century, annual average river runoff and water availability are projected [...] to decrease by 10–30 per cent over some dry regions at mid-latitudes and in the dry tropics, some of

---

1   M. L. Parry, O. F. Canziani, J. P. Palutikof, P. J. van der Linden, and C. E. Hanson, 'Summary for Policymakers,' in *Climate Change 2007: Impacts, Adaptation and Vulnerability: Contribution of Working Group II to the Fourth Assessment Report of the Intergovernmental Panel on Climate Change* (Cambridge: Cambridge University Press, 2007).

which are presently water-stressed areas. Drought-affected areas will *likely* [meaning a 66 to 90 per cent probability] increase in extent. Heavy precipitation events, which are *very likely* [90 to 99 per cent probability] to increase in frequency, will augment flood risk. In the course of the century, water supplies […] are projected to decline, reducing water availability in regions […] where more than one-sixth of the world population currently lives. The progressive acidification of oceans […] is expected to have negative impacts on marine shell-forming organisms (e.g., corals) and their dependent species. […] Many millions more people are projected to be flooded every year due to sea-level rise by the 2080s. […] At lower latitudes, especially seasonally dry and tropical regions, crop productivity is projected to decrease for even small local temperature increases (1–2°C), which would increase the risk of hunger. […] Projected climate change-related exposures are *likely* to affect the health status of millions of people, particularly those with low adaptive capacity.

The predictions of the IPCC specifically for Africa (the continent where most of the slaves came from historically) are even scarier:

By 2020, between 75 million and 250 million people [in Africa] are projected to be exposed to increased water stress due to climate change […]. Agricultural production, including access to food, in many African countries and regions is projected to be severely compromised by climate variability and change. The area suitable for agriculture, the length of growing seasons and yield potential, particularly along the margins of semi-arid and arid areas, are expected to decrease. This would further adversely affect food security and exacerbate malnutrition in the continent. In some countries, yields from rain-fed agriculture could be reduced by up to 50 per cent by 2020. […] Towards the end of the twenty-first century, projected sea-level rise will affect low-lying coastal areas with large populations. The cost of adaptation could amount to at least 5–10 per cent of Gross Domestic Product (GDP). Mangroves and coral reefs are projected to be further degraded, with additional consequences for fisheries and tourism.[1]

If we accept the carefully and conservatively worded conclusion of the IPCC, we must recognize that we are now fully aware of both the causes of climate change and its consequences. Thus, it is not possible to argue any more that our use of oil is morally neutral. Driving cars or flying *does*—however indirectly and unwittingly—hurt people now. And because emissions accumulate in the atmosphere, they will increasingly continue to do so in the future, unless somehow the trends reverse, either naturally or through human action.

For those who still disagree that climate change is hurting people, or do not believe that the climate is being significantly altered by human activity, there is still the moral as well as practical problem that by using fossil fuels we are depleting very valuable resources that are not renewable. Scholars like Jared Diamond,[2] in his book *Collapse,* have vividly shown that whole societies have disappeared from the map because they relied on a staple source of food or energy that they subsequently depleted. Britain had oil in the North Sea, much of which is now gone forever. The nation has used a resource that its children will not be able to benefit from, and because the oil and gas have been burnt in large part for leisure, commuting, and so forth, it has not replaced it by anything of similar value. The next generation will inherit the worst consequences of this cheap energy lifestyle (if we leave aside anthropogenic climate change, we could add pollution, obesity, the spread of concrete over arable land and greenbelt, and the consequent development of highly unsustainable suburbia, to the litany). One could of course rightly argue that 'human history since the dawn of agriculture is replete with unsustainable societies, some of which vanished but many of which changed their ways and survived'.[3] History is useful as it can remind us both of the ingenuity of the human species to solve problems of resource depletion in the past and at the same time can also make us acutely aware of the

---

1   Parry, 'Summary for Policymakers.'
2   Jared M. Diamond, *Collapse: How Societies Choose to Fail or Survive* (London: Allen Lane, 2005).
3   McNeill, *Something New*, p. 358.

dangers involved in depleting resources too quickly. It is also true that previous generations have often left huge debts to their children. However, anthropogenic climate change is a new problem taking place on an unprecedented scale. In any case what previous generations did cannot justify our wrongdoings now.

Similarly, how should we respond to the moral problem that in a world where poor people struggle to find enough food to feed their families, we, in the West, are increasingly burning potential food to run our cars or heat our homes? Some remorseless companies go as far as to encourage people to burn corn instead of wood pellets: 'heat your home for a bushel of corn per day' claims a Canadian company.[1] Filling up a large car's fuel tank with ethanol uses enough maize to feed a person for a year.[2] Put starkly the rich are buying up food to run cars at the expense of the world's poor.[3] We are also clearly putting our societies and our children at risk by relying so heavily on fossil fuels. In the same way as slave owners constantly worried about slaves escaping or revolting, we also worry about our suppliers of oil or gas stopping to deliver the precious liquid.[4] This scenario has happened more than once in recent times. The US, UK, and Netherlands refused to sell oil to Japan in 1941, leading to Pearl Harbor; in the 1970s, OPEC reduced their production of crude oil, triggering a worldwide fuel crisis;[5] more recently still Russia has cut off natural gas shipments to Ukraine. Industrial countries have also become involved in an increasingly violent politics of oil from Iraq, to the Sudan, to Nigeria and elsewhere.

This situation could—once more—be compared to the attitude of slave owners who benefited for a limited period of time from free labour but then left to their children the task of dealing with the dire consequences of slavery after Abolition. In the United States, African-Americans as a group continue to be disadvantaged economically and socially in many areas compared to European-Americans. It is

---

1   Caneco, http://www.ecobusinesslinks.com/corn-stoves.htm
2   'The End of Cheap Food,' *The Economist*, 6 December 2007.
3   Douthwaite, 'Sharing'.
4   Davis, *Inhuman Bondage*, p. 197.
5   Daniel Yergin, *The Prize: The Epic Quest for Oil, Money and Power* (New York and London: Pocket Books, 1991).

often difficult to separate the legacy of the segregation era from the legacy of slavery strictly speaking, but it has long been suggested, for example, that the fact that many slave men were separated from their families might be an ongoing contributory factor to the fragility of black families in contemporary American society.[1] Black families are less likely to form and more likely to break up than White, Hispanic or Asians families. As a consequence, 'although blacks account for only 12 percent of the US population, 44 percent of all prisoners in the United States are black [...] Indeed, nearly five percent of all black men, compared to 0.6 percent of white men, are incarcerated'.[2] This comes at a high cost for society as a whole which still has to be paid nearly 150 years after the Thirteenth Amendment to the United States Constitution officially abolishing slavery (1865).

One might at this point object that the comparison does not stand, because slavery is against the law, while using fossil fuel clearly is not. That is easily dismissed, as slavery *was* perfectly legal before it became banned. It only became prohibited after years of campaigning made society recognize that it was immoral. Is it completely unthinkable that one day driving inefficient vehicles might be outlawed?

Then, it is also possible to object that the harm caused by climate change is clearly unintentional. As we are causing unintentional damages, and what is more without realising it, we cannot be blamed for these damages, or at least not as severely as if they were deliberate and we knew the consequences. Therefore, as many people until very recently did not realise that by burning fossil fuels they were causing any harm at all, they cannot be blamed for it. This is a perfectly valid argument. It would be unfair and stupid to blame early twentieth-century American farmers who purchased tractors and fertilizers and saw these as an incontestable help in feeding their families and the rest of the world; or women in the 1950s or 1960s who bought washing machines to be freed from family chores. Citizens in many cities enthusiastically adopted motorised transport in the early 1900s

---

1   S. M. Elkins, *Slavery: A Problem in American Institutional and Intellectual Life* (Chicago: University of Chicago Press, 1959); D. P. Moynihan, *The Negro Family: The Case for National Action* (Washington, DC: US Department of Labor, 1965).

2   'Human Rights Watch Backgrounder,' 2003, http://www.hrw.org/backgrounder/usa/incarceration.

because they appeared as an efficient way of replacing horses which were creating numerous problems in towns.[1] It would not seem fair either to say that people who were emitting carbon dioxide a hundred, or perhaps even twenty years ago are responsible in the same way as we are now, given that we know the climatic consequences (a similar case, with hindsight, after all, could be made against them for the rate at which they were burning valuable resources, destroying eco-systems or damaging people's health by creating smog). If previous generations made a mistake by burning fossil fuel inconsiderately, they mostly did this with a clear conscience and in the good faith that they were trying to improve theirs and other people's lives. It is also true that it is more difficult for us to grasp the consequences of our actions than it was for slave owners, as the consequences of greenhouse gas emissions are indirect and most of the time mediated through a vapid media. Finally, some people remain genuinely perplexed about the causes of climate change, a huge responsibility for which rests on the fossil fuel lobbies as well as recalcitrant governments unwilling to clearly impart scientific truths to their citizens.[2]

Even so, the 'unintentional damages' argument only stands for previous generations who had no idea of the likely consequences of burning fossil fuels. For people living today it only stands as long as we are ignorant of the fact that the way we live is having devastating consequences for others. For most reasonably informed people now, it is hard to ignore the warnings of scientists. The latest IPCC report clearly states: 'most of the observed increase in the globally averaged temperature since the mid-twentieth century is *very likely* [i.e. meaning a 90 to 99 per cent probability] due to the observed increase in

---

1   McNeill, *Something New*, p. 310. McNeill interestingly reports that in 1920 'a quarter of American farmland was planted to oats, the energy source of horse-based transport' and that it took 'about 2 hectares of land to feed a horse, as much as was needed by eight people.' Clearly, getting rid of motor vehicles would create problems that are overlooked by many environmentalists.

2   See George Monbiot, *Heat: How We Can Stop the Planet Burning* (London: Allen Lane, 2006); George Monbiot, *Bring on the Apocalypse* (London: Atlantic Books, 2008); M. Bowen, *Censoring Science: Inside the Political Attack on Dr James Hansen and the Truth of Global Warming* (New York: Dutton, Penguin Group, 2008); Jeremy K. Leggett, *The Carbon War: Dispatches from the End of the Oil Century* (London: Allen Lane, 1999) for the fossil fuel lobby 'Denial Industry.'

anthropogenic greenhouse gas concentrations.'[1] Even for those who are not fully convinced of the causes of climate change, should we not be using precautionary measures if there are reasonable grounds to believe that we *might* be changing the climate? As Paul Klemperer, Professor of Economics at Oxford University recently remarked:

> Al Gore says the science on global warming is clear and there is a major problem. Vaclav Klaus, Czech president, contends that climate change forecasts are speculative and unreliable. Whose claims are scarier? [...] If our understanding of climate systems is flawed, our best guess about the dangers we face may be less pessimistic, but extreme outcomes are more likely. The continuing scientific uncertainty about the pace of climate change should make us more concerned, not less. And it is those who doubt the climatologists' models who should be the most frightened.[2]

Davidson makes a similar point when he compares the inconsistent attitude of US congressmen who decided to approve the war in Iraq but constantly refuse to act on climate change on the basis that there is, they argue, insufficient evidence that man made emissions are creating harm.

> In the context of everyday risk management, [...] the demand for 'definite conclusions' and lack of controversy before action is taken—as required by the US Congress when it comes to cutting fossil fuel consumption—is uncommon practice and in fact unprecedented. Policy-makers frequently take serious, far-reaching decisions on the basis of information generated by (economic) models that are far less reliable than the models used in climate science.[3]

If the lobbies referred to above have been so easily able to spread doubts among many intelligent people, it is perhaps because many of these people prefer to avoid the conclusions of the IPCC, not because they know a lot about the science. At root, we all have strong vested interests in not believing the climate science. Rich countries are

---

1   Parry, 'Summary for Policymakers.'
2   P. Klemperer, 'If climate sceptics are right, it is time to worry,' *Financial Times*, 28 February 2008.
3   Davidson, 'Parallels', p. 74.

mostly democracies where large sections of the general public do not want to change their lifestyles, something politicians know very well. In Eastern Europe, when parliamentary regimes were re-established after communism collapsed, environmental problems 'caused by foreigners, the military, or specific factories were often addressed and sometimes resolved. Those caused by the consumption patterns of ordinary citizens often got worse under democracy.' This seems to be a general pattern in parliamentary regimes.[1] As Upton Sinclair has put it: 'It is difficult to get a man to understand something when his salary [his standard of living] depends upon his not understanding it'.[2] Or as Al Gore has summarised, this is a very 'inconvenient truth' for all of us in the developed world.

Even then, polities and publics alike continue to clutch at available straws. IPCC predictions, for instance, that a range of 1–3°C temperature rise will see some potential for global food production, while in temperate areas [mainly in industrialised countries] 'climate change is projected to bring some benefits [on health], such as fewer deaths from cold exposure', are sometimes treated as grounds for extolling the benefits of a fossil fuel economy, *including* for future generations. This is in spite of the IPCC's overall estimation that:

> Costs and benefits of climate change for industry, settlement and society will vary widely by location and scale. In the aggregate, however, net effects will tend to be more negative the larger the change in climate [...] Overall it is expected that [the health] benefits will be outweighed by the negative health effects of rising temperatures worldwide, especially in developing countries.[3]

In the effort to claim that climate change might be a good thing, however, we once again, can hear the same kinds of self-serving justifications used by slave owners. They claimed that the work of slaves would benefit future generations; or that slaves were actually better off being slaves in the Southern USA rather than working in factories in slave-like conditions in nineteenth-century England. For example, US vice-president, John C. Calhoun, argued on the senate

---

1   McNeill, *Something New*, pp. 348, 353.
2   Quoted in Al Gore and D. Guggenheim, *An Inconvenient Truth*, Paramount, 2006.
3   Parry, 'Summary for Policymakers'.

floor on February 6, 1837: 'The Central African race... had never existed in so comfortable, so respectable, or so civilized a condition as that which it now enjoyed in the Southern States'... Slavery was not 'an evil. Not at all. It was a good—a great good'.[1]

The analogy with ourselves goes to the heart of contemporary society. Ralph Waldo Emerson speaking of slave-owners in 1863 said: 'If you put a chain around the neck of a slave, the other end fastens itself around your own'.[2] In our case it is more than simply the constant invitation to consume, like drug-addicts, ever more goods or go on vacation in remote parts of the world.[3] Our dependency on fossil fuels for energy extends to the very machines we rely on in our daily lives—the computer I am using to write this article confirms this general rule. If we cannot do otherwise, one could argue that we cannot be blamed nor can we prevent ourselves from hurting others. Slave owners, therefore, were more to blame than we are, because they could at least emancipate their slaves and choose a virtuous life.

Yet one should not under-estimate the difficulty and the struggle that it was for most slave owners to free their slaves. In the nineteenth-century American South, state laws 'restricted or in effect prohibited manumission'.[4] By the same token, we should not over-estimate our own difficulties in reducing carbon dioxide emissions. After all, while it is fairly easy to install low-consumption light bulbs, or to switch to a provider of renewable electricity, very few of us do this. If we were able to distribute an equitable share of carbon dioxide allowance per person, and to keep the overall international emissions under the threshold of what world-wide carbon sinks can safely absorb each year, our emissions would gradually slow down the rate of climate change.

There remains, however, a final objection to the slavery: fossil fuel analogy. Most definitions of slavery emphasise the idea of complete legal ownership and control by a master over a person who has to work for them.[5] By contrast, we would claim that we do not compel

1 Quoted in Davidson, 'Parallels,' p. 72.
2 Ralph W. Emerson, *Essays, First Series* (Boston: Ticknor and Fields, 1863), p. 98.
3 Jancovici and Grandjean, *Le Plein.*
4 Davis, *Inhuman Bondage*, p. 193.
5 See Davis, *Inhuman Bondage*, pp.30–31, for a useful summary of various attempts

anybody to work for us for free. Slavery denies people autonomy. Even if we are responsible for the harm of climate change, accusing us in the process of behaving like slave owners with regard to other human beings is surely untenable?

However, this objection can in turn be challenged on two grounds. Firstly, the availability of comparatively cheap energy is a required condition for the transport of foreign goods on a massive scale and over large distances. Of course, the reason why we import inexpensive products is due primarily to the fact that manpower, in the so-called 'developing countries', is much less expensive than in more advanced, richer, countries—trade-unions are weaker, standards of living lower, and so forth. To be sure, if prices of crude oil were to continue the inflationary trend they followed between 2001 and the beginning of 2008, they could reach a point where it would be too expensive to transport goods over large distances. However, as things currently stand it is comparatively inexpensive to import products to Europe or America made in often slave-like conditions, say, in east Asia, for a fraction of what it would cost to produce them in our own countries. This inexpensive energy has in a way enabled us to de-localise sub-standard working conditions far from view, yet we still rely on Chinese or Bangladeshi workers sewing our jeans or trainers. These workers have often very little or no liberty of movement, little or no choice of employer and they are often ill-treated, when they are not purely and simply inmates in state prisons. Reports of these appalling working conditions frequently appear in Western newspapers. We cannot claim that we do not know. Cheap transport, relying on fossil fuel and as a consequence contributing massively to climate change, is what makes it possible.

Secondly, the harm of climate change often amounts to violence or force against a large number of people, and will increasingly do so. Starvation or the destruction of eco-systems amounts to denying people the freedom to make decisions about their lives. Similarly, floods, droughts and sea level rise will force millions of people to become refugees. According to estimates by Norman Myers, 'when global warming takes hold, there could be as many as two hundred

---

to define slavery.

million people overtaken by sea-level rise and coastal flooding, by disruptions of monsoon systems and other rainfall regimes, and by droughts of unprecedented severity and duration'.[1] Christian Aid estimates are even more pessimistic: they predict that, 'on current trends, a further one billion people will be forced from their homes between now and 2050'.[2] Many of these refugees will end up in camps where they will not be much better off than prisoners. Forced from their homes and families, their land may be taken away from them, some of them may end up having to work for unscrupulous masters or in prostitution rings. Refugees aside, in the 'developing world' vast numbers of poor peasants in their struggle to feed their families often find themselves victims of debt bondage, a condition which The Office of the High Commissioner for Human Rights considers 'can hardly be distinguished from traditional slavery'.[3] As crop failure is a common trigger to debt bondage it seems not unreasonable to link, however indirectly, our climate change-inducing emissions to mechanisms that are reducing people to slavery.

For all of the above reasons, comparing the attitude of slave owners and our own attitude to petroleum is not as far fetched as one might initially imagine. It is in fact both adequate and useful. Useful, because virtually everybody nowadays agree that owning slaves is wrong. If we accept the comparison, it follows that we are enabled to see the iniquity of continuing to live as we currently do. It forces us to choose our camp. If we want to identify with abolitionists it is useful

1   Norman Myers, 'Environmental Refugees: A Growing Phenomenon of the 21st Century', *Philosophical Transactions: Biological Sciences*, 357 (2002), pp. 609–13.
2   Christian Aid, *Human tide: the real migration crisis*. Report, 2007.
3   Office of the High Commissioner for Human Rights, 'Fact Sheet No.14, Contemporary Forms of Slavery' (1991), http://www.unhchr.ch/html/menu6/2/fs14.htm.
    On a webpage of the University of California at Berkeley, an eye-witness report (Gupta) about bonded labourers in Tamil Nadu, India, gives a sad account of the process by which people become bonded labourers. 'After a poor monsoon season, [a family's] farm in rural Tamil Nadu failed to yield adequate harvests, causing them to fall into debt and sell their small landholdings. (...) During the rainy season, in order to make ends meet, [the parents] were forced to borrow money, thus ending their family's freedom. The conditions of the loan, which requires the family to work at the loan shark's rice mill, offer little hope of release from the burden of their debt.'

to know that the slave owner in each of us will want to resist change. Monbiot compares the power given by oil to the power given to Faust by the devil in Marlowe's story.[1]

> With the help of a flying 'chariot burning bright', [Faust] takes on a sightseeing tour around Europe. He performs miracles. He summons fresh grapes from the southern hemisphere in the dead of winter. After twenty-four years, the devils come for him. He begs for mercy, but it is too late. They drag him down to hell. If you did not know any better, you could mistake this story for a metaphor of Climate Change. Faust is humankind, restless, curious, unsated. Mephistopheles, who appears in the original English text as a 'fiery man', is fossil fuel. Faust's miraculous abilities are the activities fossil fuel permits. Twenty-four years is the period – about half the true span – in which they have enabled us to live in all voluptuousness. And the flames of hell – well, I think you've probably worked that out for yourself. Of course, the *Tragical History of Dr Faustus* is not an allegory of Climate Change. But the intention of the poet does not affect the power of the metaphor. Our use of fossil fuels is a Faustian pact.

The magical power which enabled Faust to travel on his 'flying chariot' and to eat grapes in the middle of the winter is what causes his ultimate damnation. Our abundant energy gives us an extraordinary power: as McNeill puts it 'with our new powers we banished some historical constraints on health and population, food production, energy use, and consumption generally. Few who know anything about life with these constraints regret their passing'.[2] However, we should never forget that power corrupts. If we do not change, we and our children will pay heavily the consequences of our reckless activity. Moreover, future generations will look back at us in a few years time and wonder how our twentieth- and early twenty-first century civilisation could have been so backward and live in such appalling moral blindness. Will they see that industrialised societies had some mitigating circumstances? That until relatively recently, we did not know the devastating consequences of our actions? That the vast

---

1   Monbiot, *Heat*, pp.2–3.
2   McNeill, *Something New*, p. 362.

majority genuinely thought that fossil fuels were improving the lives of most people on the planet? That we were also suffering ourselves from the fossil fuel bonanza, through obesity, pollution or loneliness and had become surreptitiously addicted to the substance? Probably not. They are more likely to curse us for the damage we will have done to the planet. Surely, they will say, these were barbarian people.

Part V: Countdown to Self-Annihilation

9. Climate Change, Resources and Future War: The Case of Central Asia

Rob Johnson

Symptoms of the End? Man and the Environment in Central Asia

When a British expedition passed through the southern fringe of Afghanistan in 1885, they found evidence of complex irrigation systems and civilisation long since abandoned. Constant attacks by impoverished raiders, and the collapse of the avenues of precious water sources through arid steppe, brought on famine and forced the human population to abandon the area. Thomas Holdich, a surveyor of the Royal Engineers commented: 'As we progressed [through Helmand] we encountered strange sights, the sights of the cities of the dead spreading out like gigantic cemeteries for miles on either side the river, gaunt relics of palaces and mosques and houses, upright and bleached, scattered over acres of debris, masses of broken pottery, mounds of mud ruins'.[1] In antiquity, in Sistan province, the jealous division of resources between Persia and Afghanistan had cut the irrigation systems in two, rendering the once fabled 'granary of Asia' a landscape of desolation. The canals that fed the wheat fields were cut off, and human habitation downstream was rendered impossible.

Historically, the margins of climate zones in Central Asia were always scenes of intense competition and the supply of water was regarded as critical. The population centres of the region lay in oases cities, or as ribbons of settlement alongside the larger rivers. Between,

---

1   T. Hungerford Holdich, *The Indian Borderland, 1880–1900*, (London: Methuen, 1901) p. 107.

traders used the safety of numbers in caravans, and steppe peoples adopted a nomadic lifestyle, carefully avoiding the overgrazing of an area whilst taking advantage of the spring-summer bloom of grass before the streams dried up and the landscape withered once again.

Sir Aurel Stein, the intrepid archaeologist of the Taklamakan Desert further east, discovered and excavated several 'lost cities' which had been similarly abandoned. These places had been subjected to invasion and denied sufficient resources to survive.[1] Stein noted that the extreme aridity of the environment had preserved a great deal, but the ruins of this Central Asian civilisation, like those in Afghanistan, were desiccated, shrivelled and dead. Stein's biographer wrote:

> Trunks of poplar avenues and orchards stood as bleached and blasted reminders of a thriving town that had gradually been abandoned to the forces of the desert – the sand had trickled in through cracks in the walls, whipped along streets and blown in through doorways ... Gradually it had filled all spaces with its slow, insidious stream, until it washed over the crumbling walls and collapsing roofs and spread in smooth undulations above, softly erasing all trace of the buildings beneath save for a few tall, ragged stumps.[2]

In the case of the Taklamakan cities, the careful management of rivers, which were fed by glaciers up in the Tien Shan and Kuen Lun mountains, had sustained the settlements of the old Silk Route for generations. However, the combined effects of war and natural climate change destroyed them. There were attacks by Huns, Tibetans, Mongols and Arab invaders, all of whom were attracted by the region's wealth, but throughout this long period the gradual warming of the climate from the end of the Ice Age eventually reduced the flow of water from glacial melt and forced the populations to retreat. The process of destruction could be swift. The town of Niya had been destroyed at the end of the third century CE when the irrigation

---

1   The exploration of the Taklamakan is vividly described in Peter Hopkirk, *Foreign Devils on the Silk Road* (Oxford:Oxford University Press, 1980) p. 81.
2   Annabel Walker, *Aurel Stein: Pioneer of the Silk Road* (London: John Murray, 1995) p. 101.

system was temporarily neglected because of the threat of attack.[1] Within a short time, the desert sands had swept over the channels and buried the settlement. As rivers receded from the towns of Loulan and Yotkan, they too were lost when deprived of water. Time and again, where war overwhelmed settlements, the climate and the environment ensured its permanent destruction. All the Silk Route cities fell into decline when the Ming Dynasty (1368–1644) rejected commercial linkages and looked inwards. This decay was accompanied by the iconoclastic destruction of the Taklamakan's Buddhist civilisation by Muslim invaders. The combination of man-made and natural environmental catastrophe ensured the final collapse of the ancient civilisation.

In the twenty-first century, these interconnected and historic themes of war for resources and climate change are more pressing than ever. Central Asia's history provides many examples where the battle for resources has been a significant factor in causing and sustaining conflict.[2] Wars and intra-state struggles will undoubtedly continue through the twenty first century, but the nexus of resources, environment and climate change will resonate with us ever more strongly.

Contemporary Lost Cities

The tomb-like relics of the 'lost cities' of Central Asia, have an eerie modern equivalent of the ancient lost cities around the Aral Sea. Rusting hulls of trawlers at Muynak, which once floated in coastal waters, now lie on sand dunes some 100 km from the dying lake. For decades, the unfolding environmental disaster was concealed. On Vozrazhdenie Island, the Soviets had built a biological weapons factory.[3] When Gary Powers flew his U2 spy plane over the Aral Sea and revealed the existence of the plant, the Russians were eager to close the region to outsiders. The sea in fact started to recede from the late

---

1 Hopkirk, *Foreign Devils,* p. 30.
2 A short, global survey of this issue is in Jeremy Black, *Why Wars Happen* (London and New York: Reaktion, 1998).
3 Anthrax and other agents were buried at the end of the Cold War and finally decontaminated by the Kazakhs in 2002. Global Security Newswire, 20 November 2002. http://www.nti.org/d_newswire/issues/newswires/2002_11_20.html.

1950s when Soviet irrigation schemes began siphoning off its waters for cash cotton crop production. The once thriving fish canning industry gradually dwindled, the 60,000 fishermen were put out of business and their boats abandoned. Today the local population face increasing infant mortality and rising cancer rates because the water supply is so badly contaminated by the leaching of pesticides, heavy metals and other pollutants.[1] Sandstorms are more frequent causing respiratory illnesses.[2] By 2020 it is estimated that the Aral Sea will have virtually disappeared, leaving a wind-blown desert, or, at best, a barren and marginal landscape unsuitable for human habitation.[3]

This is one of the greatest man-made environmental catastrophes of modern times. The construction of the Karakum canal to feed the Turkmenistani cotton fields, the impossible targets set by Soviet planners, the waste of water through unlined irrigation channels that are also open to the sun, and the construction of reservoirs upstream in Uzbekistan have all contributed to the death of the sea.[4] For years, Soviet planners were unconcerned because yields of cotton were so high. However, salination of fields have rendered many barren and the toxicity of the water supply has killed off flora and fauna in the sea and the surrounding area – and caused acute damage to human health. Soviet planners believed that they could divert water from the Ob and Irtysh rivers to refill the Aral, a project that would have required the construction of a canal 1,600 km long. The plan was badly managed by Soviet bureaucracy and never completed. Today, Uzbekistan argues that it cannot do without the fresh water supply for its cities, and Turkmenistan states that the Karakum Canal is an

---

1   The best overall study of this issue can be found in Philip Whish Wilson, 'The Aral Sea Environmental Health Crisis', *Journal of Rural and Remote Environmental Health*, I:2 (2002), pp.29–34.

2   S. L. O'Hara, G. F. S. Wiggs, B. Mamedovn, et al, 'Exposure to Airborne Dust Contaminated with Pesticide an Aral Sea Region', *The Lancet*, 355 (2000), pp. 627–28.

3   Philip Micklin, 'Water in the Aral Sea Basin of Central Asia: cause of Conflict or Co-operation?' *Post Soviet Geography and Economics*, XLIII:7 (2002), pp. 505-228. Recent efforts to refill the northern part of the Aral Sea have, so far, been a success, but there are no plans to restore the entire body of water.

4   See Philip Micklin, 'Soviet Water Diversion Plans: Implications for Kazakhstan and Central Asia' *Central Asian Survey* I/4 (1983), pp. 9-43.

economic lifeline. Both believe that they need water for their growing populations, so the sea continues to disappear.[1]

In many respects, however, the Aral Sea is simply the best-known,
if most extreme aspect of an environmental disaster affecting great
swathes of Central Asia as a consequence of intense agricultural and
industrial exploitation. For instance, the widespread storage of toxic
waste in open sites, which are invariably unprepared, has led to a
steady leakage of dangerous chemicals into the atmosphere, (as well
as into) the soil, and both underground and surface water systems.
In Kazakhstan, environmentalists have identified several 'zones of
crisis' caused by nuclear weapon testing in the years 1949–61 and
petro-chemical production.[2] At least twelve of the region's cities
with a population exceeding one hundred thousand have been and
continue to be subject to radioactive threats to health at a dangerous
level. Radioactive mining slag heaps, totalling 50 million tons, litter
the landscape and there are 267 sites where radioactive pollution lies
between 100 and 17,000 microR/hr (microRads per hour). Despite
government reluctance to acknowledge the statistics, there are evident higher than average incidences of birth defects, radiation poisoning, severe anaemia and leukaemia.[3] Kazakhs tend to regard the

---

1   For more on the rivalry between the Central Asian states at a regional level, see Rob
    Johnson, *Oil, Islam and Conflict in Central Asia since 1945* (London: Reaktion,
    2007), p. 37.
2   State Report: 'Environmental Situation of the Republic of Kazakhstan', Ministry of
    Ecology and Bioresources (Almaty, 1997); O. Ataniyazova, S. Adrian, Z. Mazhitova,
    et al., 'Workshop Report: Continuing progressive deterioration of the environment in
    the Aral Sea region: disastrous effects on mother and child health', *Acta Paediatrica*,
    90 (2001), pp. 589–591; K. Hooper, X. P. Myrto, J. Shje, et al., 'Analysis of breast
    milk to assess exposure to chlorinated contaminants in Kazakhstan: PCBs and orga-
    nochlorine pesticides in southern Kazakhstan', *Environmental Health Perspectives*,
    105 (1997), pp.1250–1254; R. Zetterstrom, 'Child health and environmental pol-
    lution in the Aral Sea region in Kazakhstan', *Acta Paediatrica* Supplement 429
    (1999):49–54; O. A. Ataniyazova, R. A. Baumann , U. A. Liem, et al., 'Levels of
    certain metals, organochlorine pesticides and dioxins in cord blood, maternal blood,
    human milk and some commonly used nutrients in the surroundings of the Aral
    Sea (Karakalpakstan, Republic of Uzbekistan),' *Acta Paediatrica*, 90 (2001), pp.
    801–808.
3   It is very hard to obtain detailed information on this problem which even local people
    regard as a shameful phenomenon. See Matthew Chance, 'Inside the nuclear under-
    world: deformity and fear', http://www.cnn.com/2007/WORLD/asiapcf/08/30/btsc.

slagheaps as a source of housing or road materials and they use them freely. Other dumps of industrial by products, some from the metallurgy sector, also threaten water supplies, soil and human health.

Kyrgyzstan has fewer radioactive slag heaps, although the town of Mailuu-Suu in the west of the country is badly affected and the mountainous nature of the state tends to funnel pollutants into areas of population. However, there are problems with the storage of dangerous pesticides throughout rural areas and environmentalists are generally concerned that seismic activity in the country makes surface storage of hazardous materials very risky.[1] The Soviet Union authorised the use of strong pesticides, but in the late 1990s tons of 'unfit' pesticides were still stored in the Central Asian republics. In Tajikistan, where pesticides have been used to increase yields in melon and cotton cultivation, there has been a sharp decline in their use in recent years, but there is still a significant correlation between their use and the appearance of malignant tumours and other illnesses. The Tajik government's environmental report admits: 'we observe growing tendencies of respiratory morbidity [and] inherent anomalies of human development'.[2] Perhaps it is not surprising, given the intensity of farming in the Ferghana Valley, the 'breadbasket' of the region, that soil and animal pollution from pesticides is also a problem for Uzbekistan.[3]

Kazakhstan has responded to its environmental damage with surveys and monitoring of pollution levels, and an agreement with China to carry out collaborative investigations into the effects of nuclear weapons tests on the region's environment. Monitoring of those localities rich in uranium ores has also been established. Kyrgyzstan and Uzbekistan have begun to reprocess or bury some of their toxic

chance.nukes/index.html 31 August 2007; State Report: 'Environmental Situation of the Republic of Kazakhstan', Ministry of Ecology and Bioresources (Almaty, 1997).

1   State of the Environment Report, Kyrgyzstan, (1997) http://enrin.grida.no/htmls/kyrghiz/soe/index.htm

2   Tajikistan State of the Environment Report, (2000), Issue 16, http://enrin.grida.no/htmls/tadjik/soe2/eng/htm/issue16.htm. The Varzob Valley has particularly dangerous levels of radioactive pollution.

3   State of the Environment Report for Uzbekistan, UNEP and GRID, (2001), http://enrin.grida.no/htmls/uzbek/env2001/content/soe/index_frame.htm .

waste. However, there is a long way to go before the long years of messy exploitation are cleared up. Central Asia is fortunate in that vast areas of austere mountains and deserts were unaffected by industrialisation. But the consequences for the centres of human population are less encouraging. The cause of this damage was the hubris of Soviet planners, who were convinced of the need to 'modernise' and industrialise, partly to leap ahead of the West, but also to support their social engineering of a 'loyal' proletariat to replace an equally mythic 'counter-revolutionary' peasantry. Ultimately, they got neither an economy to match the West, nor a loyal population. They ended up with a land that is sick. And this even before the effects of climate change are brought into the equation.[1]

There are, for instance, key socio-economic factors of importance here which have the potentiality for civil unrest. Those enriched by a bonanza of new oil wealth import European and American cars, wear designer clothes and frequent fashionable bars and hotels. They own rural properties as well as urban ones, open overseas bank accounts, and live in ostentatious luxury. By contrast, in Kyrgyzstan, the World Bank report of 2001 revealed that 68 per cent of the people lived on less than $17 a month.[2] A subsistence annual salary was calculated at $295, but the average national salary per annum was $165. GDP fell by 47 per cent between 1990 and 1996.

Poverty of itself can be a factor leading to civil disturbance. Demonstrations about housing, poverty and the absence of reform in Tajikistan were the trigger for the outbreak of a civil war (1992–96) in which an estimated 60,000 died.[3] In the event of a total breakdown of order, particularly a crisis brought on by climate change, the authorities might find themselves overwhelmed by an anarchic and acquisitive grass-roots approach to the remaining and rapidly diminishing resources. Looting is the historic manifestation of this effect,

---

1   Awareness of the environmental situation is a factor now mobilising the region's populations. There were large scale protests at Lop Nor in China in 1985, which led to rioting, and at Semipalatinsk in Kazakhstan against nuclear contamination. Johnson, *Oil, Islam and Conflict*, p. 185.
2   ICRC, *World Disaster Report, 2001* (Geneva, 2001).
3   Johnson, *Oil, Islam and Conflict*, pp. 80–95.

but so too is warlordism and protracted civil war.[1]

Running out of Water

As the UN Secretary General Dr Boutros-Boutros Ghali identified in the 1990s, water supplies are likely to prove a source of conflict in the future. The GEO (Global Environmental Outlook) group of the United Nations predicted in 1999 that 'water wars' would break out in North Africa and South West Asia between 2000 and 2025.[2] Water is likely to become a contested resource of critical importance, especially as the trend of urbanisation and industrialisation in less developed nations imposes greater strain on the available supply. There is considerable tension over the use of water from the Jordan between Israelis and Palestinians in the disputed West Bank.[3] Pakistan and India, with a long history of antagonism, may be unable to reach agreement on the Indus, nor China and Kazakhstan on the Ili. Population pressure on existing resources suggests there may be conflicts over the Brahmaputra, Tigris and Euphrates and the Ganges too.

In Central Asia, ancient irrigation systems extended or superseded by the Soviets once carried snow melt out to large cotton plantations. The independence of the republics, and civil wars in Afghanistan and Tajikistan, have disrupted many of these systems, initially causing a fifty per cent drop in supply. As a result, twenty to thirty per cent of arable land was put out of use. In Tajikistan, the figure was closer to 50 per cent. In Xinjiang, China's westernmost state, water is already a contested resource between local Uighur farmers, old settlers, new migrants and industry.[4] When Uzbekistan used the severance of gas supplies as a diplomatic lever against Kyrgyzstan and Tajikistan in the '90s, in a dispute over prices, these two countries responded

1   Warlords in Afghanistan extracted revenue from their personal fiefdoms which had been carved out in the wake of the collapse of the state and the civil war that followed. See William Maley, *The Afghanistan Wars* (London and New York: Palgrave, 2002).

2   Michael T. Klare, *Resource Wars: The New Landscape of Global Conflict* (New York: Metropolitan Books, 2001), pp. 165–173.

3   Michael T. Klare, *Resource Wars*, pp. 165–173.

4   Christian Tyler, *Wild West China: The Untold Story of a Frontier Land* (London: John Murray, 2003).

by cutting water supplies to the Uzbeks in the Ferghana Valley. A severe drought that began in 2000, and which affected Tajikistan and Afghanistan particularly badly, caused a fifty per cent fall in cereal production and left millions without an adequate diet. A further fall of 15–20 per cent in 2001 left thousands starving. In Tajikistan, people sold the doors and windows of their houses to pay for food.[1] An ongoing energy crisis in Tajikistan left the government with insufficient revenue to tackle the problem of poverty and food supply, especially in rural areas. Many are still dependent on foreign aid. In Afghanistan, the situation is very similar. School children frequently drop out of their studies because they need to take up employment in public works projects like road building to pay for food. But the absence of water doesn't just render a population poor; it makes habitation of certain areas unsustainable.

Desertification is already affecting the westernmost provinces of China. According to a Chinese government report, the area of desert in China is increasing by 6,700 km² per annum, and the trend is increasing each decade so that the current total is 1.743 million km².[2] The same recent report lamented the fact that, in marginal areas, 90 per cent of grassland has been degraded to some extent (82.5 per cent of which lies in the westernmost province of Xinjiang) and 'disastrous sandstorms' had caused considerable damage to the infrastructure. Alongside some highways, bands of trees have been planted to hold back the advancing dunes. Increased evaporation, higher temperatures, and lower precipitation will add to the effect of diminishing water reserves caused by industry and urbanisation. Perhaps settlements in the most marginal areas will once again be abandoned.

The recession of glaciers in Central Asia's mountains and increased evaporation due to climate change is also diminishing the water

---

1   UN Office for the Coordination of Humanitarian Affairs, Integrated Regional Information Network (IRIN), 'One Million People Face Starvation in Tajikistan', Dushanbe, 29 August 2001.

2   Jun Han, 'Effects of Integrated Ecosystem Management on land degradation control and poverty reduction', Workshop on Environment, Resources and Agricultural Policies in China', 19 June 2006, Beijing. www.oecd.org/dataoecd/33/57/36921383.pdf.

supply of the region.[1] The decline of the glaciers has led to a short term increase in water volume, but in the long term there will be a decline of water resources. The Fedchenko Glacier in the Pamirs in Tajikistan (the largest non-polar glacier in the world) lost 1.4 per cent of its volume in the last thirty years, and the neighbouring Skogatch Glacier lost 8 per cent. The Tuyuksu Glacier, in Kazakhstan has lost an estimated 51 million cubic metres of ice. Higher temperatures mean increased evaporation of water supplies. As a result, fresh water lakes are increasingly salinated. Lake Balkash in Kazakhstan is a case in point. Covering 18,000 square kilometres—11,250 square miles—it is one of the largest inland waters of Central Asia, but with a fall in the inflow from the Ili River, its main tributary, salination has now reached 4g/litre rendering it virtually unusable for either drinking or irrigation.[2] Climate scientists now predict that droughts, such as the ones that have affected Tajikistan and Afghanistan in recent years, will become more frequent in the region.

However, growing scientific concern about abrupt, non-linear shifts in the climate as a consequence of feedback mechanisms in the carbon cycle pose the possibility not only of steady deterioration but an entirely more radical rupture to farming economies.[3] This would mean not just the advent of short term, if disastrous incidents such as flash flooding, damaging storms, or hazardous temperature extremes but also rapid desertification, consequent mass migrations of a more permanent nature, and more sustained conflicts over water.

---

1   T. E. Khromova, M. B. Dyurgerov and R. G. Barry, 'Late-twentieth century changes in glacier extent in the Ak-Shirak Range, Central Asia, determined from historical data and ASTER imagery', (2003) http://www.agu.org/pubs/crossref/2003/2003GL017233.shtml. A small shrinkage of glaciers in the Ak-Shirak range during 1943–1977 was followed by a greater than 20% reduction during 1977–2001 in response to increases in summer and annual air temperature and decreases in annual precipitation. Studies in the northern areas of the Tien Shan mountain range show that the glaciers that help supply water to this arid region have been losing nearly two cubic km (0.47 mile) of ice per year between 1955 and 2000.

2   Stephan Harrison, 'Climate Change, Future Conflict and the Role of Climate Science', *Royal United Services Institute Journal* , 150:6 (December 2005), pp. 18-23.

3   Peter Cox, Deepak Rughani, Peter Wadhams, David Wasdell, *Feedback Dynamics & the Acceleration of Climate Change* (2007), www.apollo-gaia.org/Introduction.pdf

Already, the Chinese economy, for example, currently pays an additional $30 billion per annum to deal with water shortages. To secure future supplies, China plans to divert more water from the Ili River into Xinjiang's industry and domestic consumption. However, some climatologists think that, by 2020, precipitation in northwest China will have fallen by 20 per cent, clearly adding to the pressure on the remaining supplies.[1] This might bring China into direct confrontation with Kazakhstan, which depends on the Ili River for its own needs. If large scale movements of climate refugees are added to this scenario, then existing ethnic and clan tensions could be pushed to breaking point.

The Demand for Energy

The existence of scarce, high value hydrocarbon resources in the same region will further complicate the potentiality for both inter-group and inter-state conflict. China's energy needs largely determine its policy in Central Asia and look likely to do so with even greater importance in the future. Coal, oil and gas will be the energy sources that underpin all of China's industries for the next few decades. Coal provides 77 per cent of China's electricity capacity, and this amounted to an estimated 2.76 billion tonnes burned in 2008. China possesses 13 per cent of the world's reserves, enough to allow it to continue to exploit this resource for another 100 years.[2] Nevertheless, China appears to recognise the environmental risk this poses: small mines with low productivity, high levels of pollution and a bad record on safety have been closed, and 20 per cent of China's energy comes from renewable hydro-electricity.

However, projections of China's CO_2 emissions are less encouraging. The expansion of China's manufacturing means the trend of energy consumption is increasing, but CO_2 emissions from coal leapt from 2,363 million tonnes in 1998 to 3,809 million tonnes in 2004. Calculations that include oil and gas in the same period produced a total CO_2 emissions figure that rose from 2,940 to 4,707 million

---

1   Harrison, 'Climate Change', p. 19.
2   Peter Fairley, 'China's Coal Future', *Technology Review*, 5 January 2007.

tonnes.[1]

Shortages of coal in certain areas forced China to import coal, and, as Xinjiang's oil reserves have begun to dwindle, the projections are that, even at a conservative estimate of growth of seven per cent per year, China will have to import 45 per cent of its oil needs by 2010. Even putting aside predictions about peak oil, if China exceeds its consumption estimates it will face major problems in meeting its energy needs. This is likely to encourage a greater exploitation of its fossil fuel reserves, further adding to the damage to the environment and the biosphere.[2]

It is in this context that we can see why China has been eager to assert greater control over the hydrocarbon resources of Central Asia and will do so, perhaps more aggressively, in the future. It has purchased several oil fields, the most important of which is China National Petroleum Company's (CNPC) acquisitions in Kazakhstan for $5 billion. It has invested over $9 billion in pipelines across the Kazakh border into China and it has begun to buy a share of other companies in this arena.

Underpinning all this is an assumption on the part of China's political elite that only sustained growth can meet the basic needs of the majority, and in so doing avoid the possibility of unrest which might threaten its exclusive hold on power, and, with it, its tight internal security reins. This may explain why Beijing has put so much effort into cooperation with the Iranians for the development of China's share of Middle East oil—by 2010, 45 per cent of the world oil production will come from this region.[3] However, there is now equally the likelihood of Chinese resource wars closer to home, in or near its Central Asian borders.[4] China's priority appears to be a headlong rush to develop its economy that would enable it to deal with the con-

1 Energy Information Administration, 'Country Analysis Brief', www.eia.doe.gov/emue/cabs/china/environment.

2 Philip Andrews-Speed, 'China's Energy Woes: Running on Empty', *Far Eastern Energy Review* (June 2005). http://www.feer.com/articles1/2005/0506/free/p013.html.

3 Michael Pillsbury, 'China's Military Strategy Towards the US: A View from Open Sources', 2 November 2001, p. 2. www.uscc.gov/researchpapers/2000-2003/pdfs/strat.pdf.

4 Rob Johnson, *Oil, Islam and Conflict*, pp. 227–28.

sequences of climate change.[1] Yet it is this very issue which China, alongside Russia and the Central Asian republics neglect at their peril, not least because this is likely to be one of the most significant causes of confrontation and conflict.

What are the Trajectories to the Future?

World history provides many examples where the struggle for resources has been a major, if not deciding factor in causing and sustaining war. The scarcity and high value of certain key resources, such as spices, silk, tea, gold and silver bullion, water and land, heightened inherent tensions and conflicts within and between sociopolitical groups to the point of violence in Central Asia's history. By the middle of the twentieth century, the capacity to destroy vast numbers of human beings through Weapons of Mass Destruction did not lessen the willingness to wage either 'limited' or total war to acquire resources, fulfil ideological ambitions or to protect particular 'interests'. But to the traditional categories of inter-state war, ethnic-nationalist warfare, insurgency, intra-state unrest, and terrorism, it seems that we should now add conflicts of diminishing resources and climate change. Anxieties about energy security in hydrocarbons, (on which so many economies depend), and concerns about rising costs and increased consumption as we approach the long predicted peak production years in 2020–2030, means that states, especially emerging industrial states are likely to pursue their energy interests all the more aggressively. As a result, the Middle East—where conflicts are rising in intensity and frequency—will, according to Western strategists, assume even greater importance in the coming decades.[2] But so too will Central Asia.

---

1   'China's Energy Crisis Sends Pollution Across Asia', World Bank Press Review, 1 July 2004. http://www.cleanairnet.org/caiasia/1412/article-58739.html.
2   See, for example, Developments, Concepts and Doctrine Centre (DCDC), 'Climate Change', *Global Strategic Trends*, http://www.dcdc-strategictrends.org.uk/home.aspx ; Kurt M. Campbell, et al., *The Age of Consequences: The Foreign Policy and National Security Implications of Global Climate Change* (Washington DC: Center for New American Security and Center for Strategic and International Studies, November 2007).

The pace of climate change, combined with man-made environmental problems, has increased the desertification and evaporation of many inland lakes and seas in Central Asia, and increased
the demand for water to unsustainable levels.[1] The Aral Sea is the
most obvious indicator of that change. Land, and the food resources
it can yield, may also assume a greater importance, as areas of marginal farming retreat under the pressure of climate change, the continued abuse of exploitative and inappropriate agriculture, and conflicts. Contaminated soil and water supplies already affect Central
Asia. Man-made and climatically-induced migration could place
enormous pressure on neighbouring states and already overcrowded
urban areas, opening new fractures in addition to the broken landscape of clan, religious or ethnic identity in those societies.

The conflicts of the future, fuelled in part by this struggle for
diminishing resources or opportunities, and exacerbated by historic,
ethnic rivalries, will continue to be both intra-state and as well as
inter-state; indeed, the former may even become more frequent. The
sheer savagery of fighting which is characteristic of irregular warfare suggests that these conflicts will be far harder to resolve, and, as
the fighting in Tajikistan, Afghanistan, Azerbaijan, Georgia, Armenia
and Chechnya has indicated, will leave longer-lasting wounds. These
regions have been badly afflicted by the widespread availability of
small arms, mines and explosives. It is possible that demographic
pressures will add to the problems, not least in that large numbers of
men of military age, facing unemployment or hardship, may be more
willing to engage in combat to create a swift and decisive resolution. On the other hand, states may resort to unconventional warfare,
including trade blockades and sanctions, particularly when resources
are scarcer and overt aggression may invite retaliation from resource-
allies and associates. Uzbekistan and Russia both used restrictions on
energy resources to pressure neighbouring states in the 1990s.[2]

The trajectories of the recent past and present indicate that consumption globally will continue to increase and, given the reluctance

---

1   Tajikistan State of the Environment Report, (2000), Issue 16; http://enrin.grida.no/
     htmls/tadjik/soe2/eng/htm/issue16.htm.
2   See Developments, Concepts and Doctrine Centre (DCDC), 'Climate Change',
     Global Strategic Trends, http://www.dcdc-strategictrends.org.uk/home.aspx

of some of the most populous powers to pursue alternative energy programmes, it is very likely that fossil fuels, water and foodstuffs will be the trigger for various forms of conflict. Vulnerable resource systems and transit routes will be a prime target for the disaffected, especially terrorist groups, as attacks on dams, power stations, and oil pipelines in the Caucasus have already demonstrated.[1] Oil and gas will also be the source of intense international rivalry; they already fuel domestic corruption and heighten inequalities of wealth and opportunity. In addition, the expansion of the hydrocarbons industries threatens to repeat the environmental mistakes of the past. Sadly, the attraction of billions of dollars after years of Soviet stagnation will prove too tempting to the governments of the republics. Since independence, Kazakhstan has attracted over $40 billion in investment in its oil and gas industries. A significant amount of this national wealth has made the political elites extremely affluent, whilst the majority struggle in agriculture and a kiosk economy. The inequalities of wealth are striking. In the long term, oil and gas could be both a blessing and a curse to the region.

It is not just the causes of wars that will be affected by environmental issues, but also the way those wars are fought. The current focus of the region's major armies on counter-terrorism and on the future conventional battlefield means that consideration of the environmental setting is perhaps neglected. Armies consume vast quantities of fossil fuels on their combat or peacekeeping missions today, and wars of the future will inevitably mean greater environmental damage. In extremis chemical or nuclear contamination is a possibility, reducing diminished resources still further, and prompting mass migrations. To this should be added the damage inflicted by new biological weapons, including, perhaps, genetic-DNA attacks.[2] Deliberate

---

1   Chechen groups attacked the BTC (Baku-Tbilisi-Ceyhan) pipeline several times in 2004 and 2005. See for example, Gal Luft, IAGS, Energy Security, 'Pipeline Sabotage is Terrorists' Weapon of Choice', 28 March 2005, http://www.iags.org/n0328051.htm

2   Currently, biological attacks are extremely problematic, not least because environmental conditions and the difficulty of finding appropriate delivery system affect the feasibility of such an assault. However, there are concerns. See, for example, Colin S. Gray, *Another Bloody Century*, (London: Phoenix, 2005), pp. 278-9, 282.

assaults on resources will become strategic imperatives, with terrible consequences.

Corporate representatives and armed forces personnel from richer outside states, most obviously the USA, who stand accused of using up precious resources, in general, and those of Central Asia in particular, are also likely to become increasingly common targets of unconventional, terrorist-style attack. Flashpoints may also emerge in the regional arena which are not directly about resource control but represent a reigniting of older, dormant conflicts. It is difficult to say precisely where these flash points are likely to be, but the Caucasus, the Ferghana Valley and marginal impoverished communities in Afghanistan and Tajikistan have already become battlefields. The backdrop of increasing global temperatures, crop failures, stochastic weather patterns, and diminishing resources are clearly all factors in the equation. The consequences of these regular and irregular conflicts, fought with new technologies as well as old, are chillingly Malthusian: mass destructions through famine and killing, and the collapse of states and their entire social systems. These events are not in the far future, but near at hand, and, perhaps, have already begun.

Climate Change and its Reckonings

The conflicts of the future in Central Asia, fuelled by environmental change and by diminishing resources and opportunities will affect not only the countries of the region, but also richer, more powerful states including China and Russia. Ultimately, changes in the Asian heartland will come to affect the United States, Europe and the rest of the world.[1] For decades, whilst the Central Asian republics languished under Soviet rule, the region was little more than a backwater in the Cold War, but this has changed. Gaining their independence in 1991, the Central Asian governments, many of them staffed by former communists, had to contend with all the problems described above. However, the discovery of vast reserves of oil and gas, much of it under the Caspian Sea, brought the prospect of riches and rapid development. In the process of exploiting these resources, very little

---

1   Harrison, 'Climate Change', p. 22.

thought has been given to the question of environmental management and climate change. Yet, as the globe's resources diminish and hydrocarbon costs increase, Central Asia will become a zone of intense international competition.[1] Such an eventuality was foreseen by geostrategic thinkers like Sir Halford Makinder, who noted: 'Who rules the Heartland, commands the World-Island; Who rules the World-Island, commands the World.'[2]

New conflicts, coincident with climate change and overlaying a range of existing environmental problems, could add to the pressure on the diminished resources still available, and possibly prompt mass migrations. The impact of vast numbers of refugees in flight from such calamities will make enormous demands on already stretched economies and fuel further civil, intra-state conflict. The rising tide of religious fundamentalism, accompanied by a strong sense of political and economic injustice, is likely to intensify.[3] Deliberate assaults on resources could also become strategic imperatives for both conventional and unconventional forces with potentially disastrous results. In other words, climate change will not only cause conflicts, it will to some extent affect the way they are fought. The collapse of states, civil wars, and intense battles for the region's remaining resources are likely to mean the abandonment of what is currently inhabitable, and mass fatalities on a large scale. Is this bleak picture of the future inevitable? Are there any grounds for optimism? Does some consideration of the pressures currently facing the states of Central Asia give any more general indications of how such a future could be averted? Or do events in Central Asia indicate that we have already entered the 'Endgame'?

---

1   Michael T. Klare, *Resource Wars*, p. 97; see also Michael T. Klare, 'The New Geography of Conflict', *Foreign Affairs*, May-June, (2001), p. 49; see also John H. Ackerman, 'Climate Change, National Security and the Quadrennial Defense Review: Avoiding the Perfect Storm', *Strategic Studies Quarterly,*Spring (2008) pp.65,74, 80 and 84; Joshua W. Busby, 'Climate Change and National Security: An Agenda for Action', Council on Foreign Relations, *CSR*, 32, November (2007), p. 12.
2   Sir Halford J. Mackinder, *Democratic Ideals and Reality, A Study in the Politics of Reconstruction*, (London, 1919, reprinted., London: Constable, 1963), 194.
3   Martha Brill Olcott, 'The Caspian's False Promise', *Foreign Policy*, III (1998), p. 107.

To most of us, forecasts of the end of the anthropocene may seem implausible. Yet conflicts in the remainder of this century look likely to escalate to such a point that some existing polities will become unviable and millions will be forced to migrate. Their chances of survival in an already fractured international system, where amongst other things food security has also broken down, may well be slim. Central Asia could well be at the epicentre of this dystopian scenario for our future world.

Beyond these suggestions, current trajectories fail to give any confident guide, but perhaps a much smaller human population, jealously protective of its critical resources, in groups that the marginal environmental conditions will sustain, may be the outcome. At this 'eleventh hour', we may be able to ameliorate the worst of the effects. One thing is certain: the conflicts of the future in Central Asia will be marked by the tombstones of abandoned settlements. Like the historic 'lost cities', they will be scattered with the fossilised remnants of a once thriving civilisation, and surrounded by the eternal, restless sands of the desert.

10. On the Edge of History: the Nuclear Dimension

Dave Webb

Introduction

Anthropogenic climate change is not the only man-made threat to human history. The possibility of prematurely closing the chapter on civilisation has its roots in the industrial revolution in more ways than one. At that time scientific ideas and investigation began to shift from simply understanding nature to using or shaping it to serve humankind. We are seeing the consequences of this particular way of thinking today as the average temperature of the Earth's surface rises. However, it was also brought into sharp focus on 16 July 1945 in the desert of New Mexico with the first atomic explosion. This so-called 'Trinity Test' and the subsequent dropping of the atomic bombs on the cities and people of Hiroshima and Nagasaki in Japan on 6 and 9 August demonstrated the power and ultimate capability of human endeavour. Even before 'Trinity' took place there was concern among its scientist- initiators that it could detonate a fusion reaction which might set the entire atmosphere on fire and end all life on Earth. According to the author, Edward Sullivan:

> The scientists were later relieved when calculations showed there was only 1 chance in 3 million of the bomb igniting the atmosphere. One would think that the fact that there was any chance at all, however remote, of igniting the atmosphere would be reason enough not to detonate the bomb.[1]

Following the horror and devastation produced in Hiroshima and Nagasaki it was clear that the start of the atomic age would make

---

1   *The Ultimate Weapon: The Race to Develop the Atomic Bomb* (2007), An Interview with Author Edward T. Sullivan, Holiday House, http://sully-writer.comAuthor%20 Q&A.htm.

new demands on the way we approach war, atomic energy and the use of technology. Just as the Intergovernmental Panel of Climate Change (IPCC) was created in 1989 by the World Meteorological Organization and the United Nations Environment Program as an effort by the UN to help governments understand and deal with what is happening to the world's climate, the United Nations Atomic Energy Commission (UNAEC) was founded on 24 January 1946 by the first resolution of the UN General Assembly: 'to deal with the problems raised by the discovery of atomic energy'.[1]

In particular, an attempt to regulate the international development of nuclear technology and prevent the use of the Bomb in future conflicts was outlined by the US in the Acheson-Lilienthal Report. This report was produced to a large extent by Robert Oppenheimer, the 'father of the atomic bomb,' and later became the Baruch Plan, after Bernard Baruch, who proposed a slightly modified version to UNAEC in June 1946. However, just as it is difficult today to get industrialised countries to agree on how to cut carbon emissions, the Baruch plan failed because it relied on US- Soviet cooperation: neither side trusting each other enough to agree on an independent body controlling something they thought they might use to their own advantage.

Nevertheless, some of the scientists involved in the Manhattan Project which developed the bomb believed strongly that war between states possessing atomic weapons would become too dangerous to pursue. Joseph Rotblat, the only scientist to leave the project for moral reasons, got together with a number of leading scientists and thinkers, including Bertrand Russell and Albert Einstein, to warn of the dangers such weapons presented to the future of humankind.[2] The Russell–Einstein Manifesto was launched in 1955 in London and called for a conference at which scientists would assess the extent of the threat. The first of these 'Pugwash Conferences on Science and World Affairs' followed, in July 1957.

Similarly, scientists from the US National Academy of Scientists

---

1   United Nations General Assembly Resolution 1 Session 1, (1946) 'Establishment of a Commission to Deal with the Problems Raised by the Discovery of Atomic Energy', 24 January 1946, http://www.undemocracy.com/A-RES-1(I).
2   The 'Russell-Einstein Manifesto' was issued in London on 9 July 1955, http://www.pugwash.org/about/manifesto.htm

joined the IPCC in warning about climate change but failed to persuade President George W Bush to sign up to the 1997 Kyoto Protocol. He considered the proposed greenhouse gas emissions reductions to be unfair to the US. A common feature between the climate change and nuclear crises is that the associated problems are so large that it is difficult for individuals (even in high places) to either comprehend or feel that they can do much to prevent them.

The Midnight Hour

During the Cold War and the Nuclear Arms Race that followed the end of World War Two, the theory of nuclear deterrence led to a doctrine of Mutually Assured Destruction (MAD) in which neither side would dare initiate a nuclear war. The US and the USSR each amassed enough weapons to ensure that, even if they were subject to a first strike, they would have enough fire-power left to deliver an Earth shattering retaliatory blow. The number of nuclear weapons stockpiled rose rapidly, each side trying to outdo the other. They reached an all time high in the USA of over 32,000 in 1966 [1] and in the USSR of more than 40,000 in 1986.[2]

In 1947 'The American 'Bulletin of Atomic Scientists' recognised the severity of the situation when it first published its Doomsday Clock to indicate 'how close humanity is to catastrophic destruction' (i.e.midnight). Just six years later, following the first US test of a hydrogen bomb, the clock was set to two minutes to midnight, its closest approach so far, the Bulletin declaring that with 'only a few more swings of the pendulum …from Moscow to Chicago, atomic explosions will strike midnight for Western civilisation'. Another close encounter occurred in 1984 (3 minutes to) when US-Soviet relations reached a new low after President Reagan announced his plans for a 'Strategic Defense Initiative' or 'Star Wars.'

How close to midnight is humanity prepared to live? The total explosive power of the global nuclear arsenal at the height of the

---

1   Stephen I. Schwartz, ed., *Atomic Audit - The Costs and Consequences of U.S. Nuclear Weapons since 1940* (Washington DC: Bookings Institution Press, 1999).

2   'Archive of Nuclear Data,' from the Nuclear Program of the Natural Resources Defense Council, http://www.nrdc.org/nuclear/nudb/datainx.asp.

Cold War is estimated to be some 15,000 MT (where 1 MT represents 1 Megaton: the explosive power of 1,000,000 tons of TNT). To appreciate what this means—the total power of all the bombs used in World War Two (including Hiroshima and Nagasaki), which killed 50,000,000 people, was something like 2–3 MT and the total yield of all the explosive bombs used in every war in the history of the world so far is only around 10 MT.[1] Although from 1984 the Doomsday Clock moved gradually anti-clockwise (at the end of the Cold War in 1991, it was 17 minutes away from midnight) and the number of nuclear warheads in the world has decreased significantly, there are still enough to ensure worldwide devastation several times over and we are now steadily approaching midnight once more[2]. In fact, in 2007, climate change was added to the threats considered as the clock was advanced by two minutes to five to midnight. Simultaneous announcements were made in London and Washington DC. Astronomer Royal, Sir Martin Rees stated that 'humankind's collective impacts on the biosphere, climate and oceans are unprecedented' and emphasised that 'these environmentally driven threats—'threats without enemies'—should loom as large in the political perspective as did the East/West political divide during the Cold War era'.[3]

Modelling the Climatic Effects

The disastrous consequences of a global nuclear exchange and global warming have both been dramatically illustrated using computerised models of the climate. Fry Richardson who previously worked in the Meteorological Office was the first to suggest using mathemati-

---

1   Alan Robuck, *Climatic Consequences of Nuclear Conflict,* a 2007 presentation, http://envsci.rutgers.edu/~robock. For more information about the relevant scientific research see: http://climate.envsci.rutgers.edu/robock/robock_nwpapers.html.

2   Molly Bentley, 'Climate resets 'Doomsday Clock', 17 January 2007, http://news.bbc.co.uk/2/hi/science/nature/6270871.stm.

3   The 2008 SIPRI (Stockholm International Peace Research Institute) Handbook indicated that eight nuclear weapon states possessed a total of 25,000 nuclear warheads, almost 10,200 being operational and many thousands ready to launch within minutes. See: http://www.sipri.org.

cal modelling to predict the weather in 1922.[1] However, it was not until computers were available that it became possible to apply and develop the models usefully. Interestingly, Richardson (a Quaker and a pacifist) went on to apply similar techniques to a study of the causes of war by including such things as attitudes and moods in the modelling of international interactions.[2] His claim was that the attitudes of individuals could be averaged to provide the psychology of a whole population. As he said:

> The equations are merely a description of what people would do if they did not stop and think.

The Met Office defines the climate as 'the average, variations and extremes of weather in a region over long periods of time', while its Hadley Centre for Climate Prediction and Research provides the UK Government with assessments on natural and man-made climate change using the most sophisticated and highly developed modelling techniques. As computer power and our understanding of the physical mechanisms that determine climate increases, so the models improve and the predictions become more accurate. The latest standard models predict global average temperature rises due to increased man-made greenhouse gas emissions of 1.6–4.3°C (2.9–7.7°F).

Climate models have also been used to study the effects of a nuclear war. A 1979 report of the US National Academy of Sciences and the Office of Technology Assessment (OTA) indicated that 35–77 per cent of the US population (79–160 million people) could be killed in an all out war and:

> These calculations reflect only deaths during the first 30 days. Additional millions would be injured, and many would eventually die from lack of adequate medical care ... millions of people might starve or freeze during the following winter, but it is not possible to estimate how many... further millions ... might eventually die of latent radiation effects.[3]

---

1   Lewis Fry Richardson, *Weather Prediction by Numerical Process* (Cambridge: Cambridge University Press [1922], Second Edition, 2007).

2   Lewis Fry Richardson, *The Statistics of Deadly Quarrels* (Pacific Grove, CA: Boxwood Press, 1960).

3   'The Effects of Nuclear War,' Office of Technology Assessment, May 1979.

And there could also be serious ecological damage. In 1982 the Swedish Academy of Sciences published a report predicting that the firestorms produced would lead to a 'Nuclear Winter'.[1] Martin Hellman, an engineering professor from Stanford University, explains:

> Smoke from burning cities would absorb incoming sunlight heating the atmosphere. Dust from ground bursts would reflect sunlight back to space. But both would prevent sunlight from penetrating the atmosphere, making it cold and dark at the Earth's surface. These rapid, large surface temperature drops would make it as cold at the surface in the summer as it gets in the winter.[2]

In 1983, Richard Turco, Carl Sagan and three other scientists together produced an article on the 'Global Atmospheric Consequences of Nuclear Explosions' which became known (from the authors' initials) as the TTAPS report,[3] and which argued that the human race could be wiped out in a nuclear winter. Climate models since then have shown that these disastrous effects could result from a nuclear war involving around 1,000 nuclear warheads.[4] Interestingly there may be parallels to explain the mass disappearance of species, including dinosaurs, around 65 million years ago in what has become known as the K-T (Cretaceous-Tertiary) extinction. In this case it is thought that the ash and dust was generated by the impact of a large asteroid or comet. Although there is no overall scientific consensus on the idea of a

Available from NTIS, order #PB-296946 – and www.fas.org/nuke/intro/nuke/7906/.

1   Paul J. Crutzen and John W. Birks, 'The Atmosphere after a Nuclear War: Twilight at Noon', *Ambio*, 11:2/3 (1982), pp. 114–125.

2   Martin E. Hellman,' Risk Analysis for Nuclear Deterrence', *The Bent of Tau Beta PI, The Engineering Honor Society* (Spring, 2008), pp. 14–22.

3   Richard P. Turco, Owen B. Toon, Thomas P. Ackerman, James B. Pollack, and Carl Sagan, 'Nuclear Winter: Global Atmospheric Consequences of Nuclear War', *Science*, 222:4630 (1983), pp.1283–1292. See also Richard P. Turco, Owen B. Toon, Thomas P. Ackerman, James B. Pollack, and Carl Sagan, 'The climatic effects of nuclear war', *Scientific American*, 251 (August 1984), pp. 33–43. See also: 'Environmental consequences of nuclear war: an update – severe global-scale effects of nuclear war reaffirmed,' SCOPE ENUWAR Committee *Environment*, 29:4(1987), pp. 4–5, 46.

4   Alan Robock, Luke Oman, Georgiy L. Stenchikov, Owen B. Toon, Charles Bardeen, and Richard P. Turco, 'Climatic consequences of regional nuclear conflicts', *Atmospheric Chemistry and Physics*, 7:8 (2007), pp. 2003–2012.

nuclear winter, recent work has suggested that even a limited nuclear exchange between, for example, India and Pakistan could have devastating long-term climatic consequences from the burning of megacities and some indication that nuclear arsenals over 5 MT should be considered a 'threat to global society'.[1]

Close to the edge

The potential catastrophes of nuclear war and anthropogenic climate change operate on different timescales. The effects of a nuclear war would be felt relatively quickly after the initiating event whereas in the case of climate change there is no single initiator and the effects occur over an extended period of time. However, both possible situations are ultimately due to a failure of humans to grasp the long term consequences of our behaviour. In addition, both scenarios lie outside of the day to day experience of most people. Even though we have been provided with evidence that these dangers exist the majority of us either choose not to believe it, or ignore it, or convince ourselves that it either it won't be as bad as predicted, or that someone else will sort it out. In the case of climate change we are like a tanker moving slowly towards the edge of a waterfall. It will take a great deal of energy and a long time before we can change direction and avert destruction. For nuclear weapons however, we are like someone standing on the top of a cliff—we could keep away from the edge relatively easily but we seem to be drawn inexorably towards it.

Since 1945 there have been a number of occasions when international incidents may have led to a nuclear war. Joseph Gerson has described how the US has used nuclear weapons to preserve its global empire.[2] He lists more than twenty occasions during the Cold War when the US threatened nuclear attack against Russia, China, Vietnam, and the Middle East. Other incidents that have resulted in global nuclear alerts include the shooting down over the Soviet Union of a U-2 spy plane

---

1   Philip Webber, 'Forecasting nuclear winter', *Bulletin of the Atomic Scientists*, 63:5 (2007), pp. 5–8, http://www.thebulletin.org/ and 'Could one Trident submarine cause 'nuclear winter'? *SGR Newsletter*, 35 (Winter 2008).
2   Joseph Gerson and Walden Bello, *Empire and the Bomb* (London: Pluto Press, 2007).

and pilot Gary Powers in 1960; when the Soviet Union closed off East Berlin in 1961; the Six Day War in the Middle East in June 1967; the Soviet invasion of Czechoslovakia in 1968; the Indo-Pakistan war of 1971; the Arab-Israeli conflict in October 1973; the Soviet invasion of Afghanistan in 1979; the alert following the attempted assassination of President Reagan in 1981; and the 1991 Moscow coup d'etat attempt. For the rest of this chapter we focus on the possibility of human extinction through nuclear war or misadventure.

The Failure of Deterrence: The Cuban Missile Crisis

It is widely thought that the world came closest to all out nuclear war during the 13 days of the Cuban Missile Crisis in October 1962.

The Soviet Union probably decided to deploy Intermediate Range Ballistic Missiles (IRBMs) in Cuba for a number of reasons. The US had attempted numerous times to assassinate Fidel Castro and mounted an unsuccessful invasion at the Bay of Pigs in 1961. They had also recently deployed Jupiter IRBMs in Italy and close to the Russia border in Turkey.[1] Soviet counter-moves to position their own IRBM missiles within striking distance of the US were clearly taken by President Kennedy as a provocation. It remains unclear why the Soviets decided to install the missiles secretly, when Fidel Castro wanted it done openly. However, on the morning of 16 October 1962 Kennedy, was handed photographs taken by a US spy plane showing evidence of the Soviet IRBMs and determined that it was necessary to 'set up a chain of events' to stop the construction. Two options were considered—a sudden strike or the build up and possible escalation of an international crisis.[2] There was enormous pressure on Kennedy to invade but, unknown to him and the Executive Committee of

---

1   Stephen Twigge and Len Scott, 'The Other Missiles of October: The Thor IRBMs and the Cuban Missile Crisis', *Electronic Journal of History*, http://www.history. ac.uk/ejournal/art3.html.

2   See *The World On the Brink: John F. Kennedy and the Cuban Missile Crisis*, The Papers of John Fitzgerald Kennedy, President's Office Files, Presidential Recordings Off the Record Meeting on Cuba, The White House, Washington, 16 October 1962, 11:50 a.m. – at http://www.jfklibrary.org/jfkl/cmc/cmc_meeting_ transcript_oct16_1150am.html.

the US National Security Council, the Soviets had not only already placed battlefield nuclear weapons in Cuba, they had authorised their use in the event of an invasion by the US—without the need to consult the Kremlin.[1] If a US invasion had taken place it is likely that those nuclear weapons would have been used against US troops. And if that had happened, it would have ended, in the words of former US Secretary of Defense Robert McNamara, 'in utter disaster.'

Kennedy considered the options and thought that the USSR's response to an air strike would be to take Berlin, probably leading to a nuclear exchange. Despite arguments from his Joint Chiefs of Staff that it was a weak move, he opted for a less dangerous path and issued a demand that the Soviet leader, Khrushchev, remove all missiles and bases from Cuba backing this up on 22 October with an anti-Soviet naval blockade of the island. 'What we are doing,' he later said, 'is throwing down a card on the table in a game which we don't know the ending of'. On the night of 23 October, the Joint Chiefs of Staff instructed Strategic Air Command to go to DEFCON 2 (the Defense Condition just below maximum readiness), for the only officially verified time in history.

During the crisis, the US and USSR exchanged many formal and informal communications.[2] On 25 October, as Soviet ships approached the quarantine line, Khrushchev sent a long rambling letter that seemed to propose that the missile sites would be removed if Kennedy publicly guaranteed that he would not invade Cuba. On 27 October another letter from Khrushchev implying that the Cuban missile installations could be dismantled if the US removed its missiles from Turkey was interpreted by Kennedy's team as the result of an internal debate between Khrushchev and party officials in the Kremlin.

The whole world was aware of the Cuban Missile Crisis. It watched and held its breath as the story unfolded. It was only many years later

---

1   Laurence Chang and Peter Kornbluh, *The Cuban Missile Crisis, 1962: A National Security Archive Documents Reader* (New York: The New Press, 1998, 2nd edition).
2   See for example *Foreign Relations of the United States, 1961–1963: Volume VI: Kennedy-Khrushchev Exchanges*, (Washington DC: U.S Department of State, 1996).

that some important events came to light. In an interview with the Washington Post following a conference in Havana, Cuba, to mark the 40th anniversary of the crisis, Thomas Blanton, the executive director of the US National Security Archive, commented:

> The most surprising new evidence revealed that we were even closer to nuclear war than the policymakers knew at the time, and that's saying something, because on Saturday, October 27, Robert McNamara thought he might not live to see the sunrise. At the time, there was a crescendo of bad news: a U-2 shot down over Cuba, another U-2 straying over Siberia with US Air Force jets (also armed with nuclear air-to-air missiles) scrambling to head off possible MIG interception. The Joint Chiefs had recommended air strike and invasion of Cuba, as of 4 p.m. The Cubans were firing on all the low-level US recon flights.[1]

The conference also discovered that the USS Beale had tracked and dropped signaling depth charges on a Soviet Foxtrot-class submarine near the quarantine line. Unknown to them, the submarine was armed with a nuclear torpedo. It was also running out of air and needed to surface but was surrounded by US warships. An argument broke out on board between the captain, Valentin Savitsky, the political officer, Ivan Maslennikov, and the chief of staff of the submarine flotilla, Commander Vasily Arkhipov. The Soviet captain lost his temper and, thinking there might be a world war going on, ordered the torpedo be made ready to fire. Fortunately Commander Arkhipov was able to calm him down and avoid a catastrophe.

The submarine surfaced at just about the time that a message was issued to Khrushchev saying that if he dismantled the Soviet missile sites then the US would pledge not to invade Cuba and would also remove its missiles from Turkey, as long as that part of the deal was not mentioned publicly. The next morning Khrushchev announced that the Soviet missiles would be removed. While the US claimed that Khrushchev had backed down, both he and Kennedy had managed to avoid a full-scale conflict despite pressures from their governments and military.

---

1   'The Cuban Missile Crisis: 40 Years Later', with Thomas S. Blanton, *The Washington Post*, 16 October 2002.

Errors and False Alarms

The Cuban Missile Crisis was a particularly important incident but there have been other occasions when an error or misinterpretation of events could easily have led the world to the edge of global conflict. Throughout the Cold War the US and the USSR routinely tested each other's defences by approaching or encroaching on each other's airspace. In September 1983 flight KAL 007 from New York to Seoul disappeared somewhere over the Sea of Japan. The Boeing 747 with 269 passengers and crew on board had wandered into Soviet airspace and was probably mistaken for a US intelligence plane which was flying in the same area. It was shot down by Soviet fighters and, although the Soviets at first denied all knowledge of the event, they eventually claimed it was spying and accused the US of deliberate provocation.

The international situation at this time was extremely tense for a number of reasons. Not only was the US planning to deploy Pershing II missiles in West Germany but in March President Reagan had delivered his famous 'Star Wars' speech in which he proposed his Strategic Defense Initiative (SDI) to develop a missile shield for the US.[1] In March the previous year he had publicly called the USSR the 'evil empire'.[2] Moscow was also extremely nervous about the huge NATO 'Able Archer' exercise to be mounted in Europe in November designed to test nuclear-release procedures—which it feared could be a smokescreen for a real attack. During the exercise a temporary radio silence and the raising of alert levels of US nuclear forces in Europe almost convinced the Russians that the attack was imminent.[3] It was in the run up to this exercise that the world probably came closest to an accidental nuclear war.

---

1   Ronald Reagan's 'Star Wars' Speech, http://www.pierretristam.com/Bobst/library/wf-241.htm.
2   'President Reagan's Speech before the National Association of Evangelicals', http://www.presidentreagan.info/speeches/empire.cfm.
3   Bruce Kennedy, 'War Games: Soviets, fearing Western attack, prepared for worst in '83', CNN, http://www.cnn.com/SPECIALS/cold.war/episodes/22/spotlight/. See also 'When Armageddon Beckoned, 1983: The Brink Of Apocalypse', produced by *Channel 4*, DigiGuide Library. Broadcast January 2008.

The incident occurred near Moscow on 26 September 1983. Lt. Colonel Stanislav Petrov was in charge of the bunker at Serpukhov-15 where the Soviet early warning satellites were monitored. Just after midnight the alarm signals suddenly sounded. The *Oko* satellite Cosmos 1382 had detected the launch of a Minuteman nuclear missile from Malmstrom Air Force Base in Montana. Reports of lone rocket launches did not need to go immediately through *Krokus,* the special notification terminal, up the chain to the duty general. However, the system showed a second launch, then a third and eventually indicated that five US ICBMs had been launched. Petrov reasoned that a computer error had occurred, since the US was not likely to launch just a few missiles in an all-out attack. 'When people start a war, they don't start it with only five missiles', he recalled thinking at the time - anyway, the Soviet ground-based radars showed no evidence of an attack. He therefore decided, against strict procedure, not to raise the alarm and launch a retaliatory nuclear strike to the US.[1]

An investigation after the event identified a fault with the new Soviet detection system. It consisted of nine satellites in highly elliptical orbits monitoring the Earth for bright flashes (rocket launches). Sometimes, only one satellite at a time could observe a particular launch site and observations could not be confirmed. In this case a satellite had mistaken sunlight reflected from high altitude clouds as rocket plumes. Although Petrov had prevented a nuclear holocaust his prompt action was not acknowledged at the time and the whole incident was kept secret until 1998 when it was detailed in a book written by a fellow Russian officer subsequently leading, in 2004, to a special 'World Citizen Award' bestowed on Petrov by the Moscow-based Association of World Citizens, for his bravery and common sense.

Events such as these have generated intense controversy and illustrate that errors are all too easy to make in times of international tension.[2] They also demonstrate how the super-powers not only sus-

---

1 See G. Forde, *Reducing a Common Danger: Improving Russia's Early-Warning System* (Cato Policy Analysis No. 399, Washington DC: The Cato Institute, 2002).

2 In another incident, in July 1988, the US guided missile cruiser USS Vincennes shot down a civilian Iranian airliner (Iran Air flight IR655) over the Strait of Hormuz on its way from Bandar Abbas to Dubai. All 290 passengers and crew were killed. The

pected each other of preparing for a nuclear first strike but were also becoming increasingly aware that their nuclear missile silos were vulnerable—especially to attack from undetectable submarines—with only a few minutes warning. The consequence was silos kept in a state of high alert—ready to be activated at a moment's notice. This situation, affecting thousands of nuclear missiles, has led to considerable disquiet that a misunderstanding, false alarm, or technological fault could set off a full-scale nuclear confrontation.

As one group of analysts have noted:

> the deployments of 'fast-attack' systems with short flight times, combined with the growing complexity and automation of strategic warning and command and control systems, has given rise to the belief that during a major international crisis there would be insufficient time to distinguish false alarms from an actual warning of an enemy attack.

Examination of data on false alarms provided by NORAD similarly led them to conclude that:

> a false alarm sufficiently severe to trigger a strategic attack would occur about 50 per cent of the time during a lengthy crisis.[1]

Accidents

The specific types of accidents that could lead to an accidental nuclear war have been categorised as follows:[2]

Categories 1 and 2

Possible technology failures or malfunctions in early warning or command and control systems, either a failure to detect an actual attack (a Type I error) or a signal that an attack is occurring when it

---

US maintained that the Airbus A300 had been mistaken for an F-14 Tomcat fighter.

1   Michael Wallace, Brian Crissey and Linn Sennott, 'Accidental Nuclear War: A Risk Assessment', *Journal of Peace Research*, 23:1(1986), pp. 9–27.

2   Michael D. Intriligator and Dabobert L. Brito, *Accidental Nuclear War: An Important Issue for Arms Control*, *Proceedings of the 18th Pugwash Workshop on Nuclear Forces* (Toronto: Science for Peace/Samuel Stevens, 1990).

isn't (a Type II error).

Unidentified radar warnings are investigated at so-called 'Missile Display Conferences' and may be followed by two further stages—a 'Threat Evaluation Conference', and a 'Missile Attack Conference' (the latter would actually initiate a nuclear war and has never occurred). The total time available for all of these processes is 15 minutes—the time taken for missiles launched from offshore submarines to reach coastal targets. A 1990 analysis showed that up to 100 Missile Display Conferences were being called annually and the frequency of Threat Evaluation Conferences was directly proportional to the perceived level of tension.[1]

A list of incidents that might have accidentally started a nuclear war[2] suggests that in each case military officers were wrongly informed that their country was under nuclear attack and they had only a few minutes to decide how to respond. For example, in October 1960 NORAD received a warning of incoming warheads from the Missile Warning Squadron at Thule US Air Force Base in Greenland. Retaliatory nuclear strikes were prepared but a computer error had mistaken the moon for an incoming missile, detecting it to be 2,500 miles away rather than its actual distance of 250,000 miles.[3] In 1980 the mistaken loading of a military exercise tape into a warning system computer generated an alert that the Soviets had launched 2,200 ICBMs in an all-out attack. The false alarm was discovered just before President Carter was to be given a few minutes to decide how to react.

On another occasion, in January 1995, a Norwegian meteorological rocket was mistaken for a missile by a Russian early warning radar. Notification of the launch had not reached the early warning system personnel. President Boris Yeltsin, the Defence Minister and the Chief of Staff were informed and the 'nuclear briefcase' acti-

1 Paul Smoker.and I. Peterson, *International Tension and the Chance of Accidental Nuclear War, Proceedings of the 18th Pugwash Workshop on Nuclear Forces* (Toronto: Science for Peace/Samuel Stevens, 1990).

2 Alan F. Philips, '20 Mishaps That Might Have Started Accidental Nuclear War', NuclearFiles.org, http://www.nuclearfiles.org/menu/key-issues/nuclear-weapons/issues/accidents/20-mishaps-maybe-caused-nuclear-war.htm.

3 Intriligator and.Brito, 'Accidental Nuclear War'.

vated. The alarm was found to be false just minutes before a retaliatory nuclear strike could be launched.

Categories 3 and 4

The US Navy has defined four different types of accident involving nuclear weapons, nuclear weapons carriers or nuclear materials, ranging from Nucflash, involving a possible detonation of a nuclear weapon by US Forces, down to Dull Sword, where the incident is deemed not 'significant'.

From 1950–1993 over 50 accidents have been documented, including at least seven incidents of nuclear weapons lost or missing. Many accidents involved explosions and/or fires. In 1958 an electrical short circuit caused twelve Nike missiles to be fired the day before they were due to be fitted with nuclear warheads. The 1960 Mershon National Security Report noted 12 major accidents and stated accidental nuclear war a statistical probability. In January 1961 a B-52 bomber carrying two 24 megaton bombs crashed in North Carolina. On one of the bombs, five of six interlocking safety devices failed. The subsequent explosion would have been 1,800 times more powerful than the Hiroshima bomb.[1]

In August 2007 news broke of the first ever reported case of US nuclear weapons being moved without authorisation. Six W80-1 nuclear warheads were mounted on Cruise Missiles, loaded on a B-52 bomber and were 'lost' for 36 hours while illegally flown across the US from Minot Air Force Base in North Dakota to Barksdale Air Force Base in Louisiana. Six other missiles with dummy warheads were mounted on the plane's other wing.[2] An official report of

1   See the catalogue of accidents 1950–1996 at http://www.nuclearfiles.org/menu/key-issues/nuclear-weapons/issues/accidents/significant-nuclear-accidents.htm.   Also the additions from J. Tiwari, and C.J. Gray, 'U.S. Nuclear Weapons Accidents', http://www.cdi.org/Issues/NukeAccidents/Accidents.htm   and   'US   Nuclear Weapons Accidents: Danger in our Midst', *Defense Monitor, Center for Defense Information*, X:5 (1981), http://www.milnet.com/cdiart.htm.

2   Dave Lindorff, 'The Air Force Cover-Up of That Minot-Barksdale Nuke Missile Flight', 31 October 2007, published on 'This Can't Be Happening!', http://www.thiscantbehappening.net.

this 'Bent Spear' incident said it was a 'mistake' but did not explain how sensors, alarm systems and the requirement of the 'two man rule' failed or were bypassed. The pilots, themselves, did not apparently know that they were carrying nuclear weapons and left them unsecured on the runway in Louisiana for several hours.[1] There was no mention as to whether the nuclear weapons were operational, or whether any systems to prevent an unauthorised launch had been activated.

Category 5

The possibility of a nuclear launch due to the unpredictable and unauthorised behaviour of operational staff is a major concern. Thousands of personnel involved in operational aspects of US nuclear forces have been removed from their positions because of alcohol or drug abuse, or psychiatric problems.[2] To reduce the risk that a single deranged or unauthorised person could detonate a nuclear weapon, the US introduced a 'two-man rule' in the late 1950s which required the launch of any nuclear weapon to be initiated by two individuals acting simultaneously. In addition, in 1962, most nuclear weapons were fitted with Permissive Action Links (PALs), which required the proper sequence of numbers (known to only a few) to arm the warhead.

Category 6

Actions by third parties might sometimes be misinterpreted as the start of a nuclear confrontation. In 2002 a meeting of scientists and military personnel in Washington DC, discussed the possibility of a small asteroid accidentally triggering a nuclear war if it were mistaken for a missile strike.[3] They suggested that a global warning

---

1   John Andrew Prime, 'Barksdale bombers expand B-52 capabilities', *The Sheveport Times*, 27 August 2007, http://www.militarytimes.com/news/2007/08/gns_barksdalebombers_070826/.

2   Sean Gregory, *The Hidden Cost of Deterrence: Nuclear Weapons Accidents* (London: Brassey's, 1990), p. 156.

3   Randall Correll, 'National Security Implications of the Asteroid threat', George C. Marshall Institute, 4 February 2003, http://www.marshall.org/article.php?id=120

centre should be established to inform of asteroid impacts.

In 2008 Bruce Blair, a former Air Force nuclear launch officer,[1] highlighted another possible threat of inadvertent nuclear war – that of 'information warfare'. According to Blair, more than 20 countries have developed dedicated computer attack programs that deploy viruses to disable, confuse and delay other nations' nuclear command and warning processes.[2] Blair also cites the discovery of an unprotected electronic 'backdoor' into the naval communications network used to transmit launch orders to US Trident submarines. New launch order validation protocols have been devised but there may still be other possibilities for hackers to generate an unofficial launch order either deliberately or by mistake.

Launch on Warning

Despite the distinct possibility of an accidental nuclear war, towards the end of the Cold War the US adopted a policy of launch on warning (LOW). This provided for nuclear retaliation on just the warning of an impending Soviet attack—before the detonation of any nuclear weapons on US territory was actually confirmed. The dangers of LOW demonstrate that the two goals of a warning system, accurately warning of an attack and avoiding false alarms, can sometimes conflict. In spite of the ending of the Cold War, Russia and the US have retained their LOW strategies. In addition, fears that a nuclear war might be initiated by nuclear states in areas of tension—such as the Middle East and Asia—have increased.

Preventing an Accidental Nuclear War

Concerns that an international crisis or incident might escalate to

---

1   Bruce Blair made his name by publishing an important study on Strategic Command and Control in the mid-'80s. His Congressional Record testimony is probably the best investigation of nuclear attack launch and warning systems in the public domain.
2   Bruce Blair, 'Achieving the Vision of a World Free of Nuclear Weapons', International Conference on Nuclear Disarmament, Oslo, 26–27 February 2008, http://disarmament.nrpa.no/wp-content/uploads/2008/02/Paper_Blair.pdf

war have led to some international agreements designed to facilitate swift communication between nations and avoid the possibility of any misinterpretation or misunderstanding. The most famous of these was the establishment of a hot line between Washington and Moscow after the Cuban Missile Crisis.[1] Measures have also been taken to reduce the threat of accidental nuclear war. In 1991, a Cooperative Threat Reduction (CTR) program was initiated to assure the secure handling of nuclear weapons materials in the former Soviet Union. Additionally, in 1994, the US and Russia agreed to 'de-target' their nuclear weapons to reduce the chances of a nuclear war starting from an accidental missile launch.

A joint program between the US Departments of Defence and Energy includes a 'Nuclear Weapons System Safety Program' to monitor and safeguard the US nuclear arsenal. A Nuclear Weapons Security Standard has been established to:

> [prevent] unauthorized access to nuclear weapons; prevent damage or sabotage to nuclear weapons; prevent loss of custody; and prevent, to the maximum extent possible, radiological contamination caused by unauthorized acts.

In addition, the Defence Threat Reduction Agency (DTRA) and its partners inspect and monitor all US nuclear weapons through their 'Nuclear Weapon Status Information Systems'. However, the $1 billion spent per year on threat reduction represents less than one-third of one percent of US defence spending. Many analysts believe that these measures are not enough and the possibility of accidental nuclear war remains—especially if relations between the US and Russia continue to deteriorate over the possible establishing of US missile defence bases in Europe.[2]

---

1   'Prevention of Accidental Nuclear War', US Military History Companion, http://www.answers.com/library/US%20Military%20History%20Companion -cid-14390690.

2   At the time of writing Russia has suspended participation in the Conventional Forces in Europe (CFE) Treaty, threatened to withdraw from the Intermediate-Range Nuclear Forces (INF) treaty and threatened to re-target its nuclear weapons—indicating the possible start of a new Cold War. Also, in August 2007 President Putin announced the resumption of regular strategic flights of nuclear bombers. The possibility of nuclear armed 'training' flights was not excluded—See Victor Mizin,

In 2003 a report by the RAND Corporation described three possible scenarios for an accidental launch of a nuclear missile. These
included the intentional launch of a single missile by a rogue commander or terrorist, a training accident or system malfunction, or a
Type II error. The report concluded that the potential for an accidental nuclear missile launch in Russia or the US had grown in the previous ten years.[1] Commenting on the report, former senator Sam Nunn,
co-chairman of the Nuclear Threat Initiative (NTI), recommended
that the US and Russia take thousands of strategic nuclear warheads
off hair-trigger alert and establish a jointly developed early warning
system of sensors to monitor each other's land-based intercontinental
missiles.[2]

Another issue highlighted in the report was the deterioration of the
Russian early warning system since the end of the Cold War. This
especially relates to reports of the reduced coverage of early warning
space satellites to only seven hours a day plus significant gaps in
the ground-based early warning radar systems. A nuclear missile
could easily be launched through these radar gaps from a Trident
submarine.[3] In recognition of the problem the US and Russia set up
a joint radar centre in Moscow in 1998, to encourage collaborative
early warnings of third party attacks. However, these plans stalled
and no real progress subsequently has been made.

The development of non-nuclear weapons systems that might
appear to be nuclear is also causing problems. Commenting on a plan

---

'Russia's 'Nuclear Renaissance', *Journal of International Security Affairs*, 14
(Spring 2008), http://www.securityaffairs.org/issues/2008/14/mizin.php

1   David E. Mosher, David R. Howell, Lowell H. Schwartz and Lynn E. Davis,
'Beyond the Nuclear Shadow: A Phased Approach for Improving Nuclear Safety
and US-Russian Relations', RAND Monograph Report, 2003. This report also suggests that a combination of three factors increased the risk of accidental or unauthorised nuclear launch: 1. The large US and Russian nuclear forces that can be
delivered within minutes; 2. The dramatic decline in survivable nuclear forces and
an early-warning system in serious disrepair in Russia; and 3. The highly capable
US forces that can exploit Russian vulnerabilities.

2   'Nunn Urges Presidents Bush and Putin to Address Nuclear Dangers', *NTI* Press
Release, 21 May, 2003 http://www.nti.org/c_press/release_rand_052103.pdf.

3   Pavel Podvig, 'History and the current status of the Russian early warning system',
Science and Global Security, 10:1 (2002), pp. 21–60.

by the Pentagon to modify submarine launched Trident missiles to carry non-nuclear warheads, the Stanford University weapons specialist Pavel Podvig, along with MIT professor, Ted Postol, have suggested that the launch of any long-range non-nuclear ballistic missile could cause an automated alert and greatly increase the chances of a nuclear war.[1]

In addition, Thomas Graham, a leading US arms control expert and negotiator, pointed out in 2005 that:

> Fifteen years after the end of the Cold War, the chance of an accidental nuclear exchange has far from decreased. Yet, the United States may be contemplating further exacerbating this threat by deploying missile interceptors in space.[2]

This is not just an issue for the US military. Many other countries are also developing military space capabilities for intelligence gathering, communication and battle management roles.[3] The failure of an important satellite component in this system of 'network-centric warfare', by accidental collision or technical failure, may give the false impression of a pre-emptive strike.

Rescuing the Future

In this chapter we have focused on how we have lived close to Armageddon for over 60 years and have made some comparisons between the threats posed by nuclear war and climate change. A major feature of both is that governments and people are either not aware or ignorant of the urgency of the situation. Again, in both cases, fear, greed, mistrust, as well as ignorance, are exploited by major forces with vested interests in the military-industrial complex or the retention

---

1   E. Rosenberg, 'Experts warn of an accidental atomic war: Nuclear missile modified for conventional attack on Iran could set off alarm in Russia', *Hearst Newspapers*, 6 October 2006.

2   Thomas Graham, 'Space Weapons and the Risk of Accidental Nuclear War', *Arms Control Today*, December 2005 http://www.armscontrol.org/act/2005_12/Dec-spaceweapons.asp.

3   See, for example, Eddie F. Halpin, Philippa Trevorrow, Dave Webb and Steve Wright, eds, *Cyberwar, Netwar and the Revolution in Military Affairs* (Basingstoke: Palgrave Macmillan, 2006).

of a petroleum based economy, pushing us ever closer to the edge.

Pulling us back from that edge, in the nuclear case, has involved a proposal for a four phase plan to make nuclear war more difficult to initiate. This includes the de-targeting and de-alerting of missiles, the separation of warheads from missiles and their removal from silos.[1] These measures would give more time between thought and action— time to think over the options and find alternative ways of dealing with the situation. Even though climate change is already happening there are also plans and ideas for preventing an extinction event by this other route.

There is a further problem which presents itself, however: nuclear proliferation. Although it was recognised at the outset of the nuclear age the first major move to try and curb the spread of nuclear weapons was not made until 1968 when the Nuclear Non-Proliferation Treaty (NPT) opened for signature. Unfortunately, the treaty allowed—even encouraged—the spread of nuclear technology for the production of energy while precluding states from joining if they developed nuclear weapons at a later time (e.g. India, Pakistan, Israel and North Korea). Thus, the major problem with the treaty is that it is now seen by the more than 180 non-nuclear weapons signatories who promised *not* to obtain nuclear weapons as merely preserving the special status of the P5—the US, the Soviet Union, the UK, France and China— who already had the weapons in 1968. In other words, having not kept their side of the bargain to work 'in good faith' towards nuclear disarmament the treaty founders paradoxically set a poor example for other urgent international agreements such as those for limiting global CO2 emissions.

This would suggest that it is not simply a matter of future treaties and agreements of this kind being carefully worded or even of com-pliance being closely verified and monitored. If we are to avoid the extinction of history we will need to develop global understanding, trust and cooperation to unprecedented levels. Education and aware-ness-raising campaigns highlighting the threats *both* of nuclear war and climate change aid each other in this respect. Even so, we still need to make fundamental changes to the way we think and act. As

---

1   Bruce Blair, 'Achieving the Vision'.

long ago as 1954 Albert Einstein wrote:

> We need an essentially new way of thinking if mankind is to survive. Men must radically change their attitudes towards each other and their views of the future. Force must no longer be an instrument of politics ... Today, we do not have much time left; it is up to our generation to succeed in thinking differently. If we fail, the days of civilised humanity are numbered.[1]

He was concerned then about the nuclear threat but his words remain true today when we now have the power to destroy life on Earth in several different ways. In international relations and in the way we lead our lives, we must find new ways to resolve conflicts and build our communities. Our willingness and ability to do this must not be overcome by our apparent addiction to war and a high tech push-button life style promising instant gratification. The fatal attraction to the edge of annihilation and a belief that we can pull back at any moment may appear to have been confirmed partly through past experiences with weapons of mass destruction but it is not clear how long this will remain the case. It is also not applicable to climate change. For that we need to heed a different lesson learned from nuclear weapons—to use our intelligence and our ability to understand what the consequences of our actions might be and to ensure that history can continue by working together to make human security and global survival our top priorities.

---

1   Quoted in Ken Wilber, *A Theory of Everything* (Boston: Shambhala Publications, 2000), p. 136.

Part VI: Surviving Catastrophe: Creating Conditions for Renewal

11. On Reading History as a Mental Health Issue

Jonathan Coope

> the climate-change crisis is at its very bottom a crisis of lifestyle
> – of character, even.
>
> Michael Pollan, writing in *The Guardian*, 6 June 2008

> Where we find ourselves, then, is between stories... Our thera-
> peutic task... in this space of transition is to understand how
> these myths still shape our internal worlds, our language, and our
> defences against change...
>
> Mary-Jayne Rust, 'Climate on the Couch', 2007[1]

Introduction

This essay acknowledges Colin Feltham's point that political analysis (for example) too often overlooks 'the *psychological* dimensions of social pathology'[2] and explores whether greater psychological sophistication might help us to fruitfully rethink history in an
era of climate crisis. I begin by examining some pragmatic reasons
why greater psychological sophistication may help us understand and
address environmental problems. Second, if, as some suggest, that
crisis has psychodynamic roots, then those roots presumably have a
history; yet historians have often been suspicious of psychological
historiographies, for reasons I discuss. Third, I explore the problematic nature of 'scientism' and go on to examine the psychology of sci-

---

1. Mary-Jayne Rust, Guild of Psychotherapists Annual Lecture, 17 November 2007.
2. Colin Feltham, *What's Wrong With Us?* (Chichester: Wiley, 2007), p. 243.

entific encounters with nature, offering some historical perspectives on the 'cognitive pathologies' of science and modernity. Finally, I consider some implications for historiographic practice in relation to the pressing issue of climate change.

1. Climate Crisis and Psyche

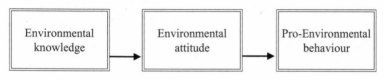

Early models of pro-environmental behaviour.[1]

The behavioural models upon which most pro-environmental campaigns have hitherto been based tended to assume that increasing environmental information leads, in a fairly straightforward 'linear' fashion, to increasingly widespread adoption of pro-environmental behaviours. However, recent climate change communications research has underlined the shortcomings of such 'rational choice' models. For example, a Government Social Research Unit report notes that:

> in a meta-analysis of pro-environmental behaviours, Fliegenschnee and Shelakovsky … found that at least 80 per cent of the factors influencing behaviour did not stem from knowledge or awareness.[2]

And a DEFRA report in 2005 concludes that 'information should not be supposed to lead to public behaviour change'.[3] Consequently, researchers are increasingly turning towards more sophisticated understandings of why people behave the way they do, drawing

---

1   Anja Kollmuss et al., 'Mind the Gap: Why Do People Act Environmentally And What are the Barriers to Pro-environmental Behavior?', *Environmental Education Research* 8:3 (2002), p. 241.

2   Andrew Darnton, *Reference Report: An Overview of Behaviour Change Models and Their Uses* (London: GSRU, 2008), p. 14.

3   Andrew Darnton, *Public Understanding of Climate Change* (London: Defra, 2005), p. 92.

insights from anthropology, consumer research, evolutionary biology, human geography, and social and environmental psychology.

For example, the WWF report *Weathercocks and Signposts: the Environmental Movement at a Crossroads* (2008), suggests that environmental campaigners need to address such intrinsic goals as 'personal growth' if they hope to effect any widespread adoption of environmentally sustainable behaviours.[1] Meanwhile, the IPPR report *Positive Energy: Harnessing People Power to Prevent Climate Change* (2007) highlights a range of influences that must be taken into account in understanding human behaviours with respect to the natural environment:

> Important internal influences that need to be taken into account include:
>
> • different psychological motivations (as defined, for example, by Abraham Maslow's 'hierarchy of human needs')...
> • emotions...
>
> Important external influences that need to be factored in include:
>
> • ...the nature of the experiences that people have (evidence suggests direct experiences are more powerful than indirect ones)...

The report's authors go on to note the potential role of *affective* (emotional, affectionate) responses to nature in motivating pro-environmental behaviour change:

> Childhood experiences of nature and of environmental destruction are among the most frequently mentioned formative experiences that research suggests lead to such sensitivity... experience of the natural world... [may be] more likely to generate an emotional connection to the natural environment, and feelings of being part of ecological processes, rather than being separate and insulated from it.[2]

The need for psychological theory to adopt a *normative* role

---

1   Tom Crompton, *Weathercocks and Signposts* (London: WWF-UK, 2008), p. 7.
2   Simon Retallack et al., *Positive Energy* (London: IPPR, 2007), pp. 10, 126–27.

for positive, affective responses to the more-than-human world around us has been highlighted by a number of theorists. For example, Abraham Maslow effectively added a sixth affective level to his well-known five-level hierarchy of human needs with his development of transpersonal psychology in the late 1960s.[1] More recently, a normative role for affective responses to nature is posited by eco-psychologists and, for instance, in the Yale School of Forestry and Environmental Studies report, *Toward a New Consciousness*.[2]

Thus, while climate crisis has often tended to be understood in predominantly scientific terms as a physical problem to be solved, recent research in climate change communications reminds us that the psychological aspects of the problem are far from immaterial. Indeed, they are a very real aspect and wholly material to any timely, *non-authoritarian* response. As a report from the Grubb Institute of Behavioural Studies puts it:

> A systemic or holistic, approach to sustainable development must pay more attention to the inner, *psycho-cultural roots of behaviour*, and how they translate into external impacts.[3]

So two points worth highlighting here are: first, the cultivation of *affective* responses to nature may have an important role to play in the development of pro-environmental dispositions and, second, environmental impacts may have complex psychodynamic roots.

2. Psyche and Historiography: Two Objections

But if, as Paul Maiteny suggests, our behaviours—pro-environmental or otherwise—may have 'inner, psycho-cultural roots' then those roots presumably have a history. Historians, however, have often been suspicious of more psychologically nuanced historiographies.

---

1   Warwick Fox, *Toward a Transpersonal Ecology* (Boston: Shambhala, 1990), pp. 294–97.
2   Anthony Leiserowitz *et al.*, *Toward a New Consciousness* (New Haven: Yale University Press, 2008).
3   Paul Maiteny, 'Psychodynamics of Meaning and Action for a Sustainable Future', *Futures*, 32 (2000), p.357.

One objection sometimes raised is that 'war and atrocities are just as much a part of the human condition' as any psychological norms we might favour. Harry Hearder thus insists that 'we can learn only from the past' as we find it 'since the past is all we have'.[1] But, as Martin Davies points out in his recent critique of the historian's trade *Historics: Why History Dominates Contemporary Society,* the problem with this kind of argument is the way it naturalises war and atrocities rather than deploring them as 'pathological symptoms' of deeper problems.[2] Such ethical myopia (as Davies terms it) can only be avoided if the historian brings something of her/his own ethical vision to bear upon the past they are studying. Our ultimate human nature doesn't *have* to be some Hobbesian nightmare: 'It depends where we look', Steven Baum observes, 'and how we aspire to be'. Indeed, Baum argues that war and atrocities cannot be effectively addressed until we begin to acknowledge the psychological dimensions of such problems. Until then, Baum insists, history will simply be doomed to repeat itself.[3]

Of course, a 'mental health' perspective on the past could never be value neutral; yet, presumably, it would never aspire to be. In any case, a lack of value neutrality in our historiography only seems problematic if we assume there exists some alternative approach or methodology that *is* capable of achieving value neutrality. However, while we all perhaps hold values that we wished everybody held as absolute, our historiographies can no more achieve neutrality than can our personal ideals of 'pro-environmental behaviour'.[4]

Another objection against more psychologically sophisticated readings of the past is the problem of *evidence.* As John Tosh puts it:

> Whereas the therapist seeks to recover the infantile experience of the patient through the analysis of dreams, verbal slips and

---

1   'Editor's foreword' in James Joll, *The Origins of the First World War* (London: Longman, 1992), p. vii.
2   Martin Davies, *Historics* (London: Routledge, 2006),p.192.
3   Steven Baum, *The Psychology of Genocide* (Cambridge: Cambridge University Press, 2008), pp. 21, 237.
4   Ideals of 'pro-environmental behaviour' are never value neutral: see, Stephen Gough, 'Whose Gap? Whose Mind?' *Environmental Education Research* 8:3 (2002), pp. 273–82.

other material produced by the subject, the historian has only the documents which are likely to contain very little, if any, material of this kind...[1]

Tosh is referring here to Freud's suggestion that verbal slips represent the outward 'projection' of inner psychic contents in individual patients. For Freud, this idea of projection offered the possibility that, even though psychic contents could not be directly examined, they might instead be amenable to indirect examination (this parallels Maiteny's suggestion that external behaviours reflect 'inner, psycho-cultural roots'). Yet, by assuming that historical traces offer little by way of psychological evidence, Tosh fails to recognise the ways in which Freud and others radically expanded the idea of projection. For, Freud realised, if our personal discourses reveal the outward projection of inner psychic contents, then so too might other aspects of culture. Indeed, Freud went on to extend the consideration of projection to religion, art and society as a whole—going so far as to suggest that civilisation itself might correlate with collective psychopathology, with the collective repression of people's innate psychic capacities and potentialities.[2]

If we pursue this idea of projection seriously, as environmental psychologists invite us to do, then we soon find Tosh's problem of evidence turned on its head. For, with regard to environmental degradation, the problem is not too little evidence but *too much*. This is the line of thinking pursued by Theodore Roszak in a pioneering text on ecopsychology in 1992:

> Freud delivered a famous series of lectures titled 'The Psychopathology of Everyday Life'... He used jokes, double-entendres, and slips of the tongue to show how these familiar experiences reveal the repressed sexual and aggressive drives of the unconscious mind.
>
> Today, a similar series of lectures might draw its material from reports of ozone depletion, toxic waste, and the greenhouse effect. These commonplace environmental problems have

---

1   John Tosh, *The Pursuit of History* (Harlow: Pearson, 2006), p.291.
2   Sigmund Freud, *Civilisation, Society and Religion* (London: Penguin, 1985), p. 338; Peter Gay, *Freud* (London: Papermac,1989), pp. 547–51.

become the psychopathology of *our* everyday life.[1]

And such 'traces' provide evidence, not only of pathology in our everyday present, but in our everyday *past* as well.

3. Modernity and the 'God Trick' of Science

Mike Hulme, founder of the Tyndall Centre for Climate Change Research, reminds us that arguments surrounding climate change encompass a plurality of often incommensurable viewpoints.[2] But when viewpoints become polarised, little inclination remains to seek any common ground of mutual understanding. And what sometimes then happens, even at an academic level, is that ardent advocates of one side or another simply set out to 'take the cudgels' to each other's viewpoints. The historian Martin Davies, however, indicates another way we might respond when confronting modernity's systemic dysfunctionalities. What we most urgently need, Davies suggests, are 'new distinctions—and new ways of making distinctions': in other words, greater *discrimination*, morally, and, perhaps, psychologically as well.[3]

Consider, for example, the sometimes polarised debates between those who insist that 'Enlightenment & modernity = Good' and those who insist that "Enlightenment & modernity = Bad'. The latter often claim that Enlightenment modernity has been complicit in developing an ecocidal mindset which has underpinned humanity's exploitation of nature, and they sometimes go on to advocate (apparently) the complete abandonment of the Enlightenment legacy as a necessary precursor to addressing environmental problems. However, in doing so, they overlook the genuine dignities of modernity: the Enlightenment virtues of equality, freedom and justice, for example, and the very real benefits bequeathed by science and technology. On the other hand, those who insist unreservedly that 'Enlightenment

---

1   Theodore Roszak, *The Voice of the Earth* (New York: Simon & Schuster, 1992), p. 13.

2   Mike Hulme, *Why We Disagree About Climate Change* (Cambridge: Cambridge University Press, 2009).

3   Davies, *Historics*, p. 31.

& modernity = Good' display a similar lack of discrimination when they downplay modernity's disasters, or insist that it is *only* through science and new technology, or *only* from the standpoint of science, that environmental problems can be resolved. As Jared Diamond asks, why should we believe that for the first time in history technology would function primarily to solve problems and no longer create new ones?[1] David Edgerton notes that the idea that future science and technology will solve our climate crisis is a common way of avoiding the kinds of change this crisis might actually require of us.[2] Why? Because the discrimination we need with regard to science, technology or any other matter of ethical moment, is a hallmark of human wisdom, not of technology or science in itself. Any truly discriminating account requires a just measure of both the dignities *and* the disasters.

Nevertheless, as Patrick Curry notes, 'Belief in technological fixes is symptomatic of a wider *faith* in modern techno-science'.[3] Curry's use of the word 'faith' here reminds us that the psychology underpinning technological optimism can appear decidedly non-rational. Indeed, Val Plumwood suggests that science and technology appear to play a distinctly *salvific* (i.e.'causing or able to cause salvation') role for many proponents: 'science,' it is sometimes claimed, 'will *save* us, provided we do not lose our nerve or our faith in techno-reason and our will to continue along our current path, however precarious it may seem'.[4]

A further psychological aspect of the matter is, I think, indicated by the fact that proponents of techno-science frequently insist that science is not just one way of being among many but the *only* true or legitimate one. This is what is meant by the term 'scientism', and the oft-perpetuated idea that science might yield 'knowledge' from some position of value neutrality has been described as the 'God trick' of science.[5] Scientism is problematic for a number of reasons.

---

1   Jared Diamond, *Collapse* (London: Penguin, 2006), p. 505.
2   David Edgerton, *The Shock of the Old* (London: Profile, 2006), p. 210.
3   Patrick Curry, *Ecological Ethics* (Cambridge: Polity, 2006), p.19.
4   Val Plumwood, *Environmental Culture* (London: Routledge, 2002), p. 6.
5   Donna Haraway, *Simians, Cyborgs, and Women* (New York: Routledge, 1991), pp. 189–95.

According to Jürgen Habermas, at the societal level, the dogmatic secularist refusal to take non-scientistic standpoints in any way seriously tends to undermine 'the very basis of *mutual recognition* which is constitutive for shared citizenship'.

> A... learning process is... necessary on the secular side... Secular citizens are expected not to exclude a fortiori that they may discover, even in religious utterances, semantic contexts and covert person intuitions that can be translated and introduced into a secular discourse. [1]

Moreover, Habermas insists, it would be a mistake for any society to pre-emptively reduce the diversity of its standpoints since we can never be sure in advance which standpoints might not afford 'scarce resources for the generation of meanings and the shaping of identities'.

Habermas's suggestion that 'scientistic consciousness' is a 'restricted' style of consciousness[2] indicates perhaps the most intractable aspect of the non-rational psychology underpinning naïve techno-scientific optimism. For, ardent advocates of techno-science may, *experientially*, know no way of responding to the world other than that afforded by a restricted objective/scientistic mode of awareness. Small wonder then that, for many proponents of scientism, discussions of affective or sensuous responses to nature are apt to sound like little more than 'transcendental twaddle'.

It is worth noting, I think, that Habermas's point—that scientistic consciousness may be too restricted for us to achieve our full human proportions—doesn't require us to perpetuate yet another tiresome polarity between, say, science on the one hand and affective responses to nature, on the other. But it does imply that in a wholesomely ordered mind, while science and objectivity have their legitimate place in our understandings of nature, so too do our sensuous, affective, or visionary responses (including experiences of delight, awe, reverence or even a sense of the sacred in the presence of the

---

1   Jürgen Habermas, 'Notes on a Post-Secular Society', lecture, University of Tilberg, 15 March 2007, http://www.signandsight.com/features/1714.html .
2   Jürgen Habermas. *Knowledge and Human Interests* (London: Heinemann, 1972), p. 316.

natural world). In other words, while science or objectivity have their rightful place in the 'spectrum of consciousness' (and, concomitantly, the spectrum of knowledge), they ought not to monopolise, nor necessarily be uppermost, in a wholesomely ordered mind.[1] Maslow's term for this wholesome ordering of the mental faculties is 'hierarchical integration'[2]—reminding us that scientific *and* affective understandings of nature both have their legitimate places within a wholesomely ordered mind (integrated hierarchically within a broader spectrum of consciousness).

The psychological shortcomings of scientism become all the more pertinent to historiography when we recall that, for the better part of three centuries, it has been to modern science that we have tended to turn for our definitive, supposedly objective, accounts of nature and reality.

4. On the Cognitive Pathologies of Modern Science

Proponents of techno-scientific standpoints frequently appear 'unconscious' of the particularity of their own values or presuppositions[3] while often tending to delegitimise those very *affective* responses to nature which are increasingly being assigned a normative role by psychologists and environmental campaigners. As Curry puts it:

> the value that proponents of science place on 'objectivity' can contribute to the ecocrisis as much as, in another way, it can help by gathering, analysing and presenting evidence. Why? One reason is the extent to which an overemphasis in this respect, and a corresponding devaluation of the value of the Earth in its sensuous particulars and emotional meanings... is itself implicated in that crisis.[4]

In other words, the *monopolising* character of techno-scientific

1   Theodore Roszak, 'Romantic at Reason's Court', *New Scientist*, 4 March 1971, pp. 484–86; Ken Wilber, *The Spectrum of Consciousness* (Wheaton: Theosophical Publishing House, 1977).
2   Abraham Maslow, *The Psychology of Science* (New York: Harper & Row, 1966), pp. 46–49.
3   Sandra Harding, *Science and Social Inequality* (Chicago: University of Illinois Press, 2006), pp. 113–32, 83–97.
4   Patrick Curry, *Ecological Ethics*, 2006), p. 19.

standpoints (or the scientific 'worldview') is implicated in devalu-
ing our affective responses to the more-than-human world around us.
Curry's remarks above remind us that the delegitimisation of our affective responses to the Earth constitutes a mental health issue of more
than merely personal concern. Indeed, according to Plumwood, our
current ecological crises represent 'the disastrous effects of the *desen-
sitisation* to nature' that has been part of the 'reductive narrative' per-
petuated by modern science.[1] Others have drawn similar conclusions:
philosopher of science, Nicholas Maxwell, insists that modern science
is 'neurotic'[2] while Maslow diagnoses science as a 'cognitive pathology'. Of course, proponents of techno-science may vigorously resist
such accusations but that may be because, as Sandra Harding suggests,
they are simply unconscious of their own presuppositions.

Historical reflection upon our environmental crises may ultimately
need to examine the extent to which their roots lie in the monopolising character of the scientific worldview. For, although science has
undoubtedly delivered innumerable benefits, it has also over the past
few centuries offered a rather bleak picture of nature and the universe
as an alien and meaningless assortment of unfeeling and inferior
objects with which we have *no conceivable ethical relation*. Such
portraits have tended to deprive nature of 'moral considerability and
thereby paved the way for a purely instrumental attitude towards the
natural world'.[3] If we choose to persist in viewing nature in this way,
we may find ourselves liable to treat the Earth with an irresponsibil-
ity we can ill afford.

Ecofeminists such as Charlene Spretnak contextualise the alien-
ative psychology of modern science within a broader patriarchal
psychology, whose predispositions include 'separateness, reactive
(defensive) autonomy, and control'.[4] In *History After Lacan*, Teresa
Brennan describes the withdrawal of sympathy between knower and
known as 'sado-dispassionate' and goes on to underline the 'negative

---

1   Plumwood, *Environmental Culture*, p. 12.
2   Nicholas Maxwell, *Is Science Neurotic?* (London: Imperial College Press, 2004),
    pp. 148–50.
3   Kate Rigby, *Topographies of the Sacred* (Charlottesville: University of Virginia,
    2004), p. 21.
4   Charlene Spretnak, *States of Grace* (San Francisco: Harper, 1991), p. 119.

aggressive emotions' which underpin 'objectifying reason' and which have 'an edge in common with sadism when it is directed towards another'.[1] Indeed, to the extent that modern science continues to perpetuate the disciplined withdrawal of sympathy between knower and known, it can be read as a form of male separation anxiety writ large: 'written, in fact, upon the entire universe'.[2]

From mental health considerations such as these, ecofeminists have traced the historical roots of contemporary environmental crisis back through the history of a patriarchal consciousness and 'reason-centred culture that is at least a couple of millennia old'.[3] Historiographies of consciousness such as these serve, among other things, to remind us of the existence of other standpoints besides secularist scientism. For if some standpoints *are* more gracefully at home in the world than others, then those ongoing efforts by proponents of scientism to monopolise our possible ways of being in the world may, *however nobly intended*, be undercutting our capacity to gain critical purchase upon modernity's 'all-encompassing systemic dysfunctionality'.[4] Undercutting, in other words, such innate capacities for moral and psychological discrimination as we may, perhaps, need if we are ever to begin seeing the wood for the trees.

5. After the 'God Trick' of History: from Metahistory to Historiographies of Consciousness

However, one reason why professional historians might be reluctant to squarely confront the psycho-historical roots of environmental crises is that modernity has often tended to peruse its *past* via the same depersonalised or 'objective' style of knowing which itself requires critique. This is one consequence of the pervasive influence of what Iggers and Wang describe as the 'cult of science' in modern historiography. This took

the progressive character of history and the superiority of

---

1   Teresa Brennan, *History After Lacan* (London: Routledge, 1993), p. 72.
2   Theodore Roszak, *The Gendered Atom* (Berkeley: Conari, 1999), p. 91.
3   Plumwood, *Environmental Culture*, p. 8.
4   See Crisis Forum, 'Crisis, What Crisis?' http://www.crisis-forum.org.uk/about_us/index.php

Western civilisation over the rest of the world for granted. Historiography was to become 'scientific'... [These] approaches... claimed that they had freed themselves from the philosophical and metaphysical assumptions of earlier historiography and that they were strictly scientific.[1]

Historians frequently attempted to emulate an 'objective' or 'dispassionate' methodological style, more commonly associated with modern science.[2] Certainly, many historians today, including many environmental historians,[3] continue to strive for objectivity in their accounts. Indeed, many historians reject the idea that history might be an *ethical* discipline or scoff at the idea that historians might have some responsibility for shedding light upon our current environmental predicaments.[4] Some continue to aver that 'history is a *scientific* discipline'.[5]

However, Hayden White's *Metahistory* (1973), among others, heralded the arrival of postmodernist understandings of historiography, which reminded historians that any historical account is inescapably the historian's own particular *representation* of the past. And, as such, no account can *ever* be value neutral, definitive or 'true' (the 'God trick' of modernist history). Historical accounts, postmodernists remind us, are always rhetorically constructed in the service of some present-centred purpose or other, and are always 'situated' culturally and politically (whether consciously or not). Postmodernist understandings have reflected a

> growing uneasiness about the conditions which modernisation had brought about, and a critique of the faith in science and in the beneficial character of modern civilisation, assumptions on which much Western historiography and social science theory and research was based.[6]

---

1   George Iggers *et al.*, *A Global History of Modern Historiography* (Harlow: Pearson, 2008), p. 120.
2   Beverley Southgate, *What is History For?* (London: Routledge, 2005), pp. 16–29.
3   J. Donald Hughes, 'The Greening of World History', in Marnie Hughes-Warrington, ed., *World Histories* (Basingstoke: Palgrave, 2005), p. 247.
4   Geoffrey Alderman, 'A Climate of Trepidation', *Times Higher Education*, 21 February 2008, p. 28.
5   Arthur Marwick, *The New Nature of History* (Basingstoke: Palgrave, 2001), p. 274.
6   Iggers, *Global History*, p. 13.

Nevertheless, postmodernism is not without its critics and some historical theorists, such as Frank Ankersmit and Eelco Runia, have suggested that even the most 'self-reflexive' postmodernist historians may have their own 'blind spots'.[1] Davies, for example, notes the failure of postmodernist historians to cognise the deeper 'social-psychological' underpinnings of modernity's crises (environmental or otherwise).[2] Charlene Spretnak, meanwhile, notes a collective 'cold-heartedness' towards our planetary habitat—on the part of both modernity *and* its postmodernist critics. Certainly, postmodernist theories often overlook the fact that culture and psyche are always *ecologically* situated.[3] If 'myth' is the way we arrange the past—'whether real or imagined, in patterns that reinforce a culture's deepest values and aspirations'[4]—then postmodernist histories have tended to perpetuate the myth that our human past can be considered *apart from* its planetary context.

To challenge myths such as these, Plumwood advocates a radical 'renarrativisation' which underlines the need for openness to 'experiences of nature as powerful, agentic and creative, making space... for an animating sensibility and vocabulary'.[5] One such narrative is offered by David Abram, who explores the historical processes 'whereby civilisation' came to isolate itself experientially 'from the breathing earth'.[6] Meanwhile, ecoanthropology reveals that many so-called 'primitive' cultures display affective 'ecoanimist' responses to nature from which modernity may have much to learn.[7] Some feminist historians, too, suggest that the imagery of ancient Earth Mother religions might usefully be read as expressions of *our own* innate capacity for sensuous engagement with nature.[8] The Gestalt therapist

---

1 Frank Ankersmitt, "'Presence' and Myth', *History and Theory* 45:3 (2006), p. 328–36.
2 Davies, *Historics*, pp.14–16.
3 Spretnak, *The Resurgence of the Real* (New York: Routledge 1999), pp. 64–73.
4 Ronald Wright, *A Short History of Progress* (Edinburgh: Canongate, 2004), p. 4.
5 Plumwood, 'Nature in the Active Voice', in Ruth Irwin, ed., *Climate Change and Philosophy* London: Continuum, forthcoming 2009), p. 14 of typescript.
6 David Abram, *The Spell of the Sensuous* (New York: Vintage, 1997), p. 263.
7 Deborah Bird Rose, *Reports from a Wild Country* (Sydney: UNSW, 2004).
8 Joan Marler, ed., *From the Realm of the Ancestors* (Manchester, CT: Knowledge Ideas & Trends, 1997).

Paul Goodman insisted that the 'therapeutic use of history' is to high-light 'what of human nature has been "lost" and, practically, to devise experiments for its recovery'.[1] If Goodman is right, then the histori-cal record may harbour reminders of our buried (or repressed) capac-ities for *affective* responses to nature—capacities whose importance is increasingly highlighted by contemporary climate change commu-nications research.

As to the historical 'roots' of environmental crises, environmental psychology traces them back to

> the ... act of breaking faith with ... Mother Earth – or whatever characterisation we might wish to make of the planetary bio-sphere as a vital, self-regulating system... the beginning of civi-lised life, the social and economic transition that rooted our spe-cies out of its original environment and relocated it to the city...[2]

Indeed, for environmental psychologists, the ever-increasing pre-dominance of urbanisation in our shared human story may itself be read as a pathological symptom or projection: an effort to estrange our human selves from close contact with the natural continuum.[3] David Loy, who terms this characteristic estrangement (between the psyche 'In Here' and nature and the world 'Out There') 'lack', argues that

> In psychotherapeutic terms: we have unconsciously projected and objectified our lack by trying to ground ourselves somewhere in the world... The history of the West, like all histories, has been plagued by the consequences of greed, ill will, and delusion. The first two are obvious enough. What is emphasised [here] is the third: the largely unconscious ways that we have tried to resolve our lack – ways that have often led to greater suffering.[4]

The topics Loy's 'history of the West' explores in this fashion include the rise of consumerism and corporate capitalism. Anthony Leiserowitz and his team similarly draw attention to the connections

---

1   Paul Goodman, *The New Reformation* (New York: Vintage Books, 1970), pp. 206–07; idem., et al., *Gestalt Therapy* (London: Souvenir, 1951), p. 311.
2   Roszak, *Voice*, p. 83.
3   *Voice*, p. 220.
4   David Loy, *A Buddhist History of the West* (New York: SUNY, 2002), pp. 1–2.

between materialism and consumerism, on the one hand, and our experiential alienation from the more-than-human realm of nature 'Out There,' on the other.[1]

Some Concluding Remarks

When it comes to 'climate crisis' we find, as Mike Hulme reminds us, a plethora of often heatedly contested viewpoints. And so when historians endeavour to identify the historical roots of that crisis, the ways in which they make sense of the past will inevitably be informed by their particular concerns or understandings here in the present. In Plumwood's work, for example, the historical roots of environmental crisis sought and identified, together with the 'renarrativisation' she offers, are contingent upon her explicit and present-centred therapeutic agenda of inviting others to open themselves to 'experiences of nature as powerful, agentic and creative'. On the other hand, those historians who continue to understand climate change in predominantly scientific terms and who dismiss its psychodynamic aspects, are liable to make sense of modernity's past in a markedly different fashion.

Yet fashion a history we surely must. As Simon Retallack suggests the 'absence of a compelling story on climate change' may be one of the major reasons why pro-environmental lifestyle choices have not yet been more widely adopted.[2] As Howard Gardner puts it, one way we might 'change minds' and perhaps alter our current trajectory is by developing compelling stories that are 'easy to identify with, emotionally resonant, and evocative of positive experiences'.[3] Consider, for a moment, Paul Maiteny's suggestion that sustainability will ultimately necessitate the replacement of many material satisfactions by non-material ones:

> The growth in psycho-therapeutic, community-based and spiritual modes of development suggests that many people are beginning to explore such possibilities, perhaps prompted by

---

1   Leiserowitz, *Toward a New Consciousness*, p. 17.
2   Retallack, *Positive Energy*, pp. 6–7.
3   Howard Gardner, cited in Leiserowitz, *Toward a New Consciousness*, p. 9.

disappointment with the adequacy of consumerism and economic growth to live up to their promise. The more individuals who shift focus in such ways, the more pressure is placed on 'second nature', secular-religious ideologies and belief in the economic 'bottom line' of human development. Individuals who take responsibility for their own transformation support a feedback effect that further supports and hastens the pace of cultural change. This further legitimises individual change, and so on.[1]

And if we individuals have such potential to hasten the pace of change, what then might be the potential for *histories* that are so minded?

---

1   Maiteny, ' Psychodynamics,' p. 358.

12. A Zoroastrian Dilemma? Parsi Responses to Global Catastrophe

Tehmina Goskar

> Think truly, and thy thoughts shall the World's famine feed
> Speak truly, and each word of thine shall be a fruitful seed
> Live truly, and thy deed shall be a great and noble creed
> —Horatius Bonar (1808–1889) Scottish churchman and poet

The Parsis, Zoroastrians of Persian origin who settled in India over the centuries following the Arab conquest of the Persian Empire, number between 75,000 and 100,000 worldwide. Like an endangered species, their numbers are in sharp decline and the threat of extinction is, for many, a tangible reality. This essay discusses how Parsi history has itself followed a contradictory cycle of crisis and success; considers the influence of Parsi custom on their development and survival; and ends by asking whether the Parsis offer a sound example for responding to impending catastrophe in a twenty-first century world.

Tradition and Culture

Whether observant of their religious traditions and practices or not, almost every Parsi Zoroastrian, when asked to sum up their beliefs, will offer a three-word answer:

> *Humata, Hukhta, Hvarashta* (Well-thought thoughts, Well-said words and Well-done deeds).

This dictum is treated as a mantra and often adorns the Fire Temple (the Zoroastrian place of worship), the home and the office. It derives from the teachings of their prophet, also teacher, sage and mystic, Zarathushtra (Zoroaster), who lived somewhere in the Central Asian Steppes in approximately 1750 BCE, after which time his teachings spread and were absorbed into existing religious practices in what is now Iran, the cradle of the Zoroastrian tradition. Zoroastrianism thrived in various hues in populations across the Persian Empire until its defeat in the mid-seventh century. The words are pronounced in the ancient tongue, *Avesta*, a contemporary of Sanskrit and ancestor of modern Farsi, but its meaning is known to all. This mantra is the heart-beat of the Parsi spirit. Whether used as a carrot or a stick, many Parsi children are counselled that following their ceremonial initiation, the *Navjote* or 'New Life' (between the ages of eight and fourteen, all their good deeds and all their bad deeds are collected in the special pocket of their gossamer-like under-vest, the *sudreh*, with which they are invested as a talisman for their personal protection at this time. Whether or not a Parsi continues to wear the *sudreh* thereafter, the memory of its function will remain with the individual forever.

The premise behind this conviction is that a Zoroastrian will treat both other people and all other aspects of creation with due respect and acknowledgement. Through meditation upon their principal god, *Ahura Mazda* (Wise Lord, God of Wisdom), a Zoroastrian is expected to realise his/her role, not as an individual, but in a partnership with their material and spiritual worlds. The seven *Amesha Spenta* (Bounteous Immortals) are the embodiment of the Wise Lord's advice to humanity, as revealed by Zarathushtra in his sacred songs, the *Gathas*. Each is responsible for reminding Zoroastrians about the different elements of earthly creation as well as a corresponding value or aspiration: *Spenta Mainyu* (Humans—Progressive Intellect); *Vohu Manah* (Animals—Good Mind); *Asha Vahishta* (Fire—Best Truth or Best Way); *Khshathra Vairya* (Metals and Minerals—Desireable Dominion); *Spenta Armaiti* (Earth—Holy Devotion); *Haurvatat* (Waters—Wholeness); *Ameretat* (Plant-life—Immortality or Perfection).[1]

Sustainability is absolutely at the core of Zoroastrian religious ideology and also what draws together the virtues of the *Amesha Spenta*. Indeed, even later eschatology embraces the idea that it is only when

---

1   For an introduction to Zoroastrianism, see Peter Clark, *Zoroastrianism. An Introduction to an Ancient Faith* (Eastbourne: Sussex Academic Press, 1998).

we, the human species, get it 'right' in terms of our relationships with others that the Earth will experience *frashokereti* (replenishment or refreshment). However, it is this heavenly goal to which many Parsis do not give a second thought, as abstract and irrelevant as it seems to modern pressures, to ways of living and working. Perhaps it is an impossible dream, yet it may turn out to be their best hope of survival, and also an inspiration to the rest of humanity which similarly struggles to understand the potentially catastrophic consequences of its actions. Is there hope here for Parsis to remind themselves, that it is meant to be in the pursuance of *frashokereti* that they can change not only their own lives, but also the future of the world itself?

The Parsis were born from their own global catastrophe. Whether you believe folk or academic history, many Persian Zoroastrians felt that they lost their world after the zealous Islamic conquest of the Sassanid Empire (with its further resonances during the Islamic Revolution in Iran of 1979). Either wishing to extricate themselves from religious and cultural persecution, or to seek prosperity away from its trauma and turmoil, through constant but tiny waves of migration to the shores of Gujarat in India, the émigrés somehow survived an economic and political crisis that could so easily have vanquished them, there and then.[1] Through a deeply-held conviction in the value of their faith to individual and community-determination, these Persians succeeded in adapting themselves in a way that allowed them to maintain an indomitable religious and cultural identity, whilst also participating fully and, in some areas, leading the socio-economic development of the sub-continent. In a small but significant way, the globalised India of today, which has such a crucial role to play in solving problems of climate change and other harbingers of global catastrophe, is a Parsi creation.

This desire within the community to continue to preserve their ethno-cultural distinction, whilst also benefitting fully from the fruits of globalisation, has generated inevitable tensions among the Parsis. Above all, a sense of vulnerability pervades concerns about falling

---

1   On the Persian settlement of north-west India, see Mani Kamerkar and Soonu Dhunjisha, *From the Iranian Plateau to the Shores of Gujarat. The Story of Parsi Settlements and Absorption in India* (Mumbai: K.R. Cama Oriental Institute, 2002).

birth rates, intermarriage and conversion. Social change has fuelled
antagonism between orthodox (traditionalist) and liberal (reformist)
Parsis. As a result, like other religious/cultural minorities, most obviously diaspora Jews, the community is divided about the best way
forward. The basis of the traditionalist Parsi view that conversion
should be prohibited, intermarriage discouraged, and the children of
mixed-race couples be not admitted to the faith, is complicated. The
oft misquoted *Qissa-i Sanjan* (a sixteenth-century epic poem describing the arrival of the Parsis in India) is used by many as evidence of
a primal promise made to the *rajah* that, in return for the new home-
land, Zoroastrians would not make converts of Hindus and Muslims.
Some argue that the essence of what it is to be a Parsi and, therefore, a
Zoroastrian, lies in their blood and therefore this essence needs to be
kept pure. Others state that the multiplicity of religions in the world
is evidence that God revealed himself in several truths and, therefore,
it would be ungodly to convert others from a faith into which they
were born. There are still others who say that the Parsis will die as a
'race' if intermarriage, in particular, is allowed to go unchecked. The
contradiction is clear. While this principle of purity has resulted in
the creation of a distinct culture and ethnicity, many orthodox Parsis
fail to acknowledge that the pursuance of such a policy in the modern
world is just as likely to compromise their survival.

Emigration is a significant contributory factor to this dilemma.
Since Indian Independence in 1947, like their Indian brothers and
sisters, Parsis migrated in greater but nevertheless small numbers
to countries across the world, but particularly the U.K. and North
America; Australia and New Zealand have also seen their communities increase in recent years. The growing Parsi diaspora in the
West has compounded several of the crises faced by those who have
remained in India. As the benefits of better living standards, higher
education and job opportunities were taken up, Parsis began to settle
in their new countries for good. Perhaps unsurprisingly, the result
was that Parsi absorption into their host societies caused their own
expectations to change. For instance, the relative liberation enjoyed
by Parsi women abroad meant that they have either remained single or
married later in life, preferring to concentrate on their careers than to

have children. Today, more couples than before are remaining childless or only having a few. If the children are from a mixed-race partnership, they are rarely initiated into the faith, although many Parsi parents in such relationships have nonetheless continued to instil a strong sense of religious and cultural identity into their children.[1]

It is against this background of rapid social and economic change that the remainder of this essay will examine two examples which represent the contradictions in Parsi society. The first explores Parsi responses to conserving their unique way of living and dying in a globalised world. The second reviews the contemporary consequences of the tension between Zoroastrian ethics geared towards ideas of sustainability set against economic gain ('progress'). For this purpose, it uses the example of the multi-national Parsi conglomerate, the Tatas. Finally, I offer some thoughts on how the Parsi example may provide inspiration for how all of humanity can create the conditions for renewal that we crave, not merely to survive, but to survive well.

Crises in life and death

The Parsis, as a distinct group of people, came to the attention of outsiders during the time of the British Raj in India. It is from British observations, dating from 1619, that some of the earliest information on the community, and the longevity of its unique customs and habits, hail. Sir James Mackintosh wrote:

> Here we see the immutable character of an Asiatic race. The remains of those Persians who three and twenty centuries ago, in the armies of Xerxes, destroyed the Temples of Idols, who were among the most ancient monotheists and iconoclasts of the world, still preserve their abhorrence of Idolatry, and shew it with peculiar force against those Idolatrous symbols which, though they are to be found from the mountains of Thibet to

---

1 For a sociological study of modern Zoroastrians, including changes in cultural attitudes of the Parsis towards themselves, see Rashna Writer, *Contemporary Zoroastrians. An Unstructured Nation* (Lanham: University Press of America, 1994).

the Appenines, are always peculiarly abhorrent from the moral
sentiments of man unperverted and undegraded by superstition.
Feelings of a very similar nature led the ancient Persian to that
peculiar mode of burial above ground which is still practised
by their descendants in this country; it must be acknowledged
that no sentiment can be more natural than the desire of insulat-
ing such repositories of the dead, of guarding them by a sort of
sacred solitude from outrage, from the eye of frigid curiosity,
and perhaps from the abhorrence of adverse sects.[1]

Mackintosh was here referring to the Parsi tradition of 'sky buri-
als', or the consignment of the dead on highly-elevated platforms for
excarnation; a tradition which had long before died out in Muslim
Iran, even among their remaining Zoroastrians.

Even today, the most iconic structures associated with the Parsis are
their Towers of Silence or *dakhma*. It is to these towers that deceased
Parsi Zoroastrians are consigned for their remains to be consumed
by scavenging carrion-eaters, principally vultures, and also desiccated by the Sun's rays. This form of disposing of the dead, *dakhmenashini,* is unique to the Parsis and, as such, is coveted all the more
by the community. Not only does *dakhmenashini* ensure certain religious obligations are fulfilled, such as avoiding the corruption of the
precious elements of earth, fire, air and water, but it is also one of the
most environmentally sound methods of disposal, should the conditions be correct. The fight to keep this timeless custom of death has
become emblematic of Parsi survival itself.

However, as a result of changes related to the ever-increasing control humans have exerted over their natural environment and rapid
demographic shifts, the future of *dakhmenashini* and the Towers of
Silence are in severe doubt. Over the last decade and a half, Asian
vulture numbers have sharply declined. For years, research suggested
that this was due to a loss of habitat and mating conditions owing
to increased urbanisation around the tower sites. In fact, the magni-
tude of the decline has now largely been attributed to their accidental

---

1   Reported in the Bombay Courier, 20 August 1808; cited in: John Hinnells, 'British
    Accounts of Parsi Religion, 1619–1843' in: *Zoroastrian and Parsi Studies. Selected
    works of John R. Hinnells* (Aldershot: Ashgate, 2000), p. 133.

poisoning, caused by the birds' consumption of the 'routine' anti-inflammatory diclofenac during feeding on animal and human carcasses. Diclofenac is a substance highly toxic for vultures. Although the Indian government has pledged to ban the use of the drug (at least in the bovine population), the problems for *dakhmenashini* remain, not least as programmes of vulture re-population and captive breeding, and the installation of solar concentrators and other measures initiated by the Bombay Parsi Panchayat—the governing council of Parsi life in Mumbai—have had limited, or no, success.

The perpetuation of *dakhmenashini* has also met acrimonious objection from without the community. Vociferous protests and threats of law-suits about intermittent odours and possible health hazards emanating from the towers by those living nearby, particularly from the highly affluent residents of the Malabar Hill area of Mumbai, are threatening this fragile tradition as much as the decline of vultures. The crisis has equally caused conflict and contradiction within the Parsi community. Undercover observation by some Parsis, concerned that *dakhmenashini* was not working well, revealed publicly the reality of consignment to the towers, such as slowly putrefying corpses, often disposed of in acid or other unholy ways. Such revelations have inevitably thrown into doubt the ethical and religious basis of this form of excarnation. The consequence has been that, while some Parsis have begun to accept other methods of disposal as religiously legitimate, others, Parsi authorities in particular, have not only denounced the doubters, but more forcefully insisted that the solution must come from within the Parsi tradition itself. In other words, the issue of *dakhmenashini* has become a litmus test of the widening rift between traditionalists (those who wish to keep Parsi customs unchanged at all costs) and reformists (those who wish to adapt Parsi customs to the modern world).

Meanwhile, diaspora Parsis who have settled in the West, have successfully adopted, and adapted to, methods of disposal used by their host communities. An example is that of the Zoroastrian burial ground at Brookwood Cemetery in Surrey, U.K. For over a century, British Parsis have been buried here, given funerary rites by their priests, with as much empathy towards the rite associated with sky burial as possible. Perhaps more promising, is the project of an American Parsi group, in association with the Universal Ethician Church in Texas, to make plans to install a Tower of Silence on farmland which is also home to a suitable vulture population. This time, precautionary tests will be conducted on the deceased to ensure harmful toxins will not endanger the bird of prey population. Working *with*, rather than *against* their surroundings has largely been a hallmark of the diaspora population; much like those early Parsis who must have adapted and invented likewise, all those centuries ago.[1]

A contradictory success

The economic precociousness of the Parsis of India has its own long history. During the British Raj, these socially-mobile people were unfettered by the caste system and other strictures which might have set them apart, such as those related to dress, diet or practice. They were already well-established as free traders, professionals and businessmen and therefore valuable to any government, being as near to 'people like us' as many British leaders could have hoped. Being also largely independent of internecine Hindu-Muslim strife, the Parsis became indispensable allies to the British both in internal affairs and foreign business, particularly with China, up to the period of Independence and Partition (1947). Once again, the instinct of Parsis to remain true to themselves and their affairs, while also participating fully in the outside world, meant that they could avoid the fate of many other inward-looking cultures which would have disappeared in the ocean of such a vast and multifarious host society. The result of this was that much of the wealth generated from commercial activities was ploughed back into the community, particularly for the foundation of new fire temples, towers of silence, hospitals, educational institutes and other charitable organisations.[2] It also provided

---

1   John Hinnells, *A Zoroastrian Diaspora. Religion and Migration* (Oxford: Oxford University Press, 2005).

2   A major success on this front comes in the form of the UNESCO-assisted 'PARZOR Foundation' (established 1999) which in turn funds the 'Preservation of Parsi Zoroastrian Heritage project', spear-headed by Parsi academic Dr Shernaz Cama. The Foundation aims to research, record, raise awareness and preserve all aspects

finances to create Parsi compounds or 'colonies', where they could live and socialise largely without recourse to other communities in the city, town or village.

The overall effect of these social developments has had its own unforeseen consequences for the community. Participation in the burgeoning globalised world has not only promoted the growth of diaspora communities, but has encouraged many Parsis to embrace the idea that individualism, often cloaked as entrepreneurship, is an acceptable way to improve one's life and that of one's family. A telling example of the negative effects of these developments is that the longer-lived, rapidly aging population of India who remain in their colonies in India—though still beloved of Parsis across the world— are suffering from unoccupied, repair-needy houses and poorly attended fire temples. The latter means that the previously strong bond between religious and social practice has been somewhat fractured, and many have reported that they no longer feel that attending the fire temple is serving their spiritual needs. The trusts which administer the colonies have, in some cases, had to resort to renting land within these special areas to non-Parsis for income, which has been met with both sorrow and chagrin by those who wish to retain Parsi exclusivity within these areas.

It poses a critical question: while the entrepreneurial activities of Parsis continue to bring untold wealth and fame to the community, has this been at the cost of forgetting their social (not to say environmental) responsibilities? The tension is well-illustrated by the example of the Tatas. From being one of India's premier industrial busi-

---

of (traditional) Parsi and Zoroastrian culture, particularly in India. It is based in Navsari, one of the quintessential Parsi ancestral towns whose aged population, environment, possessions and practices are genuinely treated as rare museum pieces for the world to see. While manuscripts are deciphered, people and buildings are photographed and rituals are recorded, the awareness of the Parsis as a distinct living people is growing, and is now greater than ever before. Indeed, the project's main aim is to spread awareness of the Parsis as a discrete cultural and ethnic group, which itself was born far back in time out of an exclusive blend of Indian, Iranian, Chinese and European civilisations. More particularly, PARZOR has been studying and spreading awareness about Parsi Zoroastrian culture as one of the distinct threads in the tapestry of multicultural India. See PARZOR Foundation website: http://www.unescoparzor.com/project/exhibitions.htm

ness houses, the still family-run firm is fast becoming a household name across the world, with 60 per cent of its business now taking place outside India. From their beginnings in the 1860s, as vigorous industrialists and innovators, Tata now employs more than 350,000 people; more than three times the world's Parsi population.[1] From tea to cars and industrial chemicals to hi-tech telecommunications, there are few areas of commerce in which Tata has not been involved. Much of its success has been put down to the high standards it insists on providing for its employees. Indeed, while most trade unions were only beginning to gather their manifestos, Tata first instituted an eight-hour day in 1912. It is little wonder, perhaps, that when Tata proposed itself as a buyer for U.K.-based Jaguar Land Rover in June 2008, it was the city of Coventry's 'preferred' option, and also that of the plant workers. The multi-national retains its commitment to always returning wealth to the communities in which its businesses are based. Its business acumen, in addition to its philanthropic contributions to its own workers and their families, and to its host communities and countries, has led to its recognition as India's most respected firm in 2006 and 2008. It was also the world's sixth most reputed company in 2008, on a par with the likes of Google, Toyota, Sweden's Ikea and Italy's Ferrero.[2]

Tata's own ethical standards, however, have not gone without challenge or question. The Indian conservationist Shayam Chainani worked for Tata for over twenty years while he campaigned for the better care of the urban environment of Mumbai (Bombay). In spite of his campaigning activities, bringing him and his employers into the public eye and also in direct opposition to the interests of Tata, they nevertheless retained him on their books.[3] Instances of vociferous opposition to Tata's rapidly expanding industrial activities were most recently brought into focus with Tata's announcement in 2008

---

1   Latest figures taken from Tata website: http://www.tata.com/ ('About us' section).
2   Full Global Pulse survey results for 2008 published by the Reputation Institute and accessible from:
    http://www.reputationinstitute.com/advisory-services/global-pulse.
3   S. Chainani, Heritage and Environment: An Indian Diary (Mumbai: Urban Design Research Institute, 2007); reviewed: http://blog.icomos-uk.org/2008/07/30/diary -of-conservation-in-india-book-review/

that it would withdraw its new car production plant in West Bengal. This impoverished Indian state was chosen by Tata as a base to produce the Tata Nano—the world's cheapest car. Farmers, forced to give up land, blockaded the plant in direct opposition to Tata and the state government. In spite of compensation offered by Tata Motors, there was no convincing the farmers and other inhabitants to lift the blockade. Tata was forced to give up ideas of completing the plant in West Bengal and, in turn, dealt a blow to the state's plan to gain from much needed inward investment. The creation of the Tata Nano itself has also raised criticism from environmentalists, who argue that what the world does not need is one of its largest populations increasing its dependency on fossil fuel car transport. But Tata also seems to take its environmental responsibilities seriously and is a major sponsor of environmentally-sound innovation, such as the development of cars which run on compressed air.

However, does Parsi ambition and passion for innovation and entrepreneurialism, so well represented by, but not limited to, the Tatas pose yet another contradiction? Can a multi-billion dollar enterprise spread over half the world use its economic strength to avert the effects of man-made climate change and other negative impacts of globalisation such as deep economic (and political) fragility? The Tatas, and indeed other Parsi enterprises, have already demonstrated an admirable tendency towards honest and ethical behaviour and good judgement, albeit with the important proviso that many of their businesses over the decades will themselves have had a detrimental impact on the natural environment, knowingly or otherwise. Also, with an unprecedented global economic recession on their door-step, will Tata and many other Parsis now suffer the results of having been overly hubristic in more halcyon days?

Rethinking Parsi Purpose in the World

The question is: do we try and change our environment so that we can continue to do the things we *think* will bring us success; or do we redefine success, and choose survival instead?

The recent terrorist attacks in Mumbai (November 2008) particularly the targets and the manner in which they were perpetrated, both shook and brought renewed purpose to many Parsis. The Taj Mahal Hotel, a key target, opened originally by Tata in 1903, is a potent symbol of both Parsi and Indian success. The immediate responses to the attacks took on a strongly religious tone as miracle stories from the events were spread colloquially via the internet, email and telephone: images of the prophet remaining on the wall of an otherwise destroyed café; the statue of Tata founder, Jamsetji Tata, remaining intact in the hall of the Taj hotel; last minute changes of plan saving whole families from almost certain peril. These all served to remind Parsis of the importance of their faith, and also that they could readily call upon a fount of hope that did not rely on material and intellectual wealth; something that many, particularly western, societies no longer enjoy. It was to retain staff morale, and that of the Parsi community, that Tata pledged to rebuild and restore the Taj Hotel when all the while they are struggling to pay back bridging loans and other debts acquired during their recent global expansion.[1]

Meanwhile, the inventiveness of the Parsi diaspora population, now in its second and third generations, has also given the community a renewed sense of purpose. On one level this is certainly about a desire to survive as a distinct cultural group. The work of international organisations such as the World Zoroastrian Organisation, founded by Parsis and Iranis in the U.K., but now serving Zoroastrians of all origins, has continued that vein of Parsi benevolence which was central to their ancestors' ethnical impulse. One of the most notable campaigns, the Gujarat Farmers' Fund, has raised considerable funds and resources to support the poverty-stricken Parsi communities of rural India where significant numbers have been largely forgotten by their aspirant urban co-religionists in the big Indian cities. But perhaps more important is that, for the first time, a cohesive Zoroastrian organisation has taken it upon itself to explicitly welcome *all* Zoroastrians and their family and friends into its community to enjoy the fruits of Parsi customs. These diaspora-inspired activities might productively be adopted by many communities around the

---

1   Parsi responses to the November 2008 bombings can be found across the internet, for example: http://parsikhabar.net/2008/11/

world, and indeed humanity itself.

No longer able to shield themselves from outside events, be they political, economic, natural or social, the Parsis face important turning-points if they are to continue to survive and respond to global catastrophe while retaining their distinctiveness. I have sought to argue that the Parsis, now living in a web of disparate geographic contexts and well-attuned to the realities of globalisation, have the potential both to imagine and realise new ways of living a good Parsi life, in partnership with the wider communities of which they are now part. It is perhaps a change in attitude among Parsis at large which has the potential to remind powerful organisations such as Tata of their responsibilities towards the earth, and that it is on meeting these responsibilities that their own survival and future prosperity depends. Indeed, the trajectory of the Tatas is a perfect microcosm for examining how even ethically-driven desires for progress and success can come to nought, and are unsustainable when not matched by the Zoroastrian emphasis on taking responsibility for one's actions, living in partnership with and taking suitable care of the earth which has hitherto provided sustenance. On the other hand, if a company like Tata was to radically change its attitude towards defining success, as suggested above, the effect on other powerful players could literally be world-changing. In other words, the Parsi contribution is not to be found in attempts to preserve their distinctiveness for themselves, but to adapt appropriately and remind themselves, and others, of their most basic ideas: to think well-thought thoughts, say well-said words and do well-done deeds. By reviving the ancient quest for *frashokereti* or replenishment as a matter of global concern, might Parsis offer a vision of the future which would be of relevance to all humankind? Their dilemma is our dilemma: how to balance the human drive for accumulation with the now urgent human need to manage and sustain the finite resources upon which we all depend.

13. How Novels Can Contribute to our Understanding of Climate Change

Peter Middleton

What would it be like to live through massive climate changes of the kind climate scientists predict will occur if carbon emissions are not reduced quickly enough? How would both ordinary people and governments respond to abrupt and severe changes of seasonal ambient temperature? What if the entire Arctic ice cap melted? What are the institutions that could be held to account for environmental degradation? Kim Stanley Robinson calls the American government institutions whose decisions most affect the environment, the 'cumulobureaucracies', a witty neologism that emphasises the interdependence of culture and nature, and he offers plausible scenarios in answer to all these questions. He suggests that a US government agency such as the National Science Foundation could lead a new research effort on climate change mitigation, and perhaps provide the platform for a new era of environmentally-aware Washington politics. Robinson is generally resistant to apocalyptic rhetoric for describing the consequences of global warming. Extreme winters brought about by sudden climate shifts need not necessarily be treated as entirely catastrophic to daily life. Inevitable power outages during extreme cold could encourage households to draw on pioneer traditions of self-sufficiency; even the most vulnerable people could survive in shelters, and a few people might even find ways to live outdoors using specialist knowledge of survival in arctic conditions. Robinson offers a vivid portrait of the frozen Potomac becoming a great open air park where 'an extraordinarily beautiful populace, every race and ethnicity on Earth represented' find themselves 'all partying together' on the ice.[1]

---

1 Kim Stanley Robinson, *Fifty Degrees Below* (London: Harper Collins, 2005), p. 363. This is the middle volume of a trilogy of novels that begins with *Forty Signs of Rain* (London: Harper Collins, 2004), and concludes with *Sixty Days and Counting* (London: Harper Collins, 2007).

Should we credit these predictions with any value for the serious business of monitoring, predicting, and mitigating climate change, and the political and social strategies that will be demanded? Robinson is not only not a scientist, he is a novelist best known for his fantasy writing and science fiction and the scenarios mentioned are all taken from novels. Our conventional wisdom tells us that novelists, especially genre writers, are not bound by truth nor committed to the dependable transmission of knowledge, they are entertainers who use narrative and character to create compelling fictions. The ice party in Robinson's novel *Fifty Degrees Below* (2005) is in fact seen through the eyes of a scientist and N.S.F. employee, Frank Vanderwal, a character who works daily with the peer review process on which good science depends. Unlike Vanderwal, Robinson's speculations are not answerable to peer review, nor are they based solely on tangible evidence and reliable predictive modelling of the future. Camping in ice-bound trees or partying on the Potomac may make good stories, but such fantasies surely have none of the credibility of solid scientific research-based knowledge. We have enough difficulty establishing accurately the nature and scope of the anthropogenic contribution to climate change, or assessing the probability and reliability of different computer-based models of rising greenhouse gases and consequent rising temperature. What possible use is a form of writing not grounded in the exacting rigours of climate science and objective evaluation of global geography? The exhaustive winnowing of theories and data by the IPCC in order to arrive at a sufficient consensus about what does constitute reliable knowledge about potential climate change is testament to the difficulty of establishing confidence sufficient to persuade governments, politicians, corporations, and publics to support initiatives that may curtail their economic and social freedoms. Such confidence is crucial and depends partly on trust. If it takes an IPCC to sift through the scientific literature before most leaders will accept the data, why should an individual creator of fictional narratives expect to be believed? Robinson might help recruit a few more campaigners, but does such literature have any value beyond grabbing the attention of readers and inciting them to go to more trustworthy sources for guidance?

Many people campaigning on global dangers would concede that novels, like films and television dramas, can play a useful part in alerting audiences to the consequences for their way of life of a catastrophe such as nuclear war. Nevil Shute's *On the Beach* (1957), Peter Watkins' *The War Game* (1965), or Stanley Kubrick's *Dr Strangelove* (1964), all did their bit to warn that the use of nuclear weapons in an international political conflict could lead to disaster. Novels about catastrophe might be considered secular equivalents of the images of apocalypse used by medieval preachers, Christian and Buddhist, trying to persuade peasants that they should support church or temple. Novels showing possible implications of current global developments could then be described as the nursery stage of political activism, learning through fantasy play. For clear facts and concepts about climate and rational arguments about strategies of response, however, we should surely graduate to the well-informed deliberately non-literary prose of expert researchers and political thinkers.

I believe that to accept such a view is a mistake. Climate change is much more than an alteration of the physics, chemistry and biology of the planet; it is a phenomenon of enormous complexity that is taking place across almost the entire range of human knowledge and experience. Fiction, like other arts, though in its own specific mode, engages in necessary intellectual inquiry capable of producing new understandings of our society, and its ethical and cognitive dilemmas. At the same time I am sympathetic to the sceptical response to the utilitarian claim that literature can address specific social needs. Novels (and indeed short stories) are at their best when they cannot be paraphrased, when they embody the complexities of lived experience, partial knowledge, passionate thought, and unresolved contradictions. However closely and skilfully one reads a novel, it cannot be fully translated into facts, formulae, conclusions, or guides to action; there will always be residual impressions that cannot be articulated. The very medium—language—that they use is made to resonate with half-glimpsed meanings and paradoxical assertions of a kind that scientific and policy discourse avoid. And yet storytelling, of which published literary fiction is only a part, does play a role in the collective creation and recreation of human knowledge on which we depend, even if our theories of literature and science are not yet very good at analysing this relationship.

Treating novels such as Robinson's as, at best, no more than the advertising of environmental risks, cuts us off from potentially valuable contributions to a better understanding of what constitutes the impending climate crisis and how to deal with it. Literary fictions constructed by writers who show some willingness to enter into a dialogue with the knowledge of the natural and social sciences, and the ethics and politics of government and campaigning, have much to offer. Mark Maslin points out that 'global warming is one of the few scientific theories which makes us examine the whole basis of modern society', and examining the whole of society, especially its lived experience, is something that novels can do well.[1] Making a similar point to Maslin, Jared Diamond argues that one crucial factor that helps determine the survival or collapse of societies for environmental reasons is 'the ubiquitous question of the society's response to its problems'. Survival of a society at risk of ecological destruction will 'depend on its political, economic, and social institutions and on its cultural values. Those institutions and values affect whether the society solves (or even tries to solve) its problems'.[2] Novels explore how such institutions and values affect who we are and where we are going in three distinct modes highly relevant to the formulation of strategies for responding to the dangers of climate change: immersive simulations of hypothetical situations, investigations of the textual consequences of our rhetorics of crisis, and examinations of the socio-cultural ramifications of global environmental stress.

Crisis fictions about the global environment are, in the simplest terms, popularisations of existing knowledge and its implications, and to this degree no different from magazine and newspaper articles, television documentaries, films, and visual art. If this was all that fiction had to offer its record would not be impressive. Ideas in popular science writings, such as Rachel Carson's *Silent Spring,* or James Lovelock's *Gaia,* have changed the way global environmental crises

---

1   Mark Maslin, *Global Warming: A very short introduction* (Oxford: Oxford University Press, 2004), p. 146.
2   Jared Diamond, *Collapse: How societies choose to fail or survive* (London: Penguin, 2005), p. 14.

are understood. Some novels have come close (John Steinbeck's *The Grapes of Wrath* (1939), or Walter M. Miller's science fiction novel warning about the long-term consequences of the use of nuclear weapons, *A Canticle for Leibowitz* (1959), for instance). However, no novel about global climate change has yet achieved this.[1] One explanation might be simply that novelists need more time to react to new developments around climate change, whose threat only began to become known in the 1980s, whilst severe damage to the biosphere has only quite recently become visible.

Robinson himself offers another explanation: 'I was interested in global warming, and I wanted to write about it, but I didn't have a handle on it as a novelist. If it was going to take 200 years, and temperatures were going to change five degrees, how do you tell that story'?[2] He only managed to conceive his trilogy when he read that abrupt climate change might be much faster, a matter of a few years not hundreds. Rapidly changing scientific projections, the tension between the novel's focus on individual lives and the vast scale of climate transformation, as well as the tendency of the genre of the novel to work best with the known dense textures of actual history rather than the imagined landscapes of the future, have so far held back writers. There is no reason, however, to think that novelists of ideas will not meet this challenge over the next few years, and produce works as powerful as the non-fiction texts already mentioned.

Significant novels are not just composed of ideas. The novel is an art form that induces a controlled daydream through textual strategies that

---

1   Steinbeck wrote vividly about the impact of the ecological damage that created the dustbowl, as well as the human cost of massive displacement of farmers. Miller's novel about a future in which scientific texts are copied and recopied in monasteries as if they were sacred writings yet are no longer understood, has caught the imagination of a number of thinkers, notably Alasdair Macintyre in *After Virtue*, who have variously applied the idea to other histories of lost meaning. The Astronomer Royal, Martin Rees repeatedly cites novels as evidence of risk, and mentions *A Canticle for Leibowitz* in a discussion of how a 'catastrophic collapse of civilisation' would destroy the continuity of knowledge. Martin Rees, *Our Final Century: Will Civilisation Survive the Twenty-First Century?* (London: Random House, 2003), p. 24.

2   Ralph Brave, 'Fear of a frozen planet: A northstate novelist tackles global climate change', Newsreview.com, 2006, http://www.newsreview.com/chico/Content?oid=46182

have been developed over the past three hundred years to make the best of our capacity to understand time, causality, and changing identities, through storytelling or what literary critics usually prefer to call narrative. An American professor of literature, David F. Bell, when asked to justify literary studies, offered this helpful analogy: 'Providing models (automatons, simulacra) and exploring and disseminating crucial information have remained at the heart of the literary enterprise since the beginning... To be deprived of literature means to be deprived of a chance to play with and test the paradigms of knowledge of a given period in a manner that is not simply mimetic'.[1] Novelists have worked hard over the life span of this broad genre to create techniques that enable the reader to feel that they are actually living through the eyes and emotions of the characters caught up in the events of a story, in what could be called the most imaginative form of modelling we have. Even popular fiction can perform this temporary immersion in a parallel world well enough to elicit cognitively worthwhile reactions from an informed reader. Novels about crisis can imaginatively simulate the impact of catastrophe on our culture, and within the frame of this big 'what if' can provide a complex experience of the emotions, differing points of view, sensations, ideas, landscapes, and lives, that would be tumbling together in an actual crisis. Immersion in the possible world of the disaster can therefore provide a stimulus for testing out existing theories and plans, and sketching new ones. One reason the novel is particularly effective at this is because the reader of a novel is a partner in the creation of this fictional world, bringing her or his own memories, emotions, and ideas to colour in the outlines provided by the novel. The more expertise a reader has in the field of climate change the more nuanced these simulations can be, and they can still be true even if some of the storyteller's science is wrong by current knowledge, because it is the enactment of experience on which the novel bases its claims to verisimilitude.

Thrillers, such as Benjamin E. Miller's *Zero Hour*, have so far been the most prevalent fictions of environmental crisis, and are generally limited by the demands of that genre.[2] One that almost tran-

---

1   David F. Bell, 'A Moratorium on Suspicion', *PMLA*, 117:3 (2002), p. 489.
2   Benjamin E. Miller, *Zero Hour* (New York: Penguin, 2003).

scends them is *Mother of Storms* by John Barnes, set in the year 2028 when a UN attack on an undersea missile site owned by the 'Siberian Commonwealth' has unexpected side-effects.[1] Methane is released into the atmosphere from seabed clathrates (gas hydrates) in such quantity that the air is explosively heated and the sea warms up, creating the perfect greenhouse for nurturing runaway hurricanes. Although Barnes attempts scientific accuracy in his treatment of abrupt climate change, and does a good job of alerting readers to the consequences in terms of severe weather, he is more interested in the ethics of spectacle that climate disasters offer (something already demonstrated in a number of recent television documentaries) than in the science of catastrophe itself. In the novel a new type of television called 'XV', that can transmit the emotions and perceptions of those on camera, has made spectacle an even more powerful influence than it is in our existing media. *Mother of Storms* therefore questions both its own permission to offer simulations of climatic violence, and some of the less conscious voyeuristic desires that may be involved in our thinking about climate crises. The end of the novel offers a redemptive vision of the transformation of 'XV' into a medium that might helps its audience grasp that the storms need to be seen within many different narrative contexts. Global climate crisis, the novel intimates, will require the combined cultural work of many heterogeneous narratives that offer diverse standpoints and hypotheses, if we are to be able to confront crisis without being seduced by its spectatorial power or cave in to a sense of fatalism.

Thrillers are by no means the only genre of recent fiction to offer self-conscious simulations of the possible effects of global warming. Children's writers have been very alert to the importance of the theme. Julie Bertagna's excellent novel for older children, *Exodus*, is set in a flooded world, where its protagonist Mara (a word with etymological roots meaning sea) discovers a colony that has survived the general inundation, only to exploit its relative safety by creating new hierarchies and excluding outsiders.[2] Images of a drowned city visible beneath the waves near the colony are especially haunting.

---

1   John Barnes, *Mother of Storms* (London: Orion, 1994).
2   Julie Bertagna, *Exodus* (London: Macmillan, 2002).

Satirists have seen the potential too. Maggie Gee's novel *The Flood* similarly explores the divisions between rich and poor that become even more visible in the face of a flooding that results from the rise of the oceans.[1] Postcolonial writers have probably been even more aware of environmental issues than novelists with an entirely Western perspective. Amitav Ghosh traces the impact of climate change on one of the most immediately vulnerable parts of the world, the Sunderban islands, in his anthropologically-informed novel *The Hungry Tide*.[2] These and other literary novels not only offer simulated experiences of environmental disasters, they explore ideas for handling them, possible actions that individuals and organisations might take, and the ethical dilemmas such challenges will create. At their best these novels can also make visible ideological commitments, intended and unintended, at work in crisis discourse itself, that could assist with the work of climate mitigation.

Crisis discourse necessarily relies on a language of threat, damage, ending, and final judgement, and in doing so it risks both inflation and importing residual ideological or religious templates into its secular vision. The long tradition of religious apocalyptic narratives readily provides a reservoir of stereotypes that can infiltrate our thinking about the future. The science journalist, Fred Pearce, notices this tendency in his book on climate change, ominously titled *The Last Generation*: 'On one plane journey, I re-read John Wyndham's sci-fi classic *The Kraken Wakes*, and was struck by the similarities between events he describes in that and predictions for the collapse of the ice sheets of Greenland and Antarctica. It is hard to escape the sense that primeval forces lurk deep in the ocean, in ice caps, in rain-forest soils and in Arctic tundra. [Jim] Hansen says that we may have only one decade, and one degree of warming, before the monsters are fully awake'.[3] Novelists have been particularly sensitive to the implications of crisis rhetoric. Michael Crichton, for instance, attacks the climate change movement in his egregious novel *State of Fear*, largely because he believes it misuses the language of crisis to gener-

---

1   Maggie Gee, *The Flood* (London: Saqi Books, 2004).
2   Amitav Ghosh, *The Hungry Tide* (London: Harper Collins, 2005).
3   Fred Pearce, *The Last Generation: How nature will take her revenge for climate change* (London: Eden Project & Transworld Publishers, 2006), p. 15.

ate unnecessary collective fear.[1]

Theorists and campaigners on climate change have certainly drawn heavily on traditional ideas of the end of the world for their rhetoric. Think of the titles of some of the most important texts such as *Collapse*, *Our Final Century*, *The Last Generation*, *Field Notes from a Catastrophe*, or Bill McGuire's explicit *Apocalypse: A Natural History of Global Disasters*.[2] What deep assumptions might be lurking in this discourse? Joanna Bourke shows in *Fear: A Cultural History*, that primary social fears have changed over the twentieth century, so that some fears of a hundred years ago now seem almost incomprehensible and in recent decades the dominant fears of nuclear attack and cancer have been largely replaced by concerns about terrorism and AIDS. She argues that the discourse of global warming has undergone its own transformation too: the rhetoric of Rachel Carson's *Silent Spring* drew heavily on images of a catastrophe that would have left much of the planet lifeless and degraded.[3] Governments, religions, and political movements, all at times deliberately heighten collective anxiety: 'fear is manipulated by numerous organisations with a stake in creating fear while promising to eradicate it. Fear circulates within a wealthy economy of powerful interest groups dependent upon ensuring that we remain scared. Theologians, politicians, the media, physicians and the psychological services depend on our fright'.[4] Are then climate campaigners trying to create coalitions of the fearful, and in doing so merely replicating older social patterns? Bourke shows that social fears are complex, and can be constructive as well as exploitative, saying with particular resonance for climate campaigners that 'fear is a great and glorious stimulant that works in direct opposition to attempts to rigidly control our environment'.[5] Shared social fear has sometimes 'produced

---

1   Michael Crichton, *State of Fear* (London: Harper Collins, 2005).
2   Bill McGuire, Apocalypse: *A natural history of global disasters* (London: Cassell Orion, 1999).
3   Joanna Bourke, *Fear: A Cultural History* (London: Virago, 2005), p. 337. Rachel Carson, *Silent Spring* (London: Penguin, [1962] 2000).
4   Bourke, *Fear*, p. 385.
5   *Fear*, p. 390.

a sense of the sacred that many people otherwise lacked'.[1] Crichton's attack on climate campaigners for using fear of disaster to recruit followers and to achieve their aims, overlooks such possibilities, and as Bourke repeatedly shows, the attachment of fear to many different types of prediction for the world does not necessarily discredit such possibilities, nor those who appeal to such rhetorically-evoked emotion. Many fears are well justified, and so are attempts to awaken them; what matters are the politics or contexts in which discourses of fear operate.

Bourke's analysis of the politics and rhetoric of fear points us to the need to be aware of the implications of this rhetoric of apocalypse that has increasingly been woven into debates about global warming. Literary fictions are well placed to assist in this task because the novel is a genre that can extrapolate and thereby make more tangible the underlying implications of the linguistic forms of ideology, belief, and lived experience. Frank Kermode argues in *The Sense of an Ending* that novels are especially sensitive to the implications of the discourse of apocalypse because the idea of an end to the world and the idea of the end of a fictional history have been bound together during the evolution of the novel. Secular beliefs about the position of a culture in time and history can therefore be more rooted in traditional religious ideas of apocalypse than exponents realise: 'there is a myth of crisis, a very deep and complex one, which we should make more sense of if we could reduce it from the status of myth to the status of fiction', because 'crisis, however facile the conception, is inescapably a central element in our endeavours towards making sense of our world'.[2] Crisis discourse is always reliant on mythic foundations. Kermode then goes on to argue that this entails that the language of crisis in the post-war period is a partially secularised transformation of earlier religious teleologies and unjustified by the events of modern history, a conclusion which is surely wrong. Just because the rhetoric of crisis and fear has been so ubiquitous does not mean, as Bourke points out, that the fears are groundless.

---

1   *Fear*, p. 387.
2   Frank Kermode, *The Sense of an Ending: Studies in the theory of fiction* (Oxford: Oxford University Press, 1967), pp. 28, 94.

Nevertheless, Kermode's theory of narrative remains valuable because it suggests another key reason why we should pay attention to fictions of world crisis. The very form of the novel has structural and ideological connections to the way cultures based on Christianity, Islam and Judaism, understand the future. Skilful novels about the risks of catastrophic climate change can reveal many of the inner workings of the collective imaginary when confronted with the future: fantasies of redemption and punishment, self-conscious experiences of living in time, and above all the pervasive need for narratives that will make sense of the connections between past, present and future as part of some greater order. The novel is always subjunctive, or hypothetical, and it unfolds in the shadow of its own end, a closure that has affinities with images of catastrophe as the end of an epoch or end of the world.

One of the finest novels to explore the complex of myths and beliefs that our culture uses to imagine global disaster is Doris Lessing's fantasy novel, *Canopus in Argos: Archives—Re: Colonised Planet 5 Shikasta* (hereafter referred to simply as *Shikasta*), which addresses a problem that shadows any radical politics based on global crisis. If we ask the obvious question of how best can crises be managed by experts within our existing political structures or through new communal ventures, we take for granted that we can and should take responsibility for the state of the world and make efforts to improve it. Many cultural critics have observed that the humanism of this seemingly reasonable self-appointment risks becoming just another expression of Western hegemony. However well-meaning, rational, scientifically-informed, and self-aware we try to be, the asymmetry of power between the rich, dominant countries of the Western World and many countries at the sharpest edge of ecological and political crises means that our discourses and actions may have unintended and potentially destructive effects. It is not enough to identify potential crises. Somehow, the inevitable distortions of perspective have to be negotiated as well.

Lessing is the author of a number of novels that deal with the challenge of understanding and living through a global environmental crisis: *The Four-Gated City*, *Briefing for a Descent into Hell*,

Memoirs of a Survivor, and then a series of science fiction novels starting with *Shikasta*. All of these novels take as their theme the difficulty of representing global crisis. Such a crisis doesn't come conveniently labelled as such, the perspective on the world of even the most far-seeing individual is restricted, collective understanding can lag far behind events, concepts for dealing with it may be inadequate, discourses about it can carry unexamined tacit assumptions, knowledge about it may be controlled by elites who may have strong sectional prejudices, and old methods of political organisation may not work in these new conditions. The protagonist of *Memoirs of a Survivor* uses the impersonal pronoun 'it' (which we might also call the 'id') to describe an enveloping international crisis, and then self-consciously rationalises this by saying: 'Perhaps, after all, one has to end by characterising "it" as a sort of cloud or emanation, but invisible, like the water vapour you know is present in the air of the room you sit in...."It" was everywhere, in everything, moved in our blood, our minds. "It" was nothing that could be described once and for all, or pinned down, or kept stationary; "it" was an illness..."it" was the price or unreliability of the electricity supply; the way telephones didn't work'.[1] This description is oddly prescient. One of the most prevalent images of global crisis today is that of an invisible gas, carbon dioxide, which is creating a new and dangerous global weather.

   Shikasta explicitly emulates the span of biblical myth and Judaeo-Christian history, starting with echoes of the story of the Elohim in Genesis, and ending in a curious post-historical world of myth. The story is presented as if it were a somewhat arbitrary collection of documents chosen from a vast archive assembled by superior beings, galactic idealists, who report on the terrible conditions on a planet they name Shikasta. This, it soon emerges, is the name given to our planet Earth by the rulers of Canopus, a self-described benevolent empire of crisis-managers trying to help the 'Native' population of Earth, an unwitting and disputed colony of several far more advanced interstellar empires, improve themselves. These almost angelic beings from Canopus cannot quite avoid the colonialist men-

---

1   Doris Lessing, *Memoirs of a Survivor* (London: Pan Books, [1974] 1976), p. 139.

tality that accompanies their officially laudable aims, an impression reinforced by the novel's unusual structure. It has no main characters in the ordinary sense, and the nearest to a leading protagonist is a galactic social worker from Canopus, Johor, who is incarnated here on Earth on several tours of duty over tens of thousands of years.[1]

In the textbook *Global Transformations*, the discussion of ecological risks begins by pointing out that crises have both objective and subjective dimensions: 'To chart or measure the globalisation of environmental degradation is simultaneously to chart or measure the construction of human perceptions and models of global environmental change'.[2] The acknowledgement of a subjective dimension is welcome, but the language here points to some severe limitations on understanding crisis. It is not only the simultaneity of objectivity and subjectivity that is difficult to handle; recognising that 'the construction of human perceptions' is unlikely to be encompassed by a process as abstract as measurement, that the metaphor of construction may be restrictive, and the reduction of human experience to perception may be inadequate, is also hard. These are just the areas of difficulty in contemplating global crises from a Western standpoint that Lessing is most interested by in her novel. Canopus represents the use of reductive strategies for representing global crisis that ignore emotion, imagination and culture, for this empire is nothing if not global in its crisis assessments, and its capacity to measure the construction of *human* perceptions: 'The long view of planetary maintenance and development, does not need, nor can depend upon, the sympathies, the empathies of the near, the partial, views'.[3] Such rationalised indif-

---

1   One of the most original features of the novel is that the Canopians don't need to travel by the mechanical means of a space ship because presumably they are so advanced (or quasi-angelic) when compared to humans, that the best way to comprehend their mode of transport would be to think of it as the re-incarnation of a soul originating from another world. Lessing is one of the few science fiction writers to have thought through the implications of speculations about an evolutionary tree on which humans are only part-way along, for the structure of the fiction itself.
2   David Held, Anthony McGrew, David Goldblatt and Jonathan Perraton, *Global Transformations: Politics, Economics and Culture* (Cambridge: Polity Press, 1999), p. 377.
3   Doris Lessing, *Canopus in Argos: Archives—Re: Colonised Planet 5 Shikasta* (London: Jonathan Cape, 1979), p. 216.

ference to lived experience permeates the outlook of Canopus, not least because its people learn, as one of them explains, 'to value ourselves only insofar as we are in harmony with the plan'.[1] Part of the brilliance of the novel is the way it suborns us into accepting these attitudes by the sheer powerful rationality of the judgements made by Canopus, until we are abruptly jolted from them.

Johor says in the opening paragraph: 'I have been sent on errands to our Colonies on many planets. Crises of all kinds are familiar to me'. The novel could be said to be the story of how crisis becomes unfamiliar to someone for whom it is a commonplace. In the Twentieth Century, he is reborn as a charismatic leader, George Sherban, and this time we witness him and the worsening global crisis indirectly, from the diary of his younger sister, Rachel. The Sherbans live through a worsening environmental crisis in North Africa, Europe's food stocks are destroyed both by the sort of pollution that Rachel Carson warned about, and by war. One of the most original sections of the novel depicts a new popular political movement based on large informal assemblies that attempt to resolve past 'racial' injustices and historical enmities in the process of reinventing democracy, and envisaging a better future. This appears to be of limited avail, unfortunately, and the environmental crises worsen further. Rachel's diary becomes a measure of the failure of Canopus to appreciate the value of human experience; through it Rachel offers a different stance towards crisis, a stance that refuses detachment, refuses the calculus of need, and emphasises empathy and imagination. Readers are unlikely to finish the novel thinking that the trouble with our world is that angelic super-beings are fighting over us (this is not a grown up version of Philip Pullman's *His Dark Materials* trilogy). They are much more likely to end up questioning the validity of all the frameworks—political, religious, scientific or mythic—by which we try to manage our world and its crises. Strange narrative points of view, alien, disembodied, and atemporal, the different modes of agency, and not least the sense that we are reading the ruins of a novel in these raw documents, fragmentary narratives, and emblematic fantasies, are all part of a diagnostics of crisis.

---

1   Lessing, *Shikasta,* p 55.

Shikasta is a meta-fiction that prefigures the Global Warming debate, but helps reveal how, like other crisis discourses, climate change is both a science in search of policy, and a site of displaced or unrealised political aspirations. Novels of global crisis are doing some of the cultural work of reconciliation between antagonistic social forces, by finding ways of representing the complex agency of the so-called multitude through narrative images of vast social complexity. Some merely offer illuminating simulations of easily grasped threats to order and justice ranging from terrorists to global warming, nuclear war, economic collapse, plagues, and alien invasions. The very best fictions of crisis do more than shine a light down into the murky affairs of the social unconscious, or give us a thrilling flight in the total reality simulator; they employ the special resources of the novel to raise issues of conceptual deficit, ethical ambiguity and failures of representation.

So are there no good novels about climate change yet? At the time of writing, there are relatively few novels explicitly about anthropogenic climate change that can be recommended. The best are probably those in the flawed trilogy by Robinson with which I began: *Forty Signs of Rain*, *Fifty Degrees Below*, *Sixty Days & Counting*, set in Washington DC. They manage to combine a typical thriller plot about a shadowy conspiracy, with a picture of how the National Science Foundation and more generally the funding of science works, and how politics intervenes in decisions about how to apply scientific knowledge to practical problems. The trilogy struggles with the task of representing science, globalism, and crisis, though I would argue that this struggle gives the novel much of its power. Robinson openly admits that for him as a novelist: 'Global warming is also a way to dramatize or symbolize the social storms coming down on us, as our way of life continues to damage the planet and exacerbate the gap between rich and poor. Stormy weather, yes, I've never been averse to committing the pathetic fallacy, I love it really. Weather is emotion as far as I'm concerned'.[1] At its best this means that Robinson is sensitive to the complexities of crisis rhetoric and largely avoids the

---

1   Nick Gevers, 'Interview with Kim Stanley Robinson', *Science Fiction Weekly* 351, 10:2 (2004), 16 January 2009, http://www.scifi.com/sfw/issue351/interview.html

sort of sensationalism that *Mother of Storms* is troubled by, so that the flooding of Washington DC and the later lethal freeze-up are presented as what Jared Diamond calls 'creeping normalcy'.

I want to conclude this discussion with a striking passage from the first novel of the series, in which Robinson explores the metaphorics of weather. Charlie Quibler, political adviser to a relatively radical senator has a fanciful vision of the clouds over the Washington government offices:

> Clouds over the White House were billowing up like the spirit of the building's feisty inhabitant, round, dense, shiny white. In the other direction, over the Supreme Court's neighborhood, stood a black nine-lobed cloud, dangerously laden with incipient lightning. Yes, the powers of Washington were casting up thermals and forming clouds over themselves, clouds that filled out precisely the shapes and colours of their spirits. Charlie saw that each cumulobureaucracy transcended the individuals who temporarily performed its functions in the world. These trans-human spirits all had inborn characters, and biographies, and abilities and desires and habits all their own; and in the sky over the city they contested their fates with each other. Humans were like cells in their bodies. Probably one's cells also thought that their lives were important and under their individual control. But the great bodies knew better.[1]

The idea of 'cumulobureaucracies' is a fitting image of the potential of fiction to contribute to climate change debate. A better understanding of what climate change demands of us will require that we understand these 'cumulobureaucracies' or collective norms and forms of life that are rooted as much in the natural world as in history. Novels at their best can do this, and we should be looking out for them and including them in what we mean by the literature on climate change.

---

1   Robinson, *Forty Signs of Rain*, p. 137.

14. Towards Transition

Robert Biel

Introduction: the problem of sustainability

Our social and economic system is now clearly in crisis. Most obviously, the environment is hitting back for decades of abuse, while available energy dries up. In this volume's final essay, I will argue that the ecological problem is linked to one *within* society: capacity is diminished, through a reduction of skills and adaptability. Intuitively, it makes sense that if a system's internal energy declines, it will compensate through excessive external energy demands. This is a simple way of stating our hypothesis.

We can look at this another way by turning the proposition upside down and focusing on *destructive* forces. The environmental problem is not just one of inputs, but of destructive *emissions*, principally greenhouse gases, the payback being climate change. It is helpful to express this destructive principle as 'entropy'.

Our quest for 'development', means wanting society to improve, for instance by reducing poverty and conflict. But according to the Second Law of Thermodynamics, the 'arrow of time' in a closed system always pushes towards greater entropy, i.e. decay or disorder (in the well-known example, a glass will break, but not reconstitute itself). The reason we can escape this dilemma is that we are not a closed system. The energy input we receive is actually a product of the sun consuming itself: the solar system as a whole therefore moves towards entropy, and in this very process furnishes a practically unlimited stream of energy.

The obvious condition for development is thus to rely essentially on solar energy.[1] But solar energy in its pure form is itself destructive: it must be mediated through an ecosystem which regulates tempera-

---

1 Nicholas Georgescu-Roegen, 'Energy and Economic Myths,' *Southern Economic Journal*, 41:3 (1975), pp. 347–81.

ture, embodies the energy in plants we can eat, and so on. We should therefore avoid a form of development which depletes that ecosystem. *This surely implies that we conserve society's internal capacity as far as possible.*

The latter condition can similarly be represented as an entropy problem, understanding entropy in this case as a loss of information. The signals within a system make sense only where there is sufficient differentiation, otherwise they degenerate into mere noise.[1] We must therefore not only nurture the ecosystem, but conserve society's internal diversity. The good news is that, if we take a long historical perspective, the two goals are positively related.

Applying the notion of information to human society we should broaden it to include knowledge and wisdom (the ability to analyse problems and improvise solutions to unfamiliar ones). It then becomes clear that, to minimise entropy with respect to the external environment we have to work *with* nature and *like* nature, which in turn requires rich and diverse sets of knowledge (and forms of social organisation to transmit it). Thus, traditional African farming systems pioneered techniques now known as intercropping and agroforestry,[2] which reproduce the characteristics of the natural forest, creating miniature ecosystems where different types of plant co-operate, and compost and mulching render digging unnecessary. It seems at first strange that the less physical effort invested the higher the yield, but this is the whole point: nature doesn't dig, but in order creatively to work like nature, an input is required not of labour, but of knowledge. Or, in animal husbandry, the characteristics of each animal are intimately known, and selective breeding offers a response to practically any challenge.[3] In a system common throughout the precolonial Americas, 'terra preta de Indio', organic waste from farming was smouldered, leaving a residue which enriches the soil and sequesters

---

1   Edgar Morin, 'La Méthode, Tome 4', *Les Idées, Leur habitat, leur vie, leurs moeurs* (Paris: Seuil, 1991).
2   Paul Richards, *Indigenous Agricultural Revolution – Ecology and Food Production in West Africa* (London: Hutchinson, 1985).
3   Zeremariam Fre, *Pastoral Development in Eritrea and Eastern Sudan*, PhD. Thesis, University of Reading (1989), Chapter 2.

carbon.[1] Clearly, this information is not just a static picture of a given environmental situation, but is above all adaptive and dynamic. For adaptation purposes, capacity must not just 'exist' within the system, but be *diffused* (widely distributed), thus cultivating the property known to cybernetics as 'redundancy', whereby multiple pathways are available if one becomes blocked (a bit like the brain's ability to respond to trauma by improvising different networks).

Where the internal equilibrium breaks down, and entropy spreads, excessive energy demands are made for fossil fuels to supply the shortfall, the resultant ejection of greenhouse gases being in some sense an export of the disorder which society can no longer manage within itself. We therefore see the sustainability problem as a relationship between two variables: where capacity is narrowed and diversity lost, the entropy imposed on the external system (environment) is bound to rise. This is our fundamental proposition.

The bad momentum of the current path of development

It is important to recognise that we are set on a wrong *course*. Encouragingly, it is not irreversible: even where the direct link with tradition is lost, we can, through concepts like permaculture, agroecology, or biodynamics, aim to restore the *spirit* of traditional ways of working with and like nature. But it is insufficient to tinker with specific methodologies unless we also correct the wrong course at a whole-system level. This involves taking a critical look at capitalism, so let's begin by addressing the relationship between capitalism and tradition.

The gender issue is a good starting point. Among women's traditionally ascribed functions was typically that of keeping alive as many strains of plants as possible.[2] In the light of our earlier discus-

---

1   A version of terra preta (under the name 'biochar') is discussed as a possible mitigator for greenhouse emissions at http://www.css.cornell.edu/faculty/lehmann/ terra_preta/TerraPretahome.htm. Controversy nevertheless surrounds this proposal. It is important to stress that *any technical solution is problematic if used as an excuse to avoid reducing consumption.*

2   Vandana Shiva, *Staying Alive – Women, Ecology and Development* (London: Zed, 1988).

sion, this resists entropy by conserving both natural diversity and the information needed to adapt the natural material to future challenges: an apparently useless strain of plant might suddenly reveal itself the best adapted to climatic change. When the forces of greed and appropriation smashed through traditional safeguards, as Carolyn Merchant shows in her important 'Death of Nature' thesis, they necessarily dismantled women's social role.[1] As a result, knowledge was 'dominated',[2] concentrated, and employed to control the producers who originally created it.[3]

In our terminology, society's internal entropy increases as the diffusion of capacity narrows. However, the revolutions accompanying the breakdown of traditional society claimed to liberate capacity and we must examine this claim carefully. The ecological literature typically blames the eighteenth century Enlightenment for destroying sustainability. I would argue, however, that we can perfectly well uphold the Enlightenment's proclamation of liberation from exploitative relations *within human society*, even while rejecting the false goal of liberation from *natural* constraints. Traditional systems had indeed 'evolved' in response to the sustainability problem. However, evolution is somewhat random: the argument that everything evolved is sacrosanct has always been a highly suspect, socially conservative one. Thus, ascribed gender roles may be functional but they limit women's fulfilment and the same could be said of caste or class, which reduce both the total capacity available to society, and its diffusion. Although diversity is good for a system, stratification is not. The claim for liberation of the human condition should therefore not be held back by the same sense of 'limits' as govern our relationship to the environment; indeed it is precisely by combating exploitation that we free up the capacity which enables society to attain a low-entropy state.

The reason things went wrong is not, therefore, the notion of social

---

1   Carolyn Merchant, *The Death of Nature* (New York: Harper, 1990).

2   F. Apffel Marglin and A. Marglin, eds, *Dominating Knowledge – Development, Culture and Resistance* (Oxford : Clarendon Press, 1990).

3   See, for example. Marie Christine Zelem, 'L'Evolution des Techniques fromagères dans le Cantal, France du XVIII au XIX Siècle', in G. Dupré, ed., *Savoirs paysans et Développement* (Paris: Karthala/Orstom, 1991).

progress as such, but rather something else: I will argue that this something is capital accumulation.

Accumulation signifies in the first place an original ('primitive') opening of the floodgates to appropriation (not just of physical resources, but information). Having broken the old order (with its mixture of social oppression, and functional grassroots sustainability), the question was whether the resultant 'development' could be contained within environmental constraints. During the Enlightenment, this preoccupied the Physiocrat school of economists gathered around François Quesnay, whom Malcolm Caldwell hailed as precursors of the radical ecological theory he sought to build.[1] The Physiocrats strove in effect to retain (albeit in an elitist way) that respect for natural cycles which the now-weakened traditional structures could no longer uphold.

But the attempt to maintain such an equilibrium was doomed. What doomed it was the other aspect of accumulation, its *continuing* character. Power is a category of both thermodynamics and of society.[2] A feedback loop results, whereby, in controlling resources, you control people, and in controlling people you grab the resources over which they previously exercised stewardship. This loop generates ongoing *circuits* which—assuming a life of their own, separate from and antagonistic to those of nature—will eventually overwhelm the latter. The promised freedom is then reduced to a removal of restrictions on accumulation. Mainstream economics falsely depicts the resultant 'free' market as a conveyor of information (through which supply connects with demand); in reality when everything is reduced to an abstract, universal measure of value, information in the true sense of concreteness, or differentiation, is lost.

People were not really equal before the supposedly universal market which claimed to have 'freed' them from the restrictions of local production-consumption. Instead, they were drawn into systems of stratification which mixed old determinants like gender with categories like colour and informality. The only universality is the right

---

1   Malcolm Caldwell, *The Wealth of Some Nations* (London: Zed, 1977).
2   Fred P. Gale, 'Theorising Power in Ecological Economics', *Ecological Economics,* 27 (1998), pp. 131–138.

of capital to infiltrate all these dualisms and extract value from them. In doing so, it creates large circuits, extracting energy (raw materials, human resources), and leaving entropy behind (depleted physical environments, social decay). At the highest level, such circuits operate on a world scale,[1] so an important form of dualistic stratification becomes the North-South divide. Here, the 'modernisation' doctrine, as Baran demonstrates, served to dismantle only those functional features of tradition which barred the way to accumulation, while retaining its oppressive and exploitative relationships as a basis upon which to graft a corrupt parody of capitalism.[2] We can further develop Baran's argument in an ecological sense: as Goonatilake shows, the imposition of a 'hegemonic cultural blanketing' reduces the diversity of responses upon which humanity can draw for future social adaptation;[3] the depletion of peripheral societies, therefore, implied a loss *not just of capacity but of variety and differentiation.*

The fallacy at the heart of capitalism

A big reason for the attack on tradition is to cover up the fact that capitalism has itself something to hide. This will be easier to understand if, instead of saying tradition we call it a 'past/future natural mode of social organisation', from which, during its capitalist era, humanity has temporarily departed.

In the person of Isaac Newton, mechanistic rationalism strangely coexisted with a lifelong obsession with alchemy. Dobbs seeks to explain this by saying that one of Newton's 'faces' looks backward to the past',[4] presumably a kind of hangover from traditional superstition. I would argue on the contrary that the alchemical 'face' is merely a representation of something characteristic of capitalism

---

1   André Gunder Frank, *World Accumulation 1492-1789* (Basingstoke: Macmillan, 1978); Samir Amin, *L'Accumulation à l'échelle mondiale: Critique du sous-développement* (Paris: Anthropos, 1970).
2   Paul A. Baran, *The Political Economy of Growth* (London: Penguin, 1973).
3   Susantha Goonatilake, *Crippled Minds – An Exploration into Colonial Culture* (New Delhi: Vikas, 1982).
4   B. J. T Dobbs, *The Janus Face of Genius, the Role of Alchemy in Newton's Thought* (Cambridge: Cambridge University Press, 1991).

throughout its life, namely a pretended escape from the entropy condition. The key delusion is to imagine an accumulation generated purely out of itself. Recent forms of this alchemy are Keynes' 'multiplier', or at an international level, Walt Rostow's Cold War ideology of *self-sustained* growth.[1]

What hidden bases of accumulation does this argument conceal? Most immediately, the exploitation of labour. But as Marx observed, labour yields a value only on condition of an underlying appropriation of nature.[2] The next step is therefore to look for the physical depletion enabling accumulation: since 'production' is really the conversion of natural resources into waste and pollution,[3] it is unsurprising that the post-war boom of 'self-sustained' growth coincided exactly with an escalation of energy inputs.[4]

But what particularly interests us is a depletion of society itself, as brought about by departing from tradition in the wrong way. It was the brilliance of Marx to subvert the rationalist illusion. In speaking of commodity *fetishism*,[5] he demonstrated that the true delusion is the *onward* motion of capital, wherein something destitute of concreteness, of information, is worshipped. In his anthropological notebooks, Marx further ironised on the supposed superiority of civilised 'asses' who, confronted by a traditional approach which they cannot comprehend, brand it as superstition.[6] Winch was spot-on in observing that the modern form of fetishism is much more alienating than the ancient one: magic in traditional society reflected a rational recog-nition of what one is not able to achieve, a limitation which we are no longer humble enough to admit.[7]

---

1   W. W. Rostow, *The Process of Economic Growth* (Oxford: Clarendon, 2nd edition, 1960).

2   Karl Marx, 'Marginal Notes to the Programme of the German Workers' Party,' *Marx and Engels, Selected Works,* Volume III (Moscow: Progress Publishers, 1970), p. 13.

3   See Joël de Rosnay, *The Macroscope* (New York: Harper & Row, 1979).

4   Jean-Marc Jancovici, *l'Avenir climatique* (Paris: Seuil, 2002), for development.

5   Karl Marx, *Capital*, Vol. I, Chapter 1, Section 4, http://www.marxists.org/archive/marx/works/1867-c1/ch01.htm#S4. Italics in original.

6   L. Krader, ed., *The Ethnological Notebooks of Karl Marx* (Assen, Netherlands: Van Gorcum, 2nd edition, 1974).

7   Peter Winch, 'Understanding a Primitive Society', in B. R. Wilson, ed., *Rationality*

Yet accumulation *needs* this thing (tradition) which it repulses. In helping us understand why, Rosa Luxemburg's contribution is essential.[1] In her view, accumulation can only proceed through the step-by-step commodification of a hinterland of hitherto non-monetarised social relations; presumably when everything is commodified, it would hit a limit.

This indeed seems a farsighted prediction of today's globalisation, whose crisis arrives at the very moment of its seeming triumph. Taking this perspective as a starting point, we must nevertheless refine it. To begin with, if we represent the depletion as entropy, what is destroyed (as fuel for accumulation) is not just the non-monetary sphere but society's information and diversity. Arguably the most persistent and fundamental economic expression of fetishism, which survived and prospered even when Keynes' and Rostow's theories were rubbished by neo-liberalism, was David Ricardo's argument for free trade.[2] Here, not only are the energy costs of long-distance transport ignored but economies are homogenised around just a few products (hence the destruction of local self-sufficiency and of diverse skill-sets) purely on the assumption of a saving self-generated miraculously from the very act of specialisation itself. It is this depletion which forms the true underpinning of globalisation.

We have seen that intra-societal diversity stands in a positive relationship with the conservation of *bio*diversity; therefore, if one is sacrificed, the other will also suffer. An example is the 'Green Revolution', a strategy initiated at the close of World War II to encourage developing countries to abandon their traditionally diverse food systems and concentrate on just a few strains of a few crops. Seeds were supplied to them by the multinationals as F1 hybrids produced by cross-pollinating two inbred parent stocks. Such hybrids possess enhanced vigour and uniformity, but only for one generation, so farmers can neither save the seed, nor, perhaps more impor-

---

(Oxford: Blackwell, 1970).
1   Rosa Luxemburg, *Die Akkumulation des Kapitals – eine Beitrag zur Ökonomischen Erklarung des Imperialismus* (Berlin: Paul Singer, 1913).
2   David Ricardo, *On the Principles of Political Economy and Taxation – The Works and Correspondence of David Ricardo,* Piero Sraffa, ed., Vol. I (Cambridge: Cambridge University Press, 1951).

tantly, *experiment* with it, and so cannot exploit its variety to refine characteristics adapted to local conditions or climatic challenges. The large repertoire of traditional varieties thus tends to fall into disuse and disappear.[1] The hands-on cultivator loses her/his position at the cutting edge of innovation while humanity, as a whole, loses both the genetic material and the associated skill-sets which could save us from future shocks. We can witness the result: agriculture itself becomes a major vehicle of accumulation circuits whereby, entirely driven by a manipulated 'demand',[2] it now falsely 'liberates' itself from the natural constraints of eating seasonal food.

Capitalism has therefore dug itself, and humanity, into a trap. The question now is: what is the way out?

Conflicting forms of adaptation in response to crisis

Crisis is a stimulus to adaptation, but not necessarily of a good kind.

Environmental literature often wrongly assumes that scarcity was only noticed in the 1970s. In reality, practical imperialism was premised on scarcity from the outset.[3] The characteristic of a zero-sum[4] conflict is that 'value is neither created nor destroyed',[5] the exact opposite of the assumption, at a *discourse* level, that growth is infinitely self-generating. At first, the great powers frantically competed against each other, and when they stopped doing this at the close of World War II, this was only to ensure a more effective *collective* control over resources, still thought of as scarce.[6] Rostow, the high priest of 'self-sustained' growth, had a parallel undercover role in

---

1   Bernhard Glaeser, ed., *The Green Revolution Revisited – Critique and Alternatives* (London: Allen and Unwin, 1987).

2   Raj Patel, *Stuffed and Starved – Markets, Power and the Hidden Battle for the World Food System* (London: Portobello, 2007).

3   See the seminal study of Harold and Margaret Sprout, *The Ecological Perspective on Human Affairs* (Princeton NJ: Princeton University Press, 1965).

4   Zero-sum, a term from game theory, means that the gains of one party exactly cancel out the losses of the other: $+ 1 - 1 = 0$.

5   Frank C. Zagare, *Game Theory – Concepts and Applications* (Beverly Hills: Sage 1984), p. 21.

6   See, for example, M. P. Leffler, 'National Security and United States Foreign Policy,' in idem., and D. S. Painter, eds, *Origins of the Cold War* (London: Routledge, 1994).

Cold War psyops,[1] thus effectively admitting the need to grab the resources which really 'sustain' growth. The notion of scarcity was therefore merely shallowly repressed, and unsurprisingly re-emerged in the 1970s crisis. The famous *Limits to Growth* report of 1972[2] was sponsored by multinationals reflecting on how to continue making money into the future. Although capitalism soon returned to its default mode—a revived discourse of no-limits growth called glo-bal-isation being superimposed upon military doctrines to grab the limited remaining resources[3]—the 1970s crisis was a wake-up call.

The most obvious response to prolonging capitalism might be to curtail depletion of the external physical environment, by introducing 'sustainable development'. But in practice—despite landmark suc-cesses in reducing CFCs, some pesticides or dioxins—mainstream sustainability notions have been too amenable to capture by finance capital (as in the carbon markets) and too narrow to respond to the really significant complex challenges such as today's food crisis (with its interrelated characteristics of soil degradation, climate, water shortage, and hedge-fund speculation on scarcity).

The less obvious adaptation may be the more interesting one: that the system might evolve in such a way as partially to regulate its own *internal* entropy.

To understand how this could happen, we have to see that the 1970s crisis in fact sparked off *two* contradictory forms of adaptation: an adaptation by capitalism, and another where the agent is humanity. The two remain basically antagonistic simply because any adaptation of capitalism must prolong its core identity: the accumulation drive, and if humanity is to survive it must get rid of this. But capitalism discovered a way to piggy-back its own adaptation onto the human survival reflex. For this reason, the two types of adaptation may be quite hard to separate in concrete cases.

We should begin to see imperialism (capitalism's highest stage) as a complex adaptive system. In a conventional reading of imperial-

1 See Gordon H., Chang, Friends *and Enemies: The United States, China, and the Soviet Union, 1948–1972* (Stanford: Stanford University Press, 1991).
2 D. L. Meadows, et al., *The Limits to Growth* (London: Earth Island, 1972).
3 Plans to invade the Middle East initiated under President Carter were later dusted off for the Iraq invasion.

ism what strikes one is its more obvious centralism. But what if the top-down, military-bureaucratic features, while still in place, were to acquire a new role: to control a partially *decentralised* system? Lenin called imperialism 'parasitic'.[1] The obvious parasitism is the dominance of finance capital over the real economy, whose ill-effects we can see today. However, I will explore a more subtle meaning, merely latent in Lenin's day: parasitism upon human ingenuity. The developmental thrust of capitalism had seemed stuck on a trajectory where all control and initiative were inexorably drawn to the centre/top, as in the Taylor management system which deliberately robbed the manufacturing operative of all initiative.[2] Left to itself, the system might never have escaped a high-entropy vortex where information and adaptive capacity disappear. But once the wider human adaptation process was triggered, this seemed to offer a way out.

The fundamental characteristics of human adaptation would include a restoration of diversity and diffuse capacity, of self-organisation and its characteristic institutional forms, such as regimes to exercise stewardship over common-pool resources. If we merely call this 'tradition', it looks like the broken glass which can't reconstitute itself. However, if these are inherent self-organisation *faculties*, we are perfectly entitled (on condition of respecting the ecosystem) to reverse the arrow of time and rebuild the broken societal order.

Capitalism somehow evolved into a form where it could parasitise upon these faculties to reduce its internal entropy. The discovery of the post-1980 neo-liberal accumulation regime was that notions of 'spontaneous order' could be used to justify not just market fundamentalism but also a co-optation of something contradictory to it: structures which access the human trait of self-organisation and relations based on reciprocity. The most obvious form of this was in the business environment. The kinds of order self-generated by decentralised, non-hierarchical systems genuinely work better than top-down imposed order, and such 'efficiency' is a seemingly neutral category, applicable to both socio-institutional systems and physical

---

1   V. I. Lenin. *Imperialism, the Highest Stage of Capitalism* (New York: International Publishers, 1939).
2   See H. Braverman, *Labour and Monopoly Capital* (New York: Monthly Review Press, 1974).

productive ones,[1] consuming less energy (or generating less waste, which is the same thing), which capitalism could then treat as profit. Thus, in management, we find structures like industrial clusters, which explore the propensity to 'happen' rather than be designed. In IT, a sphere of decentralised grassroots initiative is indispensable, or there would be no vitality. It is not at all fanciful to view open-source software as a reconstituted traditional mode, 'gift economies' supplying an explicit point of reference.[2] Here, development and creativity occur 'through a distribution, rather than a division, of labour', and are closely associated with 'production close to use.'[3]

Crisis of the system and the 'exterminist' tendency

The problem is that all this needed to be controlled. Networked systems are more difficult to destroy or capture just because there is no centre.[4] On the other hand (an insight already present in Foucault's work[5]), they can be controlled in a new way, by a power diffused within them.

This worked well enough in industry: industrial clusters are grouped into global value chains in the ultimate service of corporate or finance capital. But it is much more problematical in the sphere of politics where, the contradiction between unleashing 'tame' spontaneous order and containing it within acceptable parameters really becomes apparent. 'Civil society' (the political equivalent of the global value chains) seemingly recognises a pluralistic order more efficient than Cold War-style top-down dictatorships. In reality, as we

---

1   Göran Wall, 'Exergy, Ecology and Democracy – Concepts of a Vital Society or a Proposal for an Exergy Tax', conference paper, International Conference on Energy Systems and Ecology, Krakow July 1993, http://exergy.se/goran/eed/
2   See J. Matzan, 'The gift economy and free software', 2004, http://www.linux.com/articles/36554 .
3   Naazneen Barma, The Prospects and Pitfalls of Information Technology-Driven Development Strategies and Assistance', Conference paper: The American Political Science Association, Philadelphia, 2003, p. 15.
4   Ori Brafman and Rod A. Beckstrom, The Starfish and the Spider: The Unstoppable Power of Leaderless Organisations (London: Penguin books, 2006).
5   Michel Foucault, Society Must be Defended – Lectures at the Collège de France 1975-76 (London: Allen Lane, 2003).

see in the US 'polyarchy' doctrine,[1] the permissible degree of sponta-
neity is (in contrast to software development, for example) so slight
as to be a mere self-parody. Not surprisingly, the more capitalism co-
opts the human self-organising faculty, the more repressive it must
become in order to contain it. At some point, *the cost of containing
emergence would exceed the exploitative benefit it supplies.* I have
argued that this scenario began to materialise shortly before 9/11,
embracing the latter as a pretext.[2]

At this point, where would the system go next? Here, we can usefully explore a concept introduced by E. P. Thompson: 'exterminism'.[3]
Although his specific application of the term to late-Cold War nuclear
confrontation is debatable,[4] it remains fundamentally likely that systems can slip into a destructive dynamic which foresakes rationality.
Mark Jones, shortly before his death in 2003, began exploring an intu-
itive link between on the one hand the unbridled repressive shift, and
on the other the mindless burning-up of a shrinking stock of physical
resources.[5] Building on these insights we can redefine exterminism as
a point where repression unmoors itself from a rational linkage to the
problem of controlling emergence, and turns into a destructive reflex
whereby a doomed capitalism resigns itself to dragging humanity,
and nature, to the grave with it.

The Bush regime represented exterminism in its most single-
minded form and, educationally, this is a lesson which we should
retain because it revealed something profound about the tendencies
within the system. But Blair was actually a better representative of
the main line of capitalist development. On the one hand, the exterminist features of Blairism are clear: the use of 'depleted' uranium
in Iraq abroad, the gleeful dismantling of civil liberties at home. On

---

1   William L. Robinson, *Promoting Polyarchy – Globalisation, US Intervention and
     Hegemony* (Cambridge : Cambridge University Press, 1996).
2   Robert Biel, *El nuevo imperialismo : crisis y contradicciones en las relaciones
     Norte-Sur.*(Mexico : Siglo XXI, 2007), chapter 15.
3   Edward Thompson, 'Notes on Exterminism, the Last Stage of Civilisation,' in New
     Left Review, ed., *Exterminism and the Cold War* (London: Verso, 1982).
4   I would argue that colonialism and imperialism were always the paradigm for exter-
     minism, and the East-West conflict merely its contingent form.
5   See Mark Jones, 'Stand-off between Opec and Russia?', 20 November 2001, http://
     wsarch.ucr.edu/wsnmail/2001/msg01791.html.

the other, there is still mileage in pushing further the co-optation of the human survival reflex—in the direction of community 'empowerment'. This would go beyond the areas addressed in things like industrial clusters, and target instead the *social* economy.

Although society's 'broken glass' could not really be repaired under capitalism, it could be 'taped' in a palliative sense, *without cost to the monetary economy*. Unlike in Luxemburg's model—where the sphere of non-commodity transactions is merely destroyed by capitalist development—it now becomes clear that a social economy keeps regenerating itself as a way of keeping society alive amid the devastation. Hazel Henderson has described the economy as a cake, where two 'recognised' layers at the top—private capital (the icing), and a cherry-coloured layer of public goods—sit on top of various layers of informality, all underpinned by nature.[1] Henderson advocated the *acknowledgement* of these underlying layers but what she missed was that that they might be 'embraced' on capitalism's own, exploitative terms. We can see the results in the discourse on 'sustainable communities', a notion now enshrined in an Act of Parliament.[2] But this emergence needs to be controlled. The Blair era's extreme culture of surveillance and aggressive social inclusion are thus the inseparable partner of 'sustainable communities'. It would be too dangerous if the community response to crisis were permitted to follow its natural course.

Conclusion: can urban agriculture save the planet?

In systems theory, a system's fundamental logic derives from an 'attractor'; at moments of bifurcation, different attractors will compete. In the physical world, the attractor can be seen as an objective force embedded in the system's own networks. However, in a human system the information which is exchanged takes a special form: 'information about the future'.[3] We can interpret this to mean

---

1   See Henderson's presentation, http://www.fhs-forschung.at/fileadmin/documents/ zfz/HENDERSON_HAZEL_Konferenz_Zukunft_Lebensqualitaet_4_bis_6_ Mai_2008.pdf

2   Sustainable Communities Act 2007, http://www.opsi.gov.k/ACTS/acts2007/pdf/ ukpga_20070023_en.pdf

3   Juan G. Roederer, 'On the Concept of Information and its Role in Nature', *Entropy*,

that agency is always present in constituting attractors.

Here, it is interesting to consider the Transition Towns (TT) movement, a community initiative which, gathering remarkable momentum since its launch as recently as 2006, explicitly links input/output-reduction to the increase of capacity, skill, and diversity.[1]

The strength of such an attractor could very well draw into its orbit certain adaptations which initially appear as part of capitalism. For example, it is rational for business to minimise costly inputs and the approach called industrial ecology[2] lessens waste by using the outgoings of one process as inputs into another (such as heat which would otherwise be dissipated). Such initiatives, currently smothered within the exterminist logic which prevails at a whole-system level, could potentially act as 'plugins' for an alternative order. On the other hand, TT is, in turn, itself vulnerable to the ruling attractor, to some extent. For example, at a recent meeting on local currencies, the speaker praised the example of a privatised railway company which had paid the local community in community currency to clean up one of its stations.[3] We can critically analyse this in the language of Henderson's 'cake' model by saying that in neo-liberalism's optimistic phase the finance-capital icing fattened itself by gobbling up public goods like railways but today, when the icing is itself melting, it is frantically seeking to offset the process, by exploiting the ability of the community sector to heal the socio-environmental decay. Following this logic to its conclusion, the whole community project would be anchored into a role of supplying low-cost palliative solutions to capitalism's crisis.

But there is something solid which can pull in the opposite direction: the methodology of 'visioning' employed by TT, which we can certainly see as 'information about the future'. An interesting case study of this visioning would be one central to the transition debate: urban agriculture.

Out of all the issues for the future, food security will be the abso-

---

5, (2003), pp. 1–31.
1   See Rob Hopkins, *The Transition Handbook – from oil dependency to local resilience* (Totnes: Green Books, 2008).
2   *Journal of Industrial Ecology*, http://www.yale.edu/jie/
3   Author's participant observation.

lute fundamental: if this cannot be solved there is no point talking about a future for humanity at all. Yet the exterminist dynamic is particularly strongly embedded here, what with contempt for the precautionary principle over GM and animal disease, biofuels, the strategic scramble to buy up whole swathes of developing-country plantations, and hedge-fund speculation on scarcity.

Within agriculture too, progressive developments can occur in pockets of business practice: for example, some farmers now realise that, by adopting no-till agriculture and relying on mulches and green manures to prevent nutrients leaching from the soil, they can save money on artificial inputs, fuel and machinery.[1] But this is not much use to any transition mode unless, and until, it can be attracted in the direction of community.

A remarkable case where this is being attempted is the work of Will Allen in Milwaukee, USA. An African-American former basketball professional, Allen's central motivation is to heal social disintegration among urban youth (i.e. society's broken glass). This is achieved through a form of urban agriculture which in effect takes the city as its base to critique the *whole* of agriculture and thereby brings the notion of working like/with nature to previously-unscaled heights. The aquaponic greenhouse system is heated by the composting process, which also supplies liquid nutrients; fish swim in channels bordered by salad crops. Phoning his farm while on a speaking tour, even Allen was surprised to learn that the system had spontaneously developed a state of equilibrium, with salads purifying the water in a manner analogous to river plants.[2] By employing industrial ecology techniques like using waste hops and wood-chip for composting, such an approach survives very effectively within capitalism, while really reflecting an alternative response, of which humanity is the main agent.

Most importantly, the key educational tool of TT has been the Cuban urban agriculture experience. For the Cuban experiment, we can thank successive US administrations who, by blockading the

---

1   Rolf Derpsch, 'Economics of No-till farming, Experiences from Latin America', http://www.notill.org/KnowledgeBase/03_economics_derpsch.pdf
2   Author's notes on a Will Allen presentation.

country, incentivised it to operate on reduced inputs and become the lowest-entropy society in the world. Significantly, it represents an adaptive response *to crisis*.[1] Cuban agriculture is not only mostly organic but low input (in Britain, in contrast, organic food has much higher 'food miles' than non-organic[2]), its permaculture principles minimising not just fertiliser/fuel inputs but also labour, therefore freeing up scope for further capacity-development.

This raises important issues about the role of socialism. Interestingly, the mainstream notion of 'transition economies' was one of the most abusive distortions of transition: according to the 'end of history' discourse, 'transition' was simply equivalent to capitalism because there was supposedly no other line of development. In the current crisis, socialism should hit back by clearly explaining that the capitalist attractor is doomed anyway, and that there *can be* an alternative. This requires socialism to critique its past tendency to compete with capitalism by dominating nature more effectively. The point about the permaculture methodology shared by Cuba and TT is that it is both ecocentric, and at the same time community-centric because low entropy is a universal principle of organisation. All of this pulls the notion of sustainable community in a progressive sense. There may be a stand-off at the time of writing in 2009, but what will surely disrupt it is the growing complexity of the crisis: the adaptation of humanity can no longer be constrained within parameters unchallenging to the existing mode of production.

---

1   Peter M. Rosset, 'Cuba: Alternative Agriculture During Crisis', in L. A. Thrupp, ed., *New Partnerships for Sustainable Agriculture* (Washington DC: World Resource Institute, 1996), pp. 64–74.

2   Defra, *Joint announcement by the agricultural departments of the United Kingdom, Organic Statistics United Kingdom*, June 2005.

Humanities-Ebooks.co.uk

Full length books

Sibylle Baumbach, *Shakespeare and the Art of Physiognomy* *
John Beer, *Blake's Humanism*
John Beer, *The Achievement of E M Forster*
John Beer, *Coleridge the Visionary*
Jared Curtis, ed., *The Fenwick Notes of William Wordsworth* *
Steven Duncan, *Analytic Philosophy of Religion: its History since 1955* *
John K Hale, *Milton as Multilingual: Selected Essays 1982–2004*
Simon Hull, ed., *The British Periodical Text, 1797–1835*
John Lennard, *Modern Dragons and other Essays on Genre Fiction* *
Colin Nicholson, *Fivefathers: Interviews with late Twentieth-Century Scottish Poets*
Pamela Perkins, ed., *Francis Jeffrey's Highland and Continental Tours* *
Keith Sagar, *D. H. Lawrence: Poet* *
William Wordsworth, *Concerning the Convention of Cintra* *
William Wordsworth, *Wordsworth's Political Writings* *
The Poems of William Wordsworth: Collected Reading Texts from the Cornell Wordsworth,
3 vols.*

History Insights
ideal sixth form and college level introductions

Robert Johnson, *The British Empire: Pomp, Power and Postcolonialism*
Stuart Andrews, *Methodism and Society*
Martyn Housden, *The Holocaust: Events, Motives, and Legacy* *
Stuart Andrews, *Lenin's Revolution*
Graham Goodlad, *Oliver Cromwell*
Tim Chapman, *The Risorgimento: Italy 1814–1871*

* These titles are also available in print using links from

http://www.humanities-ebooks.co.uk

All *HEB* titles are available to libraries from Aggregators such as Ebrary
Most are available in Amazon Kindle format
Many are in Paperback